The Library in the Life of the User: Engaging with People Where They Live and Learn

This compilation is © 2015 OCLC Online Computer Library Center, Inc.

Individual copyright and licensing details related to the papers included in this compilation are noted on their respective cover pages.

October 2015

OCLC Research

Dublin, Ohio 43017 USA
www.oclc.org

ISBNs: 1-55653-500-7 (978-1-55653-500-0)
OCLC Control Number: 924929722

Please direct correspondence to:
Lynn Silipigni Connaway
Senior Research Scientist, OCLC Research
lynn_connaway@oclc.org

Suggested citation:
Connaway, Lynn Silipigni, comp. 2015. *The Library in the Life of the User: Engaging with People Where They Live and Learn.* Dublin, Ohio: OCLC Research. http://www.oclc.org/content/dam/research/publications/2015/oclcresearch-library-in-life-of-user.pdf.

We've normalized some of the references and URLs in this report for consistency. URLs that were not working at the time of publication were noted and their hyperlinks were removed from the PDF file of this report. Alternative links were included when possible. The pagination in these reports differs from the originals. Please keep this in mind when citing this work.

ACKNOWLEDGMENTS

The research represented in this compilation was made possible by several strategic partnerships as well as funding for several of the projects by the Institute of Museum and Library Services (IMLS), in collaboration with The Ohio State University and Rutgers, The State University of New Jersey, and with Jisc, in collaboration with Oxford University and the University of North Carolina, Charlotte.

Special thanks to Lorcan Dempsey for popularizing the phrase "The Library in the Life of the User" and also to the following colleagues for their help in editing and publishing this report: Melissa Renspie, Erin Hood, Linda Shepard, Brad Gauder, Jeanette McNicol, Matt Carlson and Eric Childress.

CONTENTS

Introduction, by Lynn Silipigni Connaway i

1. *Reordering Ranganathan: Shifting User Behaviours, Shifting Priorities,*
   by Lynn Silipigni Connaway and Ixchel M. Faniel 1

2. *What is Enough? Satisficing Information Needs,* by Chandra Prabha,
   Lynn Silipigni Connaway, Lawrence Olszewski and Lillie Jenkins 33

3. *"Screenagers" and Live Chat Reference: Living Up to the Promise,*
   by Marie L. Radford and Lynn Silipigni Connaway 51

4. *Sense-making and Synchronicity: Information-seeking Behaviors of Millennials and Baby
   Boomers,* by Lynn Silipigni Connaway, Marie L. Radford, Timothy J. Dickey, Jocelyn
   De Angelis Williams and Patrick Confer 79

5. *The Digital Information Seeker: Report of Findings from Selected OCLC, RIN
   and JISC User Behaviour Projects,* by Lynn Silipigni Connaway and Timothy J. Dickey . . . 97

6. *"If it is too inconvenient I'm not going after it:" Convenience as a Critical Factor
   in Information-seeking Behaviors,* by Lynn Silipigni Connaway,
   Timothy J. Dickey and Marie L. Radford 107

7. *User-centered Decision Making: A New Model for Developing
   Academic Library Services and Systems,* by Lynn Silipigni Connaway,
   Donna Lanclos, David White, Alison Le Cornu and Erin M. Hood 135

8. *Visitors and Residents: What Motivates Engagement with the Digital
   Information Environment?* by Lynn Silipigni Connaway, David White,
   Donna Lanclos and Alison Le Cornu 153

9. *"I always stick with the first thing that comes up on Google. . ."
   Where People Go for Information, What They Use, and Why*
   by Lynn Silipigni Connaway, Donna M. Lanclos and Erin M. Hood 169

10. *Meeting the Expectations of the Community: The Engagement-centered Library,*
    by Lynn Silipigni Connaway 197

INTRODUCTION

The study of user behaviors, also referred to as information behavior, information-seeking behavior research, or user studies is not a new line of inquiry. In 1931, Ranganathan wrote,

> "Perhaps the most convenient method of studying the consequences of this law will be to follow the reader from the moment he enters the library to the moment he leaves it…" (337)

This reference to "follow the reader" sounds very similar to the ethnographic studies and observations that have become more prevalent in LIS user behavior research. In 1940, when making a case for local funding of public libraries, McDiarmid stated:

> "In order to answer the question, 'What type of library service is needed in the community?'… a great deal must be known regarding the area to be served. What are the important factors in the library's community environment? What social changes have altered this environment? These are questions which require historical, geographical and social data and, hence, an important part of an effective library survey is a study of the community itself." (11)

The current economic climate, much like the environment McDiarmid described in 1940, has drawn much attention to assessment in school and academic libraries as a way to articulate the value of libraries within the academic environment. Assessment involves analyzing the data made available through educational systems to measure student success, such as retention and GPA, against service and resources provided by the library. It also involves utilizing the data generated by library systems and services, such as web analytics and feedback from those within the academic community regardless of whether they use the library. If they do use the library, it is imperative to identify how and why they use it. If they do not use the library, it is equally important to discover how and what they use to get their information and to learn why they use these services and resources instead of those provided by the library. We refer to this as user-centered assessment (Connaway 2014b).

Since the library is not the only game in town to get information and "the majority of the population does not use libraries to get information" (Connaway 2013, 83), it is important for the library to become embedded in the lifestyles of their users and potential users (those who may not or who seldom use library services).[1]

As a way to put this into a practical perspective, Dempsey (2015) discusses the importance of thinking about the library in the life of the user instead of the traditional model of thinking of the user in the life of the library. Again, this leads back to the fact that there are many more convenient and familiar ways of getting information today than from the traditional library environment. Many people do not think of the library as the first place to get their information. This may be attributed to people not knowing that the services exist or that some of the existing services are not familiar or do not fit into their workflows. Research indicates that people associate the library with books and do not consider the library in relation to online resources or reference services (Connaway, Dickey, and Radford 2011; Connaway, Lanclos, and Hood 2013; Connaway and Radford 2011; De Rosa et al. 2005; De Rosa et al. 2010; Prabha, Connaway, and Dickey 2006), which could be addressed with branding initiatives and marketing campaigns.

To address these issues we have developed an OCLC research theme titled user studies. The rationale for this research activity is that by providing the library community with behavioral evidence about individuals' perceptions, habits, and requirements, we can ensure that the design of future library services is all about the user.[2]

We have concentrated on identifying how people engage with technology and get their information for both personal and academic situations. We have learned that the context and situation of the information need often dictate how people behave and engage with technology. These also influence how and why they select to use resources, usually discovered through a web browser and that include freely available resources, such as Wikipedia; human resources; and library resources.

Our research indicates the importance of developing relationships and engaging with people. If they know us and trust us, they will seek us out when they need information and they will recommend us and our services to others. When asked to identify successful virtual reference encounters users cited instances when they did not receive an answer, but when they had a good rapport with the librarian and the librarian was kind and helpful. This exemplifies the importance of engagement and relationship building in both the online and physical environments for the development of successful and effective services.

Based on our research, the following questions were asked in the comments on "The Elusive User" blog post (Connaway 2014a).

1. If we try to identify how people find information and how and why they get their information as well as how and why they choose to engage with specific technology, could we, as librarians, provide services and systems that will meet some of these needs?

2. Is this attempting to take on more than librarians have the capacity to do, especially in today's environment of limited resources, or, is this something that we have an interest in pursuing?

3. Should we only concentrate on those who currently use our resources and services, subsequently developing personalized or "boutique" library services (Priestner and Tilley 2012)?

These are questions that need to be openly discussed in order to develop a research agenda, recommendations, and a plan for integrating the library into the life of the user. As the information environment changes, we need to envision services that will fill a gap in people's professional and personal lives. Engagement around emerging issues, such as developing data management plans and reuse practices and policies, networks of people and knowledge, and creative designs for both physical and virtual spaces provide opportunities for librarians to develop a library that fits into the lives of its users (Bannon, Guillermo, and Palfrey 2014).

This volume contains the following contributions, which represent a decade of our collaborative work in the user studies OCLC Research theme.

1. Connaway, Lynn Silipigni, and Ixchel M. Faniel. 2015. "Reordering Ranganathan: Shifting user behaviours, shifting priorities." *SRELS Journal of Information Management* 52, no. 1: 3–23. http://i-scholar.in/index.php/sjim/article/view/60392/51360.

    S.R. Ranganathan's Five Laws of Library Science provide a broad framework for designing and evaluating library programs, activities and services. Even today, the laws continue to be extensively cited suggesting their continued relevance. This paper attempts to interpret the five laws in the present day context of information abundance, digital revolution, currently available resources and services, and user behaviors. It also includes ideas for the development of library services that will better connect with users. After examining the changing roles of the Five Laws on the basis of findings of recent research, the paper suggests reordering and reframing of the Five Laws of Library Science.

2. Prabha, Chandra, Lynn Silipigni Connaway, Lawrence Olszewski, and Lillie Jenkins. 2007. "What is enough? Satisficing information needs." *Journal of Documentation* 63, no. 1: 74–89. http://www.oclc.org/content/dam/research/publications/newsletters/prabha-satisficing.pdf.

    In an "overloaded" information environment, many information users tend to experience a sense of information inadequacy and anxiety. Insight into information seeking can be gained by understanding how users seek information sources and how they choose content to meet their needs. Yet the library and information science literature has neglected to study how individuals decide what and how much information is enough to meet their needs or goals. This paper extends the information-seeking, -searching, and -gathering process to include how and when individuals stop looking for information, given a goal or a task that creates the need for information. It provides examples of satisficing information needs in relation to the academic tasks that create a need for information in the first place. Role theory and rational choice theory provide a framework for understanding why users decide to stop looking for more information when searching for information.

3. Radford, Marie L., and Lynn Silipigni Connaway. 2007. "'Screenagers' and live chat reference: Living up to the promise." *Scan* 26, no. 1: 31–39. http://www.oclc.org/content/dam/research/publications/newsletters/connaway-scan.pdf.

    "Screenagers" are defined as 12-18-year-old members of the Millennial Generation because of their affinity for electronic communication via computer, phone, television, etc. screens (see Rushkoff 1996). These young Millennials are at home in the instant messaging and chat environment. Their communication and information-seeking behaviors often are distinctly different from those of other age cohorts and radically different from those of the baby boomer generation. Libraries are providing Web-based virtual reference services (VRS) as alternatives to traditional face-to-face (FtF)

reference services to meet the information needs of virtual as well as FtF library users. This paper presents the revealing results of an international study of communication and information-seeking including a series of three focus group interviews with 12–18 year olds and analysis of a random sample of 431 live chat reference transcripts drawn from an international population. Focus group interviews with groups of urban, suburban, and rural screenagers were conducted with the cooperation of public and school librarians in collaboration with public school teachers. The findings from these interviews reveal their communication and information-seeking preferences. These groups have revealed that they use IM for socializing and collaborative homework, yet perceive library VRS differently than these other virtual encounters; they also express a preference for FtF encounters with librarians. Implications and recommendations for school library chat reference services are identified.

4. Connaway, Lynn Silipigni, Marie L. Radford, Timothy J. Dickey, Jocelyn De Angelis Williams, and Patrick Confer. 2008. "Sense-making and synchronicity: Information-seeking behaviors of Millennials and Baby Boomers." *Libri* 58, no. 2: 123–135. http://www.oclc.org/content/dam/research/publications/library/2008/connaway-libri.pdf.

   A major challenge facing today's libraries is to develop and update both traditional and digital collections and services to meet the needs of the multiple generations of users with differing approaches to information seeking. The different characteristics and information needs of Boomers and Millennials present a dichotomy for library service and system development. This paper includes the results of two research projects that investigated habits and needs of library users and potential users. Both studies employed a multi-method research design to identify how and why individuals seek and use information. The first study reports the findings of focus group interviews with seventy-eight randomly selected participants, and fifteen semi-structured interviews with a subset of these participants. The second study reports the results of focus group interviews with twenty-three Millennials, and an analysis of 492 virtual reference services (VRS) transcripts. The studies indicate that both generations consistently identify Google and human sources as the first sources they use for quick searches. The younger Millennials (Screenagers) mentioned consulting parents most frequently, while the older Millennials consult friends and professors. Boomers indicated they consult their personal libraries and colleagues. The findings have implications for the development of next generation library online catalogs, as well as services, including VRS.

5. Connaway, Lynn Silipigni, and Timothy J. Dickey. 2010. The digital information seeker: Report of findings from selected OCLC, RIN, and JISC User Behavior Projects. http://www.jisc.ac.uk/media/documents/publications/reports/2010/digitalinformationseekerreport.pdf.

   A cursory search in Library, Information Science & Technology Abstracts retrieved 2,486 items published 1958-2009 for the term user studies and 986 items published during the same time period for the term user behavior. This indicates the massive amount of literature available in the area of user behavior studies. This report is not intended to be the definitive work on user behavior studies but to identify common as well as contradictory findings reported in twelve major studies that were funded by non-profit and government agencies published 2005–2009 and specifically addressed electronic content, users' perceptions of their information-seeking behaviors, and library catalogs. The contradictory findings, may be attributed to the design of the twelve studies. The research design is a combination of large-scale quantitative studies as well as qualitative studies that provide rich portraits of specific user groups. Many of the findings presented in this meta-analysis could be used as hypotheses for subsequent testing and generalization; therefore, the next logical step is to further explore and quantify these findings by conducting large, random-sample online and interview surveys. The findings from the twelve studies indicate that users want access to even more full-text digital content. Though they value the traditional library services and human sources of information, users are adapting to new realities in the information world, and new opportunities in access to information resources.

*Note: Only the Executive Summary (pages 1–5) of this report is included in this publication.

6. Connaway, Lynn Silipigni, Timothy J. Dickey, and Marie L. Radford. 2011. "'If It Is too inconvenient I'm not going after it:' Convenience as a critical factor in information-seeking behaviors." *Library & Information Science Research* 33, no. 3: 179–190.

    In today's fast-paced world, anecdotal evidence suggests that information tends to inundate people, and users of information systems want to find information quickly and conveniently. Empirical evidence for convenience as a critical factor is explored in the data from two multi-year, user studies projects. Convenience is a situational criterion in people's choices and actions during all stages of the information-seeking process. The concept of convenience can include their choice of an information source, their satisfaction and ease of use with the source, and their allocation of time for information seeking. Convenience especially is prevalent among the millennials in both studies, but also is present in all demographic categories—age, gender, academic role, or user or potential user of virtual reference services. These two studies further indicate that convenience is a factor for making choices in a variety of situations, including both academic information seeking and everyday-life information seeking, although it plays different roles in different situations.

7. Connaway, Lynn Silipigni, Donna Lanclos, David White, Alison Le Cornu, and Erin M. Hood. 2012. "User-centered decision making: A new model for developing academic library services and systems." *IFLA World Library and Information Congress 2012 Helsinki Proceedings: Libraries Now! Inspiring, Surprising, Empowering.* http://conference.ifla.org/sites/default/files/files/papers/wlic2012/76-connaway-en.pdf.

    The Digital Visitors and Residents project is a longitudinal study that tracks US and UK participants' shifts in their motivations and forms of engagement with technology and information as they transition between four educational stages. The quantitative and qualitative methods, including ethnographic methods that devote individual attention to the subjects, yield a very rich data set enabling multiple methods of analysis. Instead of reporting general information-seeking habits and technology use, this study explores how the subjects get their information based on the context and situation of their needs during an extended period of time, identifying if and how their behaviors change.

8. Connaway, Lynn Silipigni, David White, Donna Lanclos, and Alison Le Cornu. 2013. "Visitors and Residents: What motivates engagement with the digital information environment?" *Information Research* 18, no. 1, http://informationr.net/ir/18-1/infres181.html.

    We have little understanding of what motivates individuals to use particular technologies or spaces when engaging with the information environment. This lack of understanding also makes the task of facilitating digital literacy skills challenging. There are multiple ways to engage in the information environment. Both physical and digital libraries as well as a large number of open-access choices creates a competitive information environment for schools and universities. The findings indicate that school or university resources are not necessarily the first choices of the students and other members of the academic community, who often choose the most convenient, easiest to use sources. The findings from this research can inform academic institutions of current and perspective students' expectations of services and systems based on their engagement with technology and their information-seeking behavior in different contexts and situations.

9. Connaway, Lynn Silipigni, Donna M. Lanclos, and Erin M. Hood. 2013. "'I always stick with the first thing that comes up on Google...' Where people go for information, what they use, and why." *EDUCAUSE Review Online* (6 December), http://www.educause.edu/ero/article/i-always-stick-first-thing-comes-google-where-people-go-information-what-they-use-and-why.

   Networked environments and affordable devices make it easy and convenient to access free information sources, whether human, digital, or physical. This paper utilizes the visitors and residents framework to identify ways academic communities discover, access, and evaluate digital information. The research focuses on where people look for information, what sources they use, and why they choose and return to these sources instead of other sources. One of the major findings identified in the paper is the importance of relationship building in the context of engaging with the academic community. The findings indicate that individuals do contact other people when they need help or specific information. Examples for engagement are provided.

10. Connaway, Lynn Silipigni. 2013. "Meeting the expectations of the community: The engagement-centered library." *Library 2020: Today's Leading Visionaries Describe Tomorrow's Library,* edited by J. Janes, 83–88. Lanham, MD: Scarecrow Press.

    In order for libraries to be relevant in 2020, they will need to continue to adapt and provide services for people to use, create, and curate information and content. It will be important for librarians to develop partnerships with those who create, collect, and analyze data sets in order to provide policies, systems, and services for the storage, access, preservation, and shared use of these data sets. Librarians, library users, and potential users indicate that relationships are important. This may call for a different type of librarian in the future—one who embraces change. New technologies, modes of communication, and delivery of services will continue to force librarians to rethink the services of the moment. This will require developing relationships with members of the community to provide user-centered services and systems that meet their needs and expectations.

Libraries are impacted by the ways in which individuals engage with technology; how they seek, access, contribute, and use information; and how and why they demonstrate these behaviors and do what they do. This selection of work represents a progressive line of inquiry that builds on our research findings and highlights our work in the areas of embedding the library in community workflows and engaging individuals in context. It has provided the library community with behavioral evidence about individuals' perceptions, habits, and requirements to help ensure that future library services are designed around a set of expectations that have been influenced by consumer technologies and modern research and learning environments—designed for the life of today's library user.

NOTES

1. See my blog post on *hangingtogether.org*, "The Elusive User" for more thoughts about this.
2. See the OCLC Research User Studies web page at http://www.oclc.org/research/themes/user-studies.html for more information about this theme.

REFERENCES

Bannon, Brian, Tessie Guillermo, and John Palfrey. 2014. "The Public Library Reimagined." Panel presented at Aspen Ideas Festival, 29 June, in Aspen, Colorado. http://www.aspeninstitute.org/policy-work/communications-society/our-work/dialogue-public-libraries.

Connaway, Lynn Silipigni. 2013. "Meeting the Expectations of the Community: The Engagement-Centered Library." In *Library 2020: Today's Leading Visionaries Describe Tomorrow's Library.* edited by J. Janes. Lanham, MD: Scarecrow Press, p. 83–88.

Connaway, Lynn Silipigni. 2014a. "The Elusive User." *Hangingtogether.org* (blog). http://hangingtogether.org/?p=4451.

Connaway, Lynn Silipigni. 2014b. "Why Libraries? A Call for Use-centered Assessment." *Textos Universitaris de Biblioteconomia I Documentacio* 32, http://bid.ub.edu/en/32/connaway3.htm.

Connaway, Lynn Silipigni, Timothy J. Dickey, and Marie L. Radford. 2011. "'If It Is Too Inconvenient I'm Not Going After It:' Convenience as a Critical Factor in Information-seeking Behaviors." *Library & Information Science Research* 33, no. 3: 179–190.

Connaway, Lynn Silipigni, Donna Lanclos, and Erin M. Hood. 2013. "'I Find Google A Lot Easier than Going to the Library Website.' Imagine Ways to Innovate and Inspire Students to Use the Academic Library." In *Proceedings of the Association of College & Research Libraries (ACRL) 2013 conference,* p. 289–300. http://www.ala.org/acrl/sites/ala.org.acrl/files/content/conferences/confsandpreconfs/2013/papers/Connaway_Google.pdf.

Connaway, Lynn Silipigni, and Marie L. Radford. 2011. *Seeking Synchronicity: Revelations and Recommendations for Virtual Reference.* Dublin, OH: OCLC Research. http://www.oclc.org/reports/synchronicity/full.pdf.

Dempsey, Lorcan. 2015. "From Infrastructure to Engagement: Thinking About the Library in the Life of the User." Keynote presented at *Minitex 24th Annual Interlibrary Loan Conference,* 12 May, in St. Paul. http://www.slideshare.net/lisld/from-local-infrastructure-to-engagement-thinking-about-the-library-in-the-life-of-the-user.

De Rosa, Cathy, Joanne Cantrell, Matthew Carlson, Peggy Gallagher, Janet Hawk, and Charlotte Sturtz. 2010. *Perceptions of Libraries, 2010: Context and Community.* Dublin, OH: OCLC Online Computer Library Center.

De Rosa, Cathy, Joanne Cantrell, Diane Cellentani, Janet Hawk, Lillie Jenkins, and Alane Wilson. 2005. *Perceptions of Libraries and Information Resources: A Report to the OCLC Membership.* Dublin, OH: OCLC Online Computer Library Center.

IMLS. Institute of Museum and Library Services. https://www.imls.gov/.

Jisc. https://www.jisc.ac.uk/.

McDiarmid, E. W. 1940. *The Library Survey: Problems and Methods*. Chicago: American Library Association.

Prabha, Chandra, Lynn Silipigni Connaway, and Timothy J. Dickey. 2006. *Sense-making the Information Confluence: The Whys and Hows of College and University User Satisficing of Information Needs. Phase IV: Semi-structured Interview Study.* Columbus, OH: School of Communication, The Ohio State University.

Priestner, Andy, and Elizabeth Tilley, eds. 2012. *Personalising Library Services in Higher Education: The Boutique Approach*. Farnham, England: Ashgate.

Ranganathan, Shiyali Ramamrita. 1931. *The Five Laws of Library Science*. London: Edward Goldston, Ltd.

Rushkoff, Douglas. 1996. *Playing the Future: What We Can Learn from Digital Kids*. New York: HarperCollins.

1

Reordering Ranganathan: Shifting User Behaviours, Shifting Priorities

Lynn Silipigni Connaway, Ph.D.
OCLC Research

Ixchel M. Faniel, Ph.D.
OCLC Research

A reprint of:

Connaway, Lynn Silipigni, Ixchel M. Faniel, and K. S. Raghavan. 2015. "Reordering Ranganathan: Shifting User Behaviours, Shifting Priorities." *SRELS Journal of Information Management.* 52(1), February 2015, p. 3–23. http://i-scholar.in/index.php/sjim/article/view/60392/51360.

© 2015 Sarada Ranganathan Endowment for Library Science. All rights reserved.

Reprinted with permission.

The article is an abridged version of: Connaway, Lynn Silipigni, and Ixchel M. Faniel. 2014. *Reordering Ranganathan: Shifting User Behaviors, Shifting Priorities.* Dublin, OH: OCLC Research. http://www.oclc.org/content/dam/research/publications/library/2014/oclcresearch-reordering-ranganathan-2014.pdf

The abridgement was done by Dr. K. S. Raghavan.

INTRODUCTION

When Ranganathan proposed his Five Laws of Library Science, he came out with a comprehensive framework and guideline for evaluating library programmes, library activities, and for formulating library policies and strategies. This is clearly indicated by the fact that these statements continue to be extensively cited even today, more than eight decades after their publication. Not only this, there have even been attempts at reformulating these laws to suit the present context of the Web, e-resources, multimedia resources and the resulting developments in information services. Despite the fact that even at the time these laws were formulated books were not the only kind of resources—magazines, newspapers, films, audiorecordings and even microfiche were already in use—Ranganathan stated his first law as "Books are for use." This only suggests that he used the term *'books'* as a substitute for all kinds of media that existed at that time and those that might come into existence in future. "Books are for use" is simply too powerful a statement and too succinct to warrant much improvement.

Ranganathan, like Melvile Dewey, came on the scene at a time when information was scarce; preserving library collections was a major professional concern of librarians. "Books are for use" was the driver. Dewey's classification system was essentially meant to help library users understand how to access materials. Books continue to hold a powerful place in our cultural psyche irrespective of whether it is read on paper or on a computer screen; the point is not, and never was, the medium. When we say, "I just read a great book," what is meant is that we had positive and worthwhile experience digesting new information and transferring someone else's thoughts and ideas into our own. Conversely, when we say, "Oh, it was an awful book," what is meant is that it was not worth our time. These experiences hold true for information or entertainment in any media. A Facebook like or Tweet about a research presentation or a review on Goodreads transmits the same message: "I [processed] this [content], and I would [recommend/not recommend] it to [audience]." It is essentially a new way of saying, "books are for use," "every reader his or her book," or "every book its reader." So are the following examples:

- Facebook post for a YouTube video;
- Embedded link to a scholarly article in a blog post;
- Good Google search rank on a particular phrase;
- Book cover picture on an Interest page.

The difference is that the notions of *'book'* and *'reader'* have expanded and are becoming increasingly more and more complex. Applying Ranganathan's laws to the situation obtaining now shows the difference between the time in which Dewey and Ranganathan worked and the information environment in which we operate today (table 1). We have moved from an era of content scarcity to one of incredible abundance and diversity, which is being contributed to by a multitude of channels and contributors. These differences are at the centre of what has changed the interpretations of the five laws.

TABLE 1. RANGANATHAN'S FIVE LAWS: ORIGINAL AND NEW CONCEPTIONS

	Ranganathan's original statements	New conceptions in the current environment		
First law	Books are for use	E-books are for reading	Netflix is for watching	Blackboard is for studying
Second law	Every reader his/her book	Every listener his/her iTunes	Every artist his Photoshop	Every student his/her EasyBib
Third law	Every book its reader	Every blog its reader	Every Google map its traveler	Every digital repository its researcher
Fourth law	Save the time of the reader	Save the time of the listener	Save the time of the traveler	Save the time of the researcher
Fifth law	Library is a growing organism			

Interestingly the fifth law —"Library is a growing organism"—has not changed. The library is growing given the increasingly daunting array of content facilitated by librarians for individuals to discover access and share. Libraries must provide access to not only externally produced content but also content produced within the academic community.[40] Librarians have moved beyond their doors to bring relevant content to their user community and to make visible to the outside world the content created by their user community clearly indicating an expansion in the places in which librarianship occurs and the tools librarians use to help those they serve achieve their goals. This brings us to the crucial issue being examined in this research, which is: if materials have become so abundant that "books are for use" is now less about scarcity and more about choice, availability, findability and share-ability, what does that do to the five laws? This is not to suggest that it is time to abandon the laws, which are an enormously helpful way to link the goals of librarianship with concrete programmes and activities. What is being suggested here is that a reordering of the five laws be considered in a world where information is becoming increasingly abundant in multiple formats and in a variety of settings. This will help us keep topmost in our mind the way in which the digital and Web revolutions have transformed the balance in our relationships with the user community, resources and services.

The following sections will look at what today's librarians, library researchers and information scientists have said about the changing roles of the five laws and also review relevant literature to show how the five laws still apply, but where, we believe, it's time for a change in focus and emphasis. Findings from our research on user behaviour also will be included to show how the Five Laws of Library Science are as relevant today as they were in 1931.

The new first law: save the time of the reader

Ranganathan had predicted that the fourth law, "save the time of the reader," will become more important once the requirements for the first three laws are satisfied. Given the vast array of content being offered through a multitude of information service providers, scarcity of time is the most pressing issue facing people today. It is proposed here that "save the time of the reader" has become the most important of Ranganathan's five laws and should be the lens through which to interpret the others. Recent research indicates that in the changed environment both saving time and convenience have become important to today's information seekers.[25,28] As libraries have begun to operate alongside other information service providers, such as Google, Amazon and Facebook, how people experience library services, particularly online service, has become more important.[40] Three aspects of time are discussed here:

- Time as simply time; a measure of how long it takes a user to achieve a desired outcome;
- Time as a shorthand for convenience or almost any efficiency-based value that users ascribe to their experience with a library;
- Time as stand-in for the entire service experience beyond the actual quality of content, materials, resources, etc.

EXAMINING THE LAW IN TODAY'S ENVIRONMENT

"Save the time of the reader" touches many aspects of how the library services are designed and delivered; Gorman suggests that if applied correctly, the results have the potential to be transformative.[54] While preserving, cataloguing, presenting and distributing content continue to be important aspects of librarianship, it is necessary to consider how these are carried out as patrons want to satisfy their information needs not only quickly, but also conveniently. Libraries must deliver online services that are compelling enough to attract their intended community,[51,52,64] provide meta-searching capabilities to support searching entire sets of electronic resources, and link resolvers so that readers get access to the best source.[16]

TIME AS TIME

"Time as time" is the most literal reading of the law. Its significance can be linked to rational choice theory. It is also supported by Savolainen's[91] concept of time as a context in information seeking and gratification. What is different today is that it operates within the bounds of different resources and information activities. Today, people are inundated with information requiring review and evaluation to make choices, and time has become a significant constraint as a result.[28] They also are contributing more information. Moreover, many information activities are taking place online. Students' information searches have evolved from browsing books in the stacks to submitting online queries to Google because it is quicker.[2] "Millennials, by their own admission, have no tolerance for delays."[96] They respond quickly to communications from others and expect the same in return,[75] especially from their information sources.[17,18,27,29,101] According to a Pew Research Center report, teachers report that digital technologies "encourage students to assume all tasks can be finished quickly and at the last minute."[82] Yet, librarians and instructors still are adjusting to meet the needs of students. Undergraduate and graduate students reported a preference for searching the Web instead of the online library catalogue, because the Web was fast and easy.[48] Not surprisingly, the Internet and Wikipedia are used extensively to get an initial overview of a topic.[80] Head and Eisenberg report that "almost all" of the students in their study "used course readings, library resources, and public Internet sites such as Google and

Wikipedia, when conducting courserelated research."[56] However, students' use of Wikipedia has been compared to a "covert, underground Learning Black Market"[24,25,106] as its use often is not acknowledged. In the United States and the United Kingdom, students reported citing references in Wikipedia articles, but not the actual Wikipedia articles, because they believed instructors did not value them as much as traditional information sources[24–26]. Librarians also have been adjusting their systems and services for scholars who are now required to provide better management and more accurate metadata for their scholarly works, including research data. Operating within time constraints is an issue especially in the absence of automated methods for metadata generation as these are labour-intensive and time consuming processes suggesting the need for better understanding how scholars work and providing support for improving their efficiency.[21,44] For instance, national and professional bodies in archeology have developed guidelines for data documentation to describe the types of documentation expected, preferred file formats and data points desired.[1,8,9,60,76] However, the guidelines often do not accommodate the realities of field research; so their use in the area has been limited.[47]

TIME AS CONVENIENCE

Convenience encompasses more than the time it takes to fulfill an information need. There is research to suggest that convenience is more important to people than quick service.[25,28] Convenience is defined as "1.) fitness or suitability for performing an action or fulfilling a requirement; and 2.) something (as an appliance, device, service) conducive to comfort or ease" (Merriam-Webster.com). Convenience can be physical or virtual and is based on the context and situation at the time of the need.[23,26,30,31] *Convenience* influences people's choices and actions throughout the information-seeking process.[28] Libraries do not seem to score high because of limited hours, travel time and the time needed to do their research in the library.[25,26,31,81] Search engines are preferred; they are faster and more convenient—easier to use, cost-effective and reliable (i.e., always available).[37] A set of resources may be used consistently simply because that method is now predictable and familiar.[56] A study reported that 74% of respondents did not choose the Internet because it was the best source; they chose the Internet because it was the most convenient or easiest to use (93%) and did not cost much in time or money. Simon[93] had coined the term *'satisfice'* (a combination of *satisfy* and *suffice*) to refer to this kind of user behaviour. Library catalogues have long been the point of discovery and delivery of content. However, today's patrons are more likely to find out about material using other online sources. Web searching has driven higher expectations for online library catalogues. Users expect the interface to be familiar to them, which means seeing their search results rated, reviewed and ranked by relevancy.[10,18,23,25,26,28,31,40] Library catalogues have long been the point of discovery and delivery of content. Web searching has driven higher expectations for online library catalogues. Unfortunately, libraries have not consistently employed their usage data to fully mobilize discovery services in the same way as Google[40] or Amazon. Providing seamless points of access to the content people discover through other online services could be a point of distinction for libraries. There are studies to suggest that people ranked delivery of items as important.[10,20] The library services developed with little input from end users are not easy to use and may have even alienated the users rather than engaged them. Librarians have to acknowledge that individuals have relocated much of their information activities to the Internet; therefore, librarians need to utilize the Web as a place to engage people in new and different ways. Understanding the offline and online lives of our communities will reveal opportunities to engage with them at times and in ways that are both natural and surprising. We must remember that libraries represent a very small subset of the information resources and activities people need today. And the new environment challenges librarians to move from a simple declaration of "save the time of the reader" to a more complex and interconnected priority of: **Embed library systems and services into users' existing workflows.** A library should not add procedural drag to the information activities of its community by asking users to learn separate systems for accessing separate types of media. How can librarians make that happen? Start by accepting "save the time of the reader" as the first law, then modify approaches to the other laws accordingly. Here are a few suggestions for librarians to start rethinking how to apply the spirit of the "save the time of the reader" law:

Inform users

Marketing library services is important and libraries should make the total package of library services appealing and inspiring so that they stand out as unique and essential elements of the modern information ecosystem. Users of library systems should not be required to leave one interface and go to another. Librarians should spend as much or more time working with external systems as internal systems. Librarians should understand end users' pain points and what frustrates them. Users will be inspired when the high-quality, authoritative and unique materials and services are easily found in a variety of workflows. This is an education issue for librarians as much as it is for library users.

Look upstream

Looking upstream is about seeing user needs in a much larger context and thinking broadly within the information profession and other professions related to it. There are a number of factors that might be influencing people's choices about the systems and services they use. Legal issues related to intellectual property is just one example of the kind of information support needed by our users.

CONCLUSION

Since the beginning of the Industrial Revolution, we have been looking for ways to save time. Even when libraries focus on the past as custodians of "cultural heritage" or "memory institutions" it is often at the service of forwardlooking goals. The two objectives—to serve both the materials that define our past and the people who will create our future—are not in opposition. And the balance point is where "save the time of the reader" can be most powerfully applied as a kind of skeleton key to unlock the potential for libraries to brilliantly impact the lives of our communities.

The second law

"Every person his or her book" clearly, connecting every user with the precise content they need—whether from one library's collection, the collective collection or the web collection—is of paramount importance in distinguishing libraries from other information service providers in the digital environment. There is no value in saving the time of the reader if we cannot pinpoint the information the user needs. In the last eight decades evolutionary changes in technology have impacted our world as well as our libraries. The forces reshaping the information landscape—search engines, global connectivity, cloud computing, social networking, big data, hand-held devices, to name but a few—are redefining once again what it means to be a teacher, a scholar, a business person, a student, and a librarian. Nonetheless, the basic principles of Ranganathan's second law carry well into today's world. In 1931, when he wrote his doctrine, Ranganathan's insistence on "every person" was meant to eliminate restrictions for accessing library collections. The law also was concerned with matching a person's information needs with the library resources, which were primarily books in Ranganathan's day. Ranganathan thought the books in a library collection should be based on and responsive to individual demands, accompanied by a professional, knowledgeable staff ready to guide, navigate and assist the information seeker in the information quest. How does Ranganathan's second law apply to the digital, Web-transformed world where relationships with patrons, materials and programs are vastly different? Rubin[88] interprets this law first to librarians, who "should have excellent firsthand knowledge of the people to be served," and second to collections, which "should meet the special interests of the community." "Every person" means the library will serve all people in the community; and "his or her book" refers to the content. In the following paragraphs, we will discuss the two concepts in their original context, review research as to how they apply in today's world, state our interpretation of the second law in our new digital environment and make some recommendations for how librarians can apply our interpretation to their operations. *"Every person"* exudes a strong sense of public purpose, the fervent belief in access to information for all people—a central tenet of librarianship. The efforts by librarians to bring workstations, licensed resources, web content, information literacy and Internet connections to all segments of the population in all parts of the world, even the most remote underscore the importance of available technology. However, the context is shifting and is being redefined around e-content and a multitude of user segments with differing needs of which librarians are not thoroughly knowledgeable. And in some cases, this lack of knowledge may be driving potential users to other information service providers.

THE RISE OF E-CONTENT

Noruzi[74] suggests that the second law could be "every user his or her web resource." A major challenge in fulfilling this is effectively managing the integration of electronic journals, e-books and other e-resources into library collections and making that content discoverable and accessible. Licensed e-content now is the largest collection expenditure for most academic libraries. Locally produced e-content is getting more attention and resources as print collections are moving into a shared environment for management and preservation. Local digital assets and archives are being coordinated with large-scale digital archives. Stewardship of unique assets associated with an institution, such as special collections and research data, are being given increased priority and demand increased resourcing. Librarians also face a challenge with how users perceive libraries' provision of e-content. In one study, researchers were found to "place a very high value on electronic journals, but a much lower value as yet on libraries' provision of other kinds of digital resources."[32] Studies also have reported that university resources were not the first or second choice among academic communities and were not accessed as often as open access materials.[5,13,20,105] A 2005 survey found 90% of respondents describing a search engine as a "perfect" or "good" fit for their lifestyle, whereas only 49% did so for a library and fewer still for an online library.[34] Librarians should try and eliminate the obstacles preventing users from making effective use of electronic resources.

LIBRARIES AND BIG DATA

Thanks to federal funding agency mandates, academic libraries, especially in the U.S., are increasingly being called upon to manage, curate, and/or preserve massive amounts of digital assets—images, text and data. In February 2013, the White House Office of Science and Technology Policy issued a memorandum for science agencies to develop public access policies for research outputs, including publications and data.[59] Lavoie et al.[67] present a framework describing the materials generated during scholarly inquiry now being captured before and after the dissemination of traditional published outcomes. Even though the role of the academic library in aggregating and servicing these assets is still emerging, we see libraries shifting attention from managing a narrowly defined set of materials produced at the end of the research life cycle to managing a broader range of scholarly outputs produced throughout the research life cycle. Kurt de Belder of the Leiden University Libraries (The Netherlands) has described how the library has been gearing up to provide key services related to scholarly outputs. These include virtual research environments, capacities in text and data mining, support for data management and curation, and provisions for copyright consultation and publication support. As the librarians move to becoming service experts, they have been allocated time to develop their new skills. Early signs are that the shift has been well received, with an uptake of new services, an emerging reputation of the library as a "go-to" place and the library being included as a partner in developing funding requests[33].

THE CHANGING LANDSCAPE OF INFORMATION SEEKING

Another major challenge facing libraries relates to developing and updating collections and services to meet the needs of multiple generations of users with differing approaches to information seeking. The different characteristics and information needs of Baby Boomers and Millennials present a dichotomy for library service and system development. Research also suggests that people are more familiar with search engines than with libraries.[24,25,34] Differences in the information behaviour of Baby Boomers, Millennials and screenagers have been reported. For example, Google is the first choice of Millennials and screenagers. Baby Boomers, however, consult their personal libraries first. They also read more and visit libraries. Screenagers also found online library catalogues difficult to use and so use Amazon.com as a discovery tool and then go to the library website. There are generational differences with Virtual Reference Services (VRS) as well. While Boomers' problems were technical, it was personal or hesitation to be involved in online anonymous chats for the other groups. Also, cutting across the different groups was the problem of unfamiliarity with VRS; many did not even know that such a service existed. In short, information-seeking and VRS research suggests that librarians are not necessarily fully cognizant of how faculty and students use library systems or how they view library services. A better understanding of the disparities may prove beneficial to discovering ways to integrate library services in userpreferred environments.[10,18,19]

OUR INTERPRETATION OF THE LAW

"Every person his or her book" is a demanding, and exacting task requiring knowledge of the information needs and preferences of users in the community and anticipating and matching what they will need in the future. Serving everyone with content requires greater care, effort and attention today than before. In the global, interconnected world, we propose a new interpretation of Ranganathan's second law that keeps its principles intact but recognizes these changes and extends a deeper sense of purpose for operating in today's Web-dominated world. Our modern day rephrasing of this law is: Know your community and its needs. The idea is to extend its meaning beyond the people who come to the library and to include virtual users and those who don't use the library. The interpretation of the law also extends to needs beyond physical materials and digital content into the growing demands of the diverse audiences requiring new skills, new services, or new collaborations. For example, needs may range from data management to device support to media expertise. Expanding programs and services to meet some of these new needs will maximize library impact. Understanding community needs is a critical success factor in today's digital environment where so many information service providers operate and community expectations for libraries are being set by experiences with whiz-bang consumer technologies. Failing to embrace these new challenges may drive the community elsewhere and diminish the library's role in content management and delivery.

RECOMMENDATIONS

Meeting the demands of the second law requires that today's librarians should become a part of the communities they serve and be better informed about library communities and their needs. We discuss four approaches for this:

- Performing traditional outreach: Traditional outreach allows librarians to keep a pulse on what's happening;
- Conducting user studies: User studies provide librarians with a means to take a systematic approach to getting answers to a particular question or problem, e.g., what services are used vs. not used;
- Developing collaborative work relationships with users (also known as embedded librarianship) will help librarians develop a deep and shared understanding of user needs;
- Running analytics: Analytics is an application of Big Data. It is the ability to provide forward-looking decisions based on historical data from multiple, disparate data sources. Librarians increasingly will need to partner with institutional staff and external organizations to excel at this activity.

All these approaches yield varied knowledge about which communities libraries are serving and the needs of the communities. Librarians have to think about how the knowledge can be purposefully applied to improving the library. They must know the issues facing the community and understand, from the researchers' perspective, why the community is facing a particular issue. Librarians always have been needs focused.[38,65,86,92,107] However, we propose that librarians focus their engagement with faculty and students in three key ways:

- Start farther upstream in the research cycle at the point when researchers are planning their studies;
- Focus attention on the research processes as well as the research products; and
- Consider the perspectives of those reusing as well as those producing the data.

The focus should be on understanding how the research unfolds and how the data are generated, documented and re-used with respect to the researchers' workflows.

CONCLUSION

Ranganathan's second law is clearly applicable today and carries with it an expanded charge in the new digital environment in which libraries are operating. "Every person his or her book" is now know your community and its needs, with the reinterpretation calling for new services from libraries and new skills from librarians along with continuing the key practices of today. Knowing your community and its needs is a key step in developing these new programs and moving in new directions will help libraries remain transformational places, as central to our shared future as they have been to our shared past. The needs of the 21st century demand that librarians, who serve the public good, develop new habits and mindsets to go along with the traditional roles they have played. It is imperative to expand and extend the library's presence in the community by delivering new, needed services to changing user groups. Moving from "every person his or her book" to know your community and its needs presents an opportunity to bring considerable value to our communities through leadership, collaboration and a range of supporting services.

The new third law: books are for use

This emphasized the importance of *use* vis-à-vis *preservation* and implied that all library procedures and actions and the attitude and behaviour of library staff should be geared to realize this goal. However, many of the facilities considered novel during Ranganathan's time are commonplace today and are taken for granted. Librarians operating in today's increasingly complex information and technology infrastructure must provide proactive, reliable service[28] and must connect with users not merely within the physical library building but also on the Internet so that current and prospective users know how to reach the library and what resources exist beyond books. In this section we discuss the opportunities and challenges of rethinking and expanding the physical and technical infrastructure—the bricks and mortar facility and the browser-based digital doorway— to extend access beyond books and to boost the library's impact in the digital era.

EXAMINING THE LAW IN TODAY'S ENVIRONMENT

Four simple words, "books are for use," elicit a wide range of commentary from scholars on what Ranganathan really meant in 1931 and its contemporary relevance. Some emphasize the service role of the librarian, while others focus on the evolution of newer resource formats and delivery mechanisms.[4,6,16,51,52–54,64,74,102] Carr says that Ranganathan's first law "is, in effect, declaring that a library is a technology."[12] The perception of books as the brand of the modern library endures.[18,22,23,25,34,36] In a national survey of Americans 16 years or older, 80% responded that borrowing books is a "very important" service libraries provide and 73% who had visited a library or bookmobile in the last year did so to borrow print books.[110] This indicates that books and book lending still are very important. However, as librarians continue to extend their content and service offerings, they must be careful that the library isn't identified only as a source and provider of books.

Move beyond books

E-content and improved access are key. Libraries have never been about just books and even at the time of Ranganathan's writing, books were not the only materials libraries collected; the law is not about books per se but about acquiring and making materials available for use.[54] Current scholars emphasize this point, going so far as to replace the word "books" with terms that encompass the variety of content available including digital content.[16,20,51,74] The digital content extends beyond e-journals and e-books to collections that contain such things as older literature, sheet music, art images, biological specimens, archaeological finds and scientific research data.[22,46,47] These days, users—academics in particular—expect everything to be accessible online and are easily frustrated when something is not.[85]

Research data are for use

Driven by demands to increase access to the results of state-sponsored research, librarians have begun to develop services to ensure research data are for use.[14,15,38,62,73,77] Studies by Association of Research Libraries (ARL) and by Association of College and Research Libraries (ACRL) report that finding relevant data and developing data management plans are among current research data services provided by libraries.[95,98] Just as Ranganathan argued that books should be freely available to all, contemporary scholars are calling to make all content openly, freely and easily accessible.[16,51,74] As libraries move beyond books to create better access to physical and digital materials, librarians have had to rethink the infrastructure to keep up with changing times and to manage users' social engagement with experts and peers in virtual environments as well as Face-to-Face (FtF). Ranganathan had stressed improvements to different aspects of the physical infrastructure. While the same holds true today, librarians also must consider designing space for change. Information commons (or learning commons) at the University of Southern California and the University of Iowa in the 1990s were early attempts to provide technology-enabled spaces where students could collaborate and seek help from library and computer services staff.[68] There is no one-size-fits-all approach and more recent reconfigurations of space have emphasized flexibility in the face of changing and, at times, competing user needs.[78,89] Some emphasize experimentation, such as the University of North Carolina at Charlotte, that targeted the 11-day final exam period as "a key time to support—and engage—stressed students."[58] A committee of nine library staff and faculty members implemented changes to space and activities to BLAST the stress from students, including bouncing ball activities, such as ping-pong and indoor sponge basketball; lounging opportunities in comfortable seating and low tables; art activities with coloring books, Play-Doh® and puzzles, etc. Maker spaces or creativity spaces are another example of places where students can access specialist equipment to build, create and craft. By providing physical space and tools, people can share resources and knowledge while engaging in hands-on experimentation.[49]

Change user perceptions

A major challenge is that users may not know the range of skills and services librarians can offer and their failure to acknowledge the role librarians have in the online information-seeking process. Users often do not recognize that the services they value are courtesy of the library. Studies report that college and university students and faculty who value online library catalogues and databases such as LexisNexis, PubMed and MEDLINE don't associate them with the library.[18,23,34,36,80] Perceptions of the user community also have affected the effectiveness of institutional repositories which remained practically empty given social, organizational and technical barriers, including a poor understanding of faculty and student motivations and incentives.[72,90] Disciplinary data repositories face similar barriers.[44,99,100]

OUR INTERPRETATION OF THE LAW

Ranganathan promoted the use of books and other library resources when the practice at the time was to store and preserve them. He was not against the storage and preservation of books, but he believed these activities should be conducted in order to make the resources available for individuals to use them. It is safe to say that the core meaning of "books are for use" is about access, and access remains a key issue more than 80 years since it first was identified by Ranganathan. Today, freeing books from their chains takes on new meaning. Our interpretation of the law is: **Develop the physical and technical infrastructure needed to deliver physical and digital materials** as it is not just the availability of physical and digital materials that matters, but more so the infrastructure—both physical and technical—that libraries put in place to capture and deliver them. Today's users often lack awareness of library offerings, whether materials, technology, or services. The lack of awareness seems to rise in parallel with the increase in library alternatives. There also are users who are accessing materials but don't realize the materials are being made available by the library. One way librarians can build user awareness is through a revamped physical and technical infrastructure; redesigning physical space in the library to offer creative areas open to the research and learning community as purposefully redesigned spaces are what get people to come to the library. Once in the door, opportunities present themselves to ramp up users' awareness of the physical and digital resources available in and accessible through the library. There are opportunities to introduce them to new equipment and technologies and to provide assistance during use. It is also important to ensure that users trust their virtual environment and its offerings. Trust can take on different meanings based on the situation of use. While Millennials may want assurances about who is monitoring Virtual Reference Services (VRS) before deciding to use them, scholars sharing and reusing data through a digital repository may want assurances that the data are being preserved and the repository is sustainable. Taking heed of the social dynamics at play in users' decisions to use and adopt technologies also must be part of the solution if libraries are to be successful.

RECOMMENDATIONS

As librarians continue to build infrastructure, it is important to build users' awareness of the changes as well as to maintain their trust. Although libraries enjoy a strong institutional reputation within the communities they serve, that doesn't necessarily translate into increased library usage. We outline several recommendations for librarians to consider:

- Provide a warm transfer: By working FtF with individuals, library staff can help increase trust on a personal level and can positively influence future library visits. A way to leverage and extend the bond created between users and librarians in the physical environment is to demonstrate online systems and services during in-person encounters.[18]
- Understand and internalize users' interests: Identification plays a role in building trust in organizations. How does an organization demonstrate that it identifies with its users? An idea that is applicable even beyond the initial development cycle is to have users participate in the development of library systems and services.[103] Libraries also can show a commitment to internalizing users' interests at the point of need, e.g., by installing pop-up chat services on library websites and in online catalogues when users are idle or their search retrieves no sources.[18] Some college and university librarians provide video introductions to themselves on the library website or YouTube that are linked to the library website.[69]
- Be visible: The value librarians create across a range of activities also must be made more visible so that librarians' expertise is identified and eventually internalized.[40] As library services continue to evolve, we recommend incorporating explicit promotion of librarians' expertise as faculty services specialists, as academic partners. A study found that faculty at the University of Houston expressed surprise that librarians could offer research data services beyond traditional library instruction (Peters and Dryden, 2011).[77]
- Leverage the power of social influence: The library needs to have a presence, both physically on campus and virtually through social media and a Web presence, which can be difficult with limited resources. People who didn't use VRS indicated that they would try it if it were recommended by a trusted librarian, colleague or friend.[18]

CONCLUSION

Despite an explosion of new formats and various delivery methods, printed books appear to have a secure future in libraries. People still want them and actively search for them, especially known titles. However, the library is not the first place people go for help with their personal and academic information needs. This should not be viewed as a failure but an opportunity. It's an opportunity for librarians to promote and develop new ways to engage, get to know and create relationships with their communities. The opportunity starts with the recognition that "books are for use" encompasses more than the content that needs to be preserved and organized for access. The library Ranganathan knew has undergone dramatic changes in scope, mission and service models. Today, libraries must enable users to move between two worlds—the physical and the virtual.

The new fourth law: every book its reader

"Every book its reader" depends entirely on the previous law "every reader his or her book." While librarians always have had to make collection development choices based on both budgets and the needs, or perceived needs, of the communities they serve, doing so from a judgmental, restrictive stance has rarely been well received in the long run. Now that we have opened up the definition of what "book" means to include any possible medium, including raw data and transactional information of all kinds, "every book" means, essentially, every single, possible piece of communicative material that anyone, anywhere might find useful. Debates about what kind of materials libraries should store and provide access to and on issues related to how these decisions could be a form of censorship are not new. Although controversial, Ranganathan believed the librarian cannot reduce the content made available to the end users. Even though we do not know what materials may be important to a particular student, researcher, author or community, librarians no longer are legitimately able to say, "we don't cover that topic" or "we can't help you with that question." In the networked world of the Web, there are many other information options and anyone a library turns away will seek answers elsewhere, often satisficing and taking sources that may not be authoritative. The three values that are broadly applicable are:

- Discoverability
- Access
- Use

Librarians provide personal service in order to help maximize all of the above. We know that:

- Every book has a reader;
- Every TV show has its fans (and critics); and
- Every piece of data is useful to some researcher.

What we can do is apply modern tools to help connect the community to information and services as efficiently and elegantly as possible.

EXAMINING THE LAW IN TODAY'S ENVIRONMENT

It is difficult to determine how best to get relevant and authoritative content into the hands of users since preferred media change over time, access points evolve and social and cultural environments differ greatly from person to person. Today librarians are faced with the challenge of developing and updating collections and services to meet the needs of multiple generations of users with differing approaches to information seeking.[27] Research in the area of information-seeking behaviour suggests three broad focus areas that hold the potential to provide a framework on which we can move forward to interpret the law:

- Understanding the flow in workflow;
- Acknowledging the role of online social interaction; and
- Paying more attention to context.

USER WORKFLOWS—CONNECTING THE DOTS

Addressing the learning goals of the user communities has been at the heart of library collection development. However, in recent decades the tools with which users address their needs have changed. Some tools are clearly more universal. For example, many information seekers, regardless of demographics, make heavy use of Web information sources, such as Wikipedia and Google.[20,22,57,80] On the other hand, college students rate libraries significantly higher than all respondents in terms of lifestyle fit, for both online and for physical libraries[35] and journal articles are reported as the main resource of interest to researchers.[85] These are fairly consistent with most investigations of information-seeking behaviours. When looked at from the point of *matching every book to its reader,* however, these issues provide points within a workflow, not examples of actual workflows. For example, while college students are inclined to rely more heavily on the library, the library is the *who* of their flow, not the *what* or the *how*. Are they using the library for high-speed wifi access? For meeting and social space? For access to print materials? Similarly researchers value journal articles and the articles are the *what*. But how do they find them? Any information workflow relies on some combination of these elements and to add value, we should understand the relationships between them and how they are changing. The distance between any information need and the right book is a function of the difference between a successful, efficient workflow and one with dissatisfying results. Improving and enhancing the workflow experience for users is essential to how libraries interact with their communities. Librarians are mediators, helping to bridge the gap by connecting the dots between user requirements and available resources. Earlier most materials used to be available only through libraries, now users can find them directly online. Libraries need to employ new kinds of mediation that support discovery, access and use. Archives, libraries and cultural heritage institutions have used social networking technologies such as Facebook, Twitter and blogs with some success. For example, the library at the University of Nevada, Reno brought their special collections to life by creating pages for several students who attended the university in the early 1900s.[42] However, the issue is that the library's Facebook pages, Twitter streams and blog posts are not part of the users' workflow in the same way as Google or Wikipedia.[24,25] Several academic libraries have increased discovery of their collections by adding links to Wikipedia.[43,66,97] The approach should be to create options that allow users to craft personal workflows that are flexible and efficient.

Social media

The role of social networking and social media in information seeking has been studied in the past decade. This phenomenon is interesting in part because of the volume. But we also are interested because these traces of social behaviour are both expressible and quantifiable in very granular ways. People always have been social about their learning and the most natural first step for information seeking is to ask the people with whom one is already in contact.[83] The tendency to trust peers and peer-based evaluations of information sources is strong. Online social media and networking activities differ from traditional interactions in one important way: they leave more permanent marks (think of Amazon reviews vs. simply asking your friends for a recommendation for a good book). The former is available for wider dissemination, can be used (essentially) forever and can be merged with other ratings to provide an average score. Online, social interactions are another set of important dots that information seekers will use to connect to what they need.

Complex Contexts

Connecting the right dots: When there is a profusion of resources and information services available, some of them will be, for whatever reason, wrong for a particular information seeker. It is important that the information seeker has the context to make that decision in this increasingly complex information environment, which is exemplified in the evidence that academic researchers increasingly reuse each other's data.[11,45–47,87,111] As information professionals librarians need to provide services that make access to deeper, more authoritative sources of content available in ways that users can adopt into their workflows. Connaway and Dickey[20] suggest that online library catalogues should operate more like search engines, but that is only part of the story. "… The poor usability, high complexity, and lack of integration of many electronic resource discovery systems have raised the … barrier to information search and retrieval [and] distract users from focusing on the content; analysis and evaluation that would help them learn and make sense of what they have discovered." The ability to use a search engine does not mean that one is able to find quality information.[108] Users can't easily discern whether the content ranked high by a search engine is indeed relevant. Here, libraries are at an advantage with their staff acting as what Ranganathan[84] called "canvassing agents."

OUR INTERPRETATION OF THE LAW

It was mentioned earlier that our interpretation of Ranganathan's third law goes back to three areas that help connect "every book" to "its reader": **Increase the discoverability, access and use of resources within users' existing workflows.** Factors and judgments that influence decisions to reuse colleagues' data are identified in a study of data reuse within the Earthquake Engineering (EE) community.[46] All three goals of this law—discoverability, access and use—are wrapped up in issues of workflow, social connections and context. Understanding not only what context people need but also how they get it and what they use it for will be important in determining how to best support them:

- Finding relevant information—the discovery process, which is attached to workflow and social connections;
- Getting it—accessibility, which is often a factor of both workflow and context; and
- Understanding and trusting it enough to be able to decide to use it and have ways of doing so that are convenient and consistent with their goals. Here workflow, context and social connections come into play.

Workflow appears across all three goals. The tasks that Ranganathan used to illustrate how these could be enhanced are important. However, they are limited to what can be done within the library's walls and do not consider users' workflows. For example, making a catalogue look and behave more like Google won't make it as popular as Google. Improving the shelving to the point where it is as attractive and useful as any retail store display won't get the resources in front of users. And the largest set of journals is worthless if a researcher's peers are Tweeting and linking elsewhere. There also are other factors identified in the literature regarding the importance understanding users' workflows.[80] "Every book its reader" is a simple phrase, but there are now trillions of pieces of information and every user is no longer just a reader, but a judge, reviewer, channel, content creator and, often, even a librarian. There are signs that libraries have begun to adapt to a flood of new workflows and are finding new ways to support this law, ways that adhere both to its original intent as well as new ones given the new environment.

RECOMMENDATIONS

For the three areas we've discussed throughout this chapter—discoverability, access, use—we have some specific ideas about how to apply our interpretation:

- Increase discovery through partnerships: That there is lateral thinking among content creators and providers with a view to maximize the reach of their materials is obvious. For example, it is not uncommon for a publisher to provide content related to a work in different media; the growing number of popular books that are released with video trailers on YouTube indicates this. These also may be discussed and shared in social media. Thus, it is no longer enough to think in terms of *'writer to publisher to book store (or library) to reader.'* Librarians need to consider the points at which content can intersect with users' preferred workflows. Librarians need to establish partnerships outside the "normal" scope of librarianship. Libraries should not rely heavily on users coming to library-specific places for "every book" to be discovered by "its reader." This might manifest as:
  - Working with technology companies to expose library metadata into more and vastly different user workflows;
  - Teaming with logistics companies to solve issues of shared print collections, such as transportation and delivery of physical materials; and
  - Making library data compatible with other formats, such as linked data.

- Increase access through redundancy: Having materials in one format may not be enough when serving users with widely diverse needs and workflows. Of course, traditionally libraries often have been the only places where information seekers with barriers to accessibility can get to relevant materials in a variety of formats. But today it is not just whether the material can be accessed but whether it will be.[79] The mere availability of some material does not mean that it will be highly valued as an information source by audiences who have many other options. Librarians must provide more pathways and deliver material in multiple ways. For example:
  - When providing reading lists, librarians could link to open-source options when available; provide access to the audio versions of the book; link to reviews on Amazon, to the Facebook pages and Twitter accounts of authors and to Wikipedia pages with information about the series or other works by the author;
  - Libraries can make the online library catalogue and website available on multiple platforms and tablet- and mobile-friendly; and
  - Librarians should let users know about alternatives to the library's offerings, such as local book stores, subject experts, listservs, Facebook groups, etc.

- Increase use through marketing and social networking: Lack of knowledge of what the library has to offer is one of the largest barriers to library use. Marketing research has shown that frequency (how often a message is seen) and how recently a message has been seen are keys to effective advertising. Simple advertising campaigns such as providing ongoing messaging in those places where users are getting their information and engaging with others should be considered. Advertising not only will help promote *every book* within users' workflows but will also enhance the library's brand as an information source.

CONCLUSION

The information that meets a user's need always has been context dependent; but more so in today's complex information environment when so many people are using so many powerful, new tools to discover, access and use information. We have come to the point at which the provision of information resources at unheard of scales has become somehow both incredibly useful and yet, at the same time, mundane.

- Routine Google searches turn up millions of results;
- Wikipedia hosts, as of April 2014, more than 32 million pages;
- HathiTrust provides open access to more than 11,145,244 volumes;[55]
- Half of all adult Facebook users have more than 200 friends in their networks;[94] and
- LinkedIn, as of April 2014, has professional profiles for more than 277 million people, which is more than the adult population of the United States.

The figures are huge; however, for a researcher about to add data to a study, an author promoting her work on YouTube or a community loading articles online as they try to maintain transparency about a public works program, the *"book"* in *"every book its reader"* has moved from a record of something in the past to an active part of an important project with goals that reach into the future. Ranganathan recommended extensive cross-referencing to make accessible the contents of *every book*. In the present day context "every book" no longer means "every one of the books of the library" but applies to content across all kinds of formats and media. Drawing from Ranganathan's reference to the role of librarians as *canvassing agents,* we suggest that librarians work towards finding ways to connect people to the "10% that's not crud" from each user's point of view. This view provides both a sobering limitation on what we can expect from our technology and an encouraging vision about the future importance of library staff in an expanding information environment.

The new fifth law: a library is a growing organism

What does it mean for libraries to grow in today's content-rich, time-poor, attention-driven environment? Ranganathan focused his discussions of growth on the size of four factors—books, staff, readers, and the library's physical infrastructure—because he believed growth and change in any one of them affected the others. In the next section, we consider recent growth and change in these four factors. Then we discuss our interpretation of the law. Unlike prior chapters, our interpretation of the law does not include a rephrasing of the law itself. Instead, we propose an additional factor libraries may want to consider growing.

EXAMINING THE LAW IN TODAY'S ENVIRONMENT

A number of researchers and writers have reflected on Ranganathan's ideas of growth and generally agree that the law is still useful, especially when enhanced with new examples and clarifications. In the following paragraphs we examine the four factors that Ranganathan had focused on in today's environment.

The Collection

Kwanya, Stilwell and Underwood[64] explain that electronic materials, digitization efforts, services and new kinds of infrastructure for remote access all need to be included in any definition of growth. The sheer number of books, articles, databases, movies, maps, etc. provided by most libraries today will dwarf the collections that were available in the early 20th century. More recently there is growth in the research data, a relatively new type of material, being generated by the academic communities. Noruzi[74] suggests that providing access to content may involve a more intense and wide ranging winnowing process on the part of librarians adding an important editorial element to the idea of the library collection that encompasses not just what the library owns, licenses and holds, but also what it values.

Library staff

Libraries throughout the world are facing the problem of lack of funds for creating new positions and hiring new personnel. The roles of librarians change with changes in user needs and demands and the technology employed. A survey conducted for Research Libraries UK found skill gaps in nine key areas in which subject librarians could be supporting researchers' needs[3]. Even though many librarians may want to hire new staff with these skills, a survey found that the reality for most will be training existing staff. This emphasizes the importance of continuing education programs and workshops focused on skill development.[61]

The infrastructure

Growth of infrastructure is not just about growth in the volume of content, but it is growth in resources necessary to meet service demands. Changes in the information environment necessitate rethinking the role of the library to explore how it can become more about collaborating, learning, teaching, creating, playing, relaxing, studying and researching with the aid of physical space, people, media and technology. We have discussed cases in which space has been successfully repurposed into study areas, learning commons and maker spaces. As use of the collection has shifted to electronic resources, we have seen changes in the library's physical and technical infrastructure. Library space, e.g. space earlier occupied by print resources, is being repurposed.

Patron use

Kwanya, Stilwell and Underwood[64] define "growth as extending beyond the simplicity of numbers and size and incorporating complexities relating to diverse user needs and wants." The objective is to apply the knowledge gained about users toward improvements in existing services as well as the creation of new services. In order to determine what collections to maintain in which formats, how to allocate and design infrastructure and what roles and responsibilities to assign staff and how to train them, it is imperative to know how people use the collections and infrastructure and where they need assistance and education from the library staff. Growth within shifting contexts means growing whatever elements of collection, staff, infrastructure and patron use that are currently part of our users' expectations. Definitions of library services will change. We need to grow the ways users can engage with whatever they value from libraries, whether papyrus rolls, maker spaces or data management instruction.

OUR INTERPRETATION OF THE LAW

We agree that "a library is a growing organism." There is a need for continual evolution of the library based on the needs and behaviours of current and prospective users. While we offer no reinterpretation of the law, we do want to expand what growth means in today's highly connected, competitive and shifting information environment. Drawing from Ranganathan's metaphor, we propose another major area of a library that is capable of growth:

Share of attention

Media analysts use the term to describe the total amount of time a person has available to spend on activities and materials of choice.[7,41] Television has experienced a decline in share of attention relative to online activities such as Facebook. What portion of individuals' time is spent using library services and resources? We believe share of attention is essential to promoting growth and change in libraries across all the other dimensions—collection, staff, infrastructure, and patron use. Toward that end, we discuss three ways to think about nurturing its growth:

- Relevance;
- Visibility; and
- Unique capabilities.

These metrics suggest a dramatic difference in how libraries need to measure growth and success. Since we have suggested that the most important of Ranganathan's laws today is "save the time of the reader," we need to find ways that factor time, convenience and usefulness into library metrics.

Relevance

Before trying to measure the relevance of any service, it is important to have a good idea of what library resources and services are used, or not used, and more importantly, why are they used or not used? Carr[12] suggests enabling users to select materials—referred to as Demand-Driven Acquisition (DDA)—giving the users a degree of control that entices them to try library services and resources as another way to grow the library. The library is just one of many information service providers and, as such, needs to consider providing an "inside-out" library experience.[40] To be considered relevant within people's share of attention, libraries need to be discovered not only by their local community through library services but also by the larger Web population through external sites and services.

Visibility

Most people do not know the library services being offered or the various formats of material available for use.[34] Research suggests a library's value can be demonstrated through various marketing activities, such as promotion of collections and services, advertisement of the library brand and resources and integration with external services users employ, such as Web browsers, Facebook, Twitter and Wikipedia.[28] Several initiatives that have been quite creative in raising the visibility of libraries and library resources have been mentioned when discussing laws 1–4. We provide three additional examples below:

- **Wikipedian in Residence Projects:** Host Wikipedians to help contribute entries to Wikipedia related to the institution's resources and services to serve as a liaison between the institution and the Wikipedia community;

- **Slam the Boards and Enquire Initiatives:** With Slam the Boards, librarians participate in answer boards and Social Question and Answer (SQA) sites to answer questions during pre-determined times. At the end of each answer users are told that a librarian provided the information. The objective is to let users know that libraries and librarians are a viable alternative for users information needs.[63]
- **Building and Analyzing Online Audiences through Twitter:** Yep and Shulman[109] found that the Richard Stockton College of New Jersey's Bjork Library's Twitter account served as a gateway for information within and outside the library, which raised the library's visibility.

Unique capabilities

What is the Unique Selling Point (USP) of libraries vis-à-vis other information service providers? The term USP, coined by marketers and advertisers, showcases an organization's competitive advantage which other organizations simply cannot offer. In the past, an important USP for libraries was that their materials were freely and centrally available in an environment where resources were scarce and costly. While this selling point is still true, it is no longer unique.[39] Libraries are unique in today's information environment in that they have, in most cases, a very strong community or institutionally-based physical presence. This sets them apart from almost all online information choices. One cannot simply walk into Amazon or call up Facebook and ask a question. Nobody from LinkedIn will sit with you and help you design your resume. Librarians contribute an overwhelmingly positive aspect to the library brand. They are a major USP that should be promoted as the library's most valuable resource. Their ability to develop ongoing relationships in person and online should be leveraged.[18] Their expertise is unique, valuable, and can be applied to entirely new areas of research support.[50,70,71] Recently, the Association of Research Libraries (ARL) has partnered with the Association of American Universities (AAU) and The Association of Public and Land-grant Universities (APLU) around a SHared Access Research Ecosystem (SHARE) to ensure compliance with funding agency mandates and to meet the needs of its stakeholders.[104] Reference already has been made to librarians' role in developing and offering research data.

RECOMMENDATIONS

Librarians need to consider how to increase the library's share of attention in addition to the collection, staff, infrastructure and patron use. We provided three ways to nurture share of attention by identifying the relevance, increasing the visibility, and promoting the unique capabilities of library services. In this context it is important to remember that for most people the library is not the first or main choice to get information[31]. Recommendations for measuring these three ways of increasing share of attention follow.

Relevance

For relevance, librarians should leverage the strengths of non-library services. Librarians need to know what users already value as part of their workflows in order to influence or try to change their choices and practices. Understanding the differences and user preferences provide good cues on how to improve library services. Connaway and Radford[18] suggest that library tools should be integrated into the services and resources people use making library services and resources conveniently discoverable and accessible. Librarians should make sure real world use of services is being examined, rather than how librarians use it or think their communities use it. In focus group interviews with WorldCat.org users and librarians,

Connaway and Wakeling[19] found that librarians judge library services in light of their own interaction with the tools rather than considering actual users' expectations and judgments.

Visibility

Librarians should measure the ways in which users find and learn about library services by tracking the number of clicks or views on websites and conducting brand awareness surveys and interviews. Librarians also may want to measure connections from services most used by users, connections to most used services, and connections to other libraries as no one library has all the answers.

Unique capabilities

It has been mentioned earlier that unique capabilities refer to those services libraries are providing that simply are not available anywhere else. Libraries are unique among many information services in that they provide real, live people and physical and virtual spaces. Users are much more likely to use and recommend services to others if a trusted librarian introduces them.[18] Google never knows if it provides the right link and Amazon can't tell if a book purchased for a new mother taught her something important. But a librarian has the opportunity to interact with people making it possible to provide services and sources that meet their needs and expectations. Librarians should measure the effectiveness of services based on the users' perceptions of success. Librarians also should move beyond surveys of how library space is being used and should conduct structured observations and interviews with the people using the space. It is not enough to know that the various spaces, whether physical or virtual, are busy. Librarians need to understand when and how the spaces are being used. Librarians have a unique set of skills that can be applied to a variety of services, yet many faculty and students can't think of librarians beyond book and journal provision. It's not enough to have the skills; librarians have to showcase them through instruction, consultation and collaboration. Being nice to customers is important as it translates into positive experiences.[18] It is important for librarians to incorporate basic customer service metrics as a growth goal.

Conclusion

The "inside-out" library[40] is an inversion of traditional metrics in many ways. Most content is not gathered in a centralized storage area inside the library; it is out there, and the librarians' job is to help users find it. In a world where Ranganathan's fourth law, "save the time of the reader," is the most important, our measurements of growth need some "inside–out" thinking too. Librarians need to change how they think about growth. A set of nice, simple, linear graphs that show how collections, staff and infrastructure grow over time relative to the size of the communities they serve is comforting. It's easy to communicate, but is flawed. The process of guiding library growth needs to be one in which experimentation is not just tolerated or accepted but actively sought out and brought into planning processes and everyday work. The information environment and social networking landscape we are living in is so new, so big and changes so quickly that anything less than an experimental plan is doomed to fail, because by the time we think we understand, say, MySpace, it's all about Facebook. If Ranganathan's fifth law, "a library is a growing organism," is to remain true, we need to decide what growth means. How do we measure it in an environment where convenience is king and where being as invisible as possible within our users' information searches is a sign of success? We've suggested librarians consider growing share of attention. There probably are other areas of growth that also should be considered, and we encourage the profession to discuss and suggest additional ones, because one thing is for sure: if we don't know how to describe our growth and success, we will not know whether our results are positive or negative. Our interpretation and reordering of Ranganathan's five laws is given in the table below.

Ranganathan's original conception	Our interpretation and reordering
Save the time of the reader	Embed library systems and services into users' existing workflows
Every person his or her book	Know your community and its needs
Books are for use	Develop the physical and technical infrastructure needed to deliver physical and digital materials
Every book its reader	Increase the discoverability, access and use of resources within users' existing workflows
A library is a growing organism	

Conclusions

The purpose and scope of OCLC's Research activity area "User Behavior Studies & Synthesis," centers on how users engage with technology and content. Ranganathan's *Five Laws of Library Science* has greatly influenced our thoughts on the work of libraries and librarians. We realized the five laws provide a framework for our research activity area as well as a lens through which to view the information environment. The intent here is to help interpret the five laws in the context of currently available resources and services, and user behaviours when engaging with them. The idea has been to suggest how libraries and librarians can better connect to those behaviours. Our intent here is not to include all user behaviour research, which would be virtually impossible given the significant amount of work done in the area. The objective is to shape the direction of our research and put it within a context that would be timely and relevant for librarians, library researchers and information scientists as they think about making changes in practice and developing an agenda for future research. In view of the fact that it is the lack of time, not content, that is one of the most pressing issues people face, we consider "save the time of the reader" the most important law today; therefore, as we set up goals for our libraries to grow and improve, we need to consider how to save users time, in more places and in ways that are convenient and familiar to them. We have identified *convenience* a moving target, dependent on the situation individuals find themselves in when they need information and on the context of the specific situation. Surprisingly, in our studies of Virtual Reference Services (VRS), we found that many people who were asking questions through VRS actually were sitting in the library! Why did they choose VRS and not Face-to-Face (FtF) reference services? There are multiple reasons—not wanting to lose their seat or table, not feeling like moving or getting up from the chair, not wanting to leave personal belongings to get an answer to their questions, or not feeling comfortable asking the question FtF. Regardless of the reason, in this instance, many people saw VRS as being more convenient and faster than FtF. There is no value in saving the time of the reader if the content needed cannot be found and accessed, which is why "every person his or her book" is next in our list. Librarians are redefining the communities they serve around e-content and a wide range of needs and demographics. Our world has been transformed by the Web, changing the way people interact with the information environment and making it necessary for librarians to change the way materials and programs are developed and delivered. One size fits none, so it is important that there are multiple options for discovery and access to resources and content based on each individual's context and situation at the time of his or her need. It requires a difficult balance between personalized and generalized service, which is why we believe it is imperative to constantly collect, analyze and discuss data to help librarians know their communities and their needs. This transitions us to the laws "books are for use" and "every book its reader." We believe these laws are interconnected and build on each other. "Books are for use" pertains to the ongoing evaluation and assessment of the library's physical and technical infrastructure in relation to the target users' behaviours and needs. It involves looking beyond the content and its containers to the infrastructure that provides access to the content. Providing content people want depends upon the reliability and integrity of the library's systems that make it discoverable and accessible. Our interpretation of "every book its reader" focuses on increasing the discoverability, access and use of resources and doing so within users' workflows. It is dependent on the provision of resources and systems addressed in discussions about the "books are for use" law. Interestingly, in the midst of a multitude of technically mediated delivery channels, our findings show that human sources still play a huge role in users' information activities. Librarians have an opportunity to become part of users' social networks and to put resources in the context of users' information needs. This brings us to the final law, which underlies the previous four: "A library is a growing organism." While we do not attempt to reinterpret this law, we do discuss *share of attention* as another area librarians should consider growing by elevating their relevance, visibility and unique capabilities in the eyes of their users. We find library growth and change most readily apparent in library approaches to exposing content created within their institutions, from digitized special collections to research data. Not only are collections growing in size and type, but library staff is experiencing growth by retooling existing skills, hiring new people with new areas of expertise and changing users' perceptions of librarians' capabilities. The infrastructure is changing as librarians work more closely with their offices of research and information technology, researchers on their campuses, and build external relationships with other academic institutions. Patron use also is changing with increased demand for developing new kinds of literacy, new forms of engagement with librarians and new services that support their research needs. Ranganathan's laws—even taken verbatim, with no changes or additions—are as helpful today as they were when Ranganathan formulated these. They provide a framework that keeps us focused on the core values of librarianship that have remained remarkably consistent across a time that has seen incredible changes in information technology. It is equally remarkable that the laws still are as relevant to small public libraries as they are to the largest research institutions in the world. It should be obvious to any reader of this report that we hold Ranganathan's work and his laws in great esteem. Our intent is to reflect on them, not to supplant them. In all probability, others will continue to use his laws in this way for another hundred years, and our particular thoughts at this point in time will become helpful (hopefully) footnotes. These laws will continue to serve as a sign post.

NOTES

1. Aitcheson, K. 2009. "Standards and guidance in archaeological archiving: The work of the archaeological archives forum and the institute for archaeologists." *The Grey Journal* 5, no. 2: 67–71. http://www.greynet.org/images/Contents_TGJ.V5.N2.pdf.

2. Alves, J. 2013. "Unintentional knowledge: What we find when we're not looking." *The Chronicle of Higher Education: The Chronicle Review* (23 June). http://chronicle.com/article/Unintentional-Knowledge/139891/?cid=cr&utm_source=cr&utm_medium=en.

3. Auckland, M. 2012. *Re-skilling for Research*. London: Research Information Network. http:// www.rluk.ac.uk/files/RLUK%20Re-skilling.pdf.

4. Barner, K. 2011. "The library is a growing organism: Ranganathan's Fifth Law of library science and the academic library in the digital era." *Library Philosophy and Practice*. http://unllib.unl.edu/LPP/barner.htm.

5. Beetham, H; McGill L; Littlejohn, A. 2009. *Thriving in the 21st century: Learning literacies for the digital age* (LLiDA Project). Glasgow: The Caledonian Academy, Glasgow Caledonian University. http://www.academy.gcal.ac.uk/llida/LLiDAReportJune2009.pdf (inaccessible 26 October 2015).

    Alternative URL http://www.caledonianacademy.net/spaces/LLiDA/uploads/Main/LLiDAreportJune09.pdf (accessed 26 October 2015).

6. Bhatt, R.K. 2011. "Relevance of Ranganathan's Laws of Library Science in library marketing." *Library Philosophy and Practice*. http://unllib.unl.edu/LPP/bhatt.htm.

7. Blanchard, O. 2006. "The continuing shift from 'market share' to 'attention share'." *Corante*. http://marketing.corante.com/editorial/archives/2006/09/post_5.php. (inaccessible 26 October 2015)

8. Brown, A.; Perrin, K. 2000. *A model for the description of archaeological archives*. Forth Cumberland: English Heritage Centre for Archaeology. http://www.eng-h.gov.uk/archives/archdesc.pdf. (inaccessible 26 October 2015).

9. Brown, D.H. 2007. *Archaeological archives: A guide to best practice in creation, compilation, transfer and curation*. n.p.: Archaeological Archives Forum. http://www.archaeologyuk.org/archives/.

10. Calhoun, K; Cantrell, J; Gallagher, P; Hawk, J. 2009. *Online Catalogs: What Users and Librarians Want: An OCLC report,* OCLC, Dublin.

11. Carlson, S; Anderson, B 2007. "What are data? The many kinds of data and their implications for data re-use." *Journal of Computer-Mediated Communication* 12, no. 2: 635–661. Do i:10.1111/j.1083-6101.2007.00342.

12. Carr, P.L. 2014. "Reimagining the Library as a Technology: An Analysis of Ranganathan's Five Laws of Library Science within the Social Construction of Technology Framework." *Library Quarterly* 84, no. 2: 152–164.

13. Centre for Information Behaviour and the Evaluation of Research. 2008. *Information Behaviour of the Researcher of the Future: A CIBER Briefing Paper.* CIBER: London.

14. Choudhury, G.S. 2008. "Case study in data curation at John Hopkins University." *Library Trends* 57, no. 2: 211–220.

15. Choudhury, G.S. 2010. "Data curation: An ecological perspective." *College & Research Libraries News* 71: 194–196.

16. Cloonan, M.V. and Dove, J.G. 2005. "Ranganathan online: Do digital libraries violate the Third Law?" *Library Journal* 130, no. 6: 58–60.

17. Connaway, L.S, Radford, M.L. 2007. "Service sea change: Clicking with screenagers through virtual reference." *Sailing into the Future: Charting our destiny: Proceedings of the Thirteenth National Conference of the Association of College and Research Libraries,* March–April 2007, Baltimore, edited by Hugh A. Thompson. Chicago: Association of College and Research Libraries. http://www.oclc.org/research/publications/archive/2007/connaway-acrl.pdf.

18. Connaway, L.S; Radford, M.L. 2011. *Seeking Synchronicity: Revelations and Recommendations for Virtual Reference.* OCLC Research. Dublin. http://www.oclc.org/reports/synchronicity/full.pdf.

19. Connaway, L.S.; Wakeling, S. 2012. *To Use or Not to Use WorldCat.org: An International Perspective from Different User Groups.* Unpublished report, 26 April 2012.

20. Connaway, L.S. and Dickey, T.J. 2010. *The Digital Information Seeker: Report of Findings from Selected OCLC, RIN, and JISC User Behavior Projects.* Higher Education Funding Council for England (HEFCE). http://www.jisc.ac.uk/media/documents/publications/reports/2010/ digitalinformationseekerreport.pdf. (inaccessible 26 October 2015).

    Alternative URL http://www.webarchive.org.uk/wayback/archive/20140615023510/http://www.jisc.ac.uk/media/documents/publications/reports/2010/digitalinformationseekerreport.pdf .

21. Connaway, L.S. and Dickey, T.J. 2010. "Towards a profile of the researcher of today: What can we learn from JISC Projects?" *Common Themes Identified in an Analysis of JISC Virtual Research Environment and Digital Repository Projects.* http://ie-repository.jisc.ac.uk/418/2/VirtualScholar_themesFromProjects_revised.pdf.

22. Connaway, L.S.; Prabha, C. and Dickey, T.J. 2006. "Sensemaking the information confluence: The whys and hows of college and university user satisfying of information needs. Phase III: Focus group interview study." *Report on National Leadership Grant LG-02-03-0062-03,* Institute of Museum and Library Services, Washington. Columbus: School of Communication, The Ohio State University.

23. Connaway, L.S.; White, D.; Lanclos, D.; Le Cornu, A. 2013. "Visitors and Residents: What motivates engagement with the digital information environment?" *Information Research* 18, no. 1. http://informationr.net/ir/18-1/infres181.html.

24. Connaway, L.S.; Lanclos, D.M. and Hood, E.M. 2013. "I always stick with the first thing that comes up on Google ... Where people go for information, what they use, and why." *EDUCAUSE Review Online.* http://www.educause.edu/ero/article/i-always-stick-first-thingcomesgoogle-where-people-go-information-what-theyuse-and-why. (inaccessible October 2015).

    Alternative URL http://er.educause.edu/articles/2013/12/i-always-stick-with-the-first-thing-that-comes-up-on-google---where-people-go-for-information-what-they-use-and-why (accessed 26 October 2015).

25. Connaway, L.S.; Lanclos, D.M. and Hood, Erin, M. 2013. "I find Google a lot easier than going to the library website. Imagine ways to innovate and inspire students to use the academic library." *Proceedings of the Association of College & Research Libraries (ACRL) 2013 conference, Chicago: Association of College & Research Libraries,* 10–13 April, Indianapolis, p. 293. http://www.ala.org/acrl/sites/ala.org.acrl/files/content/conferences/confsandpreconfs/2013/papers/Connaway_Google.pdf.

26. Connaway, L.S.; Lanclos, D.M.; White, D.; Le Cornu, A. and Hood, E.M. 2013. "User-centered decision making: A new model for developing academic library services and systems." *IFLA Journal* 39, no. 1: 30–36.

27. Connaway, L.S.; Radford M.L.; Dickey, T.J.; De Angelis, JW. and Confer, P. 2008. "Sense-making and Synchronicity: Information-seeking Behaviors of Millennials and Baby Boomers." *Libri* 58, no. 2: 123–135. http://www.oclc.org/resources/research/publications/library/2008/connaway-libri.pdf.(inaccessible 26 October 2015).

28. Connaway, L.S.; Dickey, T.J.; Radford, M.L. 2011. "If it is too inconvenient I'm not going after it: Convenience as a critical factor in information-seeking behaviors." *Library & Information Science Research* 33, no. 3: 179–190. http://www.oclc.org/content/dam/research/publications/library/2011/connaway-lisr.pdf.(inaccessible 26 October 2015)

29. Connaway, L.S. 2008. "Make room for the Millennials." *NextSpace,* 10: 18–19. http://www.oclc.org/nextspace/010/research.htm.

30. Connaway, L.S. 2013. "Findings from user behavior studies: A user's world." *ALA Midwinter Meeting and Exhibits,* 28 January 2013, Seattle.

31. Connaway, L.S. 2013. "Why the Internet is more attractive than the library." *The Serials Librarian* 64, no. 1-4: 41–56.

32. Consortium of University Research Libraries and Research Information Network. 2007. *Researchers* 39.

33. De Belder, K. 2012. "Session 1: Directly supporting researchers." *Libraries rebound: Embracing mission, maximizing impact,* 5–6 June, Philadelphia. https://www.youtube.com/watch?v=R9qUoVSD7HA&feature=youtu.be.

34. De Rosa, C.; Cantrell, J.; Cellentani, D.; Hawk, J.; Jenkins, L. and Wilson, A. 2005. *Perceptions of Libraries and Information Resources: A Report to the OCLC Membership.* OCLC Online Computer Library Center, Dublin.

35. De Rosa, C.; Cantrell, J.; Hawk, J. and Wilson, A. 2006. *College students' perceptions of libraries and information resources: A report to the OCLC Membership,* OCLC Online Computer Library Center, Dublin.

36. De Rosa, C.; Cantrell, J.; Carlson, M.; Gallagher, P.; Hawk, J. and Sturtz, C. 2010. *Perceptions of libraries, 2010: Context and community.* OCLC Online Computer Library Center, Dublin.

37. De Rosa, C. 2005. *Perceptions of libraries and information resources: A report to the OCLC Membership,* OCLC Online Computer Library Center, Dublin.

38. Delserone, L.M. 2008. "At the watershed: Preparing for research data management and stewardship at the University of Minnesota Libraries." *Library Trends* 57, no. 2: 202–210.

39. Dempsey, L. 2008. "Always on: Libraries in a world of permanent connectivity." *First Monday* 14, no. 1. http://www.firstmonday.org/htbin/cgiwrap/bin/ojs/index.php/fm/article/view/2291/207.

40. Dempsey, L. 2012. "Thirteen ways of looking at libraries, discovery, and the catalog: Scale, workflow, attention." *EDUCAUSE Review Online.* http://www.educause.edu/ero/article/thirteen-ways-looking-librariesdiscovery-and-catalog-scale-workflow-attention. (inaccessible 26 October 2015).

    Alternative URL http://er.educause.edu/articles/2012/12/thirteen-ways-of-looking-at-libraries-discovery-and-the-catalog-scale-workflow-attention (accessed 26 October 2015).

41. Dennis, S.P. 2011. "Share of Attention." *Steve Dennis' Blog: Zen and the Art & Science of Customercentricity.* http://stevenpdennis.com/2011/06/09/share-of-attention-2/.(accessed 26 October 2015).

42. DeSantis, N. 2012. "On Facebook, librarian brings 2 students from the early 1900s to life." *Wired Campus.* http://chronicle.com/blogs/wiredcampus/on-facebook-librarian-brings-twostudents-from-the-early-1900s-to-life/34845.

43. Elder, D; Westbrook, R.N. and Reilly, M. 2012. "Wikipedia lover, not a hater: Harnessing Wikipedia to increase the discoverability of library resources." *Journal of Web Librarianship* 6, no. 1: 32–44. DOI:10.1080/19322909.2012.641808.

44. Faniel, I.M. 2009. *Unrealized potential: The socio-technical challenges of a large scale cyberinfrastructure initiative.* National Science Foundation, Arlington. http://hdl.handle.net/2027.42/61845.

45. Faniel, I.M.; Kriesberg, A. and Yakel, E. 2012. "Data reuse and sensemaking among novice social scientists." *The annual meeting of the American Society for Information Science and Technology.* 26–31 October, Baltimore.

46. Faniel, I.M. and Jacobsen, TE. 2010. "Reusing scientific data: How earthquake engineering researchers assess the reusability of colleagues' data." *Computer Supported Cooperative Work* 19, no. 3-4: 355–375.

47. Faniel, I.; Kansa, E.; Kansa, S.W.; Barrera-Gomez, J. and Yakel, E. 2013. "The challenges of digging data: A study of context in archaeological data reuse." *JCDL 2013 Proceedings of the 13th ACM/IEEE-CS Joint Conference on Digital Libraries.* New York: ACM, p. 295–304. http://dx.doi.org/10.1145/2467696.2467712.

48. Fast, K.V.; Campbell, D.G. 2004. "I still like Google: University student perceptions of searching OPACs and the web." *Proceedings of the ASIS&T Annual Meeting* 41: 138–146.

49. Fisher, E. 2012. "Makerspaces move into academic libraries." *ACRL Tech Connect.* http://acrl.ala.org/techconnect/?p=2340.

50. Gabridge, T. 2009. "The Last Mile: Liaison Roles in Curating Science and Engineering Research Data." *Research Library Issues: A Bimonthly Report from ARL, CNI, and SPARC* 265: 15–21. http://www.arl.org/bm~doc/rli-265-gabridge.pdf. (inaccessible 26 October 2015).

    Alternative URL http://publications.arl.org/rli265/16 (accessed 26 October 2015).

51. Glassmeyer, S. 2010. Ranganathan 2.0. *AALL Spectrum* 14, no. 3: 22–24.

52. Goldup, S.J. 2010. *Public libraries in the digital age: Investing the implementation of Ranganathan's Five Laws of library science in physical and online library services.* School of Information Management, Victoria University of Wellington, February 2010.

53. Gorman, M. 1995. "Five new laws of librarianship." *American Libraries* 26, no. 8: 784–785.

54. Gorman, M. 1998. "The five laws of library science: Then and now. (Excerpt of *Our singular strengths* by Michael Gorman)." *School Library Journal* 7: 20–23.

55. HathiTrust. 2014. Statistics information. *Hathi Trust Digital Library.* http://www.hathitrust.org/statistics_info (accessed 28 May 2014).

56. Head, A.J. and Eisenberg, M.B. 2009. "Lessons learned: How college students seek information in the digital age." *Project Information Literacy Progress Report.* The Information School, University of Washington. http://projectinfolit.org/images/pdfs/pil_fall2009_finalv_yr1_12_2009v2.pdf.

57. Head, A.J. and Eisenberg, M.B. 2010. "How college students evaluate and use information in the digital age." *Project Information Literacy progress report,* The Information School, University of Washington, Seattle.

58. Hiebert, J. and Theriault, S. 2012. "BLASTing the zombies! Creative ideas to fight finals fatigue." *College and Research Libraries News* 73, no. 9: 540–569.

59. Holdren, J.P. 2013. Memorandum for the Heads of Executive Departments and Agencies. *Washington, DC: Office of Science and Technology Policy,* 2013. http://www.whitehouse.gov/sites/default/files/microsites/ostp/ostp_public_access_memo_2013.pdf.

60. Institute for Archaeologists. 2009. *Standard and guidance for the creation, compilation, transfer and deposition of archaeological archives.* n.p.: Institute for Archaeologists. http://www.archaeologists.net/sites/default/files/node-files/Archives2009.pdf. (inaccessible 26 October 2015)

61. Jahnke, L.; Asher, A.; Keralis, S.D.C. 2012. "The Problem of Data." *With an introduction by Charles Henry,* Washington, DC: Council on Library and Information Resources.

62. Johnston, L. and Hanson, C. 2010. "e-Science at the University of Minnesota: A collaborative approach." *International Association of Scientific and Technological University Libraries, 31st Annual Conference.* http://docs.lib.purdue.edu/iatul2010/conf/day2/3.

63. Kearns, A.J. 2012. "Slam the Boards! Predatory Reference and the Online Answer Sites." *OCLC Webjunction.* http://www.webjunction.org/documents/webjunction/Slam_the_Boards_Predatory_Reference_and_the_Online_Answer_Sites.html.

64. Kwanya, T.; Stilwell, C.; Underwood, P.G. 2010. "Library 2.0 Principles and Ranganathan's Fifth Law." *Mousaion* 28, no. 2: 1–16.

65. Lage, K.; Losoff, B. and Maness, J. 2011. "Receptivity to library involvement in scientific data curation: A case study at the University of Colorado Boulder." *Portal: Libraries and the Academy* 11, no. 4: 915–937.

66. Lally, A.M. and Dunford, C.E. 2007. "Using Wikipedia to extend digital collections." *D-Lib Magazine* 13, no. 5/6. http://www.dlib.org/dlib/may07/lally/05lally.html.

67. Lavoie, B.; Childress, E.; Erway, R.; Faniel, I.; Malpas C.; Schaffner, J. and van der Werf, T. 2014. *The Evolving Scholarly Record.* Dublin, OH: OCLC Research, 2014. http://www.oclc.org/content/dam/research/publications/library/2014/oclcresearch-evolving-scholarly-record-2014.pdf.

68. Lippincott, J.K. 2010. "A mobile future for academic libraries." *Reference Services Review* 38, no. 2: 205–213.

69. Lippincott, JK. and Duckett K. 2013. "Library space assessment: Focusing on learning." *Research Library Issues: A Report from ARL, CNI, and SPARC* 284: 12–21. http://publications.arl.org/rli284/.

70. Luce, R.E. 2008. "A New Value Equation Challenge: The Emergence of eResearch and Roles for Research Libraries" *No Brief Candle: Reconceiving Research Libraries for the 21st Century.* Washington, DC: Council on Library and Information Resources.

71. National Science Foundation. 2006. "To Stand the Test of Time: Long-term Stewardship of Digital Datasets in Science and Engineering." *A Report to the National Science Foundation from the ARL Workshop on New Collaborative Relationships: The Role of Academic Libraries in the Digital Data Universe.* National Science Foundation, Arlington, 2006. http://www.arl.org/bm~doc/digdatarpt.pdf.(inaccessible 26 October 2015).

    Alternative URL
    http://www.arl.org/storage/documents/publications/digital-data-report-2006.pdf. (accessed 26 October 2015).

72. Nelson, B. 2009. "Data sharing: Empty archives." *Nature* 461, no. 7261: 160–163. http://www.nature.com/news/2009/090909/pdf/461160a.pdf.

73. Newton, MP.; Miller, C.C. and Marianne, S.B. 2010. "Librarian roles in institutional repository data set collecting: Outcomes of a research library task force." *Collection Management* 36, no. 1: 53–67. Doi: 10.1080/01462679.2011.530546.

74. Noruzi, A. 2004. "Application of Ranganathan's Laws to the Web." *Webology* 1, no. 2. http://www.webology.org/2004/v1n2/a8.html.

75. Oblinger, D.G. and Oblinger, J.L. eds. 2005. *"Educating the net generation." EDUCAUSE.* http://www.educause.edu/content.asp?PAGE_ID=5989&bhcp=1. (inaccessible 26 October 2015).

    Alternative URL https://net.educause.edu/ir/library/pdf/PUB7101.pdf (accessed October 2015).

76. Parks Canada. 2005. *Archaeological recording manual: Excavations and surveys.* n.p.: Parks Canada. http://www.pc.gc.ca/eng/docs/pc/guide/fp-es/index.aspx.

77. Peters, C and Dryden, A.R. 2011. "Assessing the academic library's role in campus-wide research data management: A first step at the University of Houston." *Science & Technology Libraries* 30, no. 4: 387–403. http://www.tandfonline.com/doi/pdf/10.1080/0194262X.2011.626340.

78. Pierard, C and Lee, N. 2011. "Studying space: Improving space planning with user studies." *Journal of Access Services* 8: 190–207. Doi:10.1080/15367967.2011.602258.

79. Popova, M. 2011. "Accessibility vs. Access: How the Rhetoric of 'Rare' is Changing in the Age of Information Abundance." *Nieman Journalism Lab* (23 August 2011), http://www.niemanlab.org/2011/08/accessibility-vs-access-how-the-rhetoric-of-rare-is-changing-in-the-age-of-information-abundance/.

80. Prabha, C.; Connaway, L.S. and Dickey, T.J. 2006. "Sensemaking the information confluence: The whys and hows of college and university user satisficing of information needs. Phase IV: Semi-structured interview study." *Report on National Leadership Grant LG-02-03-0062-03, to Institute of Museum and Library Services,* The Ohio State University, Washington, DC. Columbus, OH: School of Communication.

81. Pullinger, D. 1999. "Academics and the new information environment: The impact of local factors on use of electronic journals." *Journal of Information Science* 25, no. 2: 164–172.

82. Purcell, K.; Rainie, L.; Heaps, A.; Buchanan, J.; Friedrich, L.; Jacklin, A.; Chen, C.; and Zickuhr, K. 2012. *How teens do research in the digital world.* Washington DC: PEWInternet & American Life Project. http://pewinternet.org/Reports/2012/Student-Research.aspx.

83. Radford, M.L. and Connaway, L.S. 2008. "Seeking synchronicity: Evaluating virtual reference services from user, non-user and librarian perspectives: IMLS final performance report." *Report on Grant LG-06-05-0109-05,* Institute of Museum and Library Services, Washington, DC. Dublin, OH: OCLC Online Computer Library Center.

84. Ranganathan, S.R. 1931. *The five laws of library science.* London: Edward Goldston, Ltd., 313.

85. Research Information Network. 2006. *Researchers and discovery services: Behaviour, perceptions and needs.* London: Research Information Network, p. 5.

86. Research Information Network. 2008. *To share or not to share: Publication and quality assurance of research data outputs.* London: Research Information Network.

87. Rolland, B. and Lee, C.P. 2013. "Beyond trust and reliability: Reusing data in collaborative cancer epidemiology research." *Collaboration and sharing in scientific work.* New York: ACM, p. 435–444.

88. Rubin, R.E. 2004. *Foundations of Library and Information Science.* New York: Neal-Schuman Publishers, p. 251.

89. Sadler, S. 2012. "Session 3: Exploiting space as a distinctive asset." Presented at *Libraries rebound: Embracing mission, maximizing impact,* 5–6 June, in Philadelphia, PA. https://www.youtube.com/watch?v=AmEtdVPro54&feature=youtu.be.

90. Salo, D. 2008. "Innkeeper at the roach motel." *Library Trends* 57, no. 2: 98–123.

91. Savolainen, R. 1993. "The sense-making theory: Reviewing the interests of a user-centered approach to information seeking and use." *Information Processing & Management* 29, no. 1: 13–28.

92. Scaramozzino, J.M.; Ramirez, M.L. and McGaughey, K.J. 2012. "A study of faculty data curation behaviors and attitudes at a teaching-centered university." *College and Research Libraries* 73, no. 4: 349–365. http://crl.acrl.org/content/73/4/349.full.pdf+html.

93. Simon, H.A. 1957. "A behavioral model of rational choice." *Models of man: Social and rational.* New York: John Wiley & Sons.

94. Smith, A. 2014. "6 New Facts About Facebook." *Fact Tank* (3 February 2014), http://www.pewresearch.org/fact-tank/2014/02/03/6-new-facts-about-facebook/.

95. Soehner, C.; Steeves, C. and Ward, J. 2010. *e-Science and data support services: A study of ARL member institutions.* http://www.arl.org/bm~doc/escience_report2010.pdf.(inaccessible 26 October 2015).

    Alternative URL
    http://www.arl.org/storage/documents/publications/escience-report-2010.pdf (accessed 26 October 2015).

96. Sweeney, R. 2006. *Millennial behaviors and demographics.* http://certi.mst.edu/media/administrative/certi/documents/Article-Millennial-Behaviors.pdf.

97. Szajewski, M. 2013. "Using Wikipedia to enhance the visibility of digitized archival assets." *D-Lib Magazine* 19, no. 3/4. http://www.dlib.org/dlib/march13/szajewski/03szajewski.html.

98. Tenopir, C.; Birch, B. and Allard, S. 2012. *Academic libraries and research data services: Current practices and plans for the future. An ACRL white paper.* Chicago: Association of College and Research Libraries.

99. Van House, N.A.; Butler, M.H. and Schiff, Lisa R. 1998. "Cooperative knowledge work and practices of trust: Sharing environmental planning data sets." *Proceedings of the 1998 ACM Conference On Computer Supported Cooperative Work.* Seattle, WA: ACM, p. 335–43. Doi:10.1145/289444.289508.

100. Van House, N. 2002. "Digital libraries and practices of trust: Networked biodiversity information." *Social Epistemology. A Journal of Knowledge, Culture and Policy* 16, no. 1: 99. Doi:10.1080/02691720210132833.

101. Van Scoyoc, A.M. and Caroline, C. 2006. "The electronic academic library: Undergraduate research behavior in a library without books." *Portal: Libraries and the Academy* 6, no. 1: 47–58.

102. Walter, S. 2012. Ranganathan redux: "The 'Five Laws' and the future of college and research libraries." *College and Research Libraries* 73, no. 3: 213–215.

103. Walter, V.A. and Mediavilla, C. 2005. "Teens are from Neptune, librarians are from Pluto: An analysis of online reference transactions." *Library Trends* 54, no. 2: 209–227.

104. Walters, T. and Ruttenberg, J. 2014. "Shared Access Research Ecosystem." *EDUCAUSE Review Online* 49, no. 2: 56–57. http://www.educause.edu/ero/article/shared-access-research-ecosystem.

105. Warwick, C.; Galina, I.; Terras, M.; Huntington, P. and Pappa, N. 2008. "The Master Builders: LAIRAH Research on Good Practice in the Construction of Digital Humanities Projects." *Literary and Linguistic Computing* 23, no. 3: 383–396. http://discovery.ucl.ac.uk/13810/.

106. White, D. 2011. "The learning black market." *TALL Blog* (30 September), http://tallblog.conted.ox.ac.uk/index.php/2011/09/30/the-learning-black-market/.

107. Witt, M.; Carlson, J.; Brandt, D.S. and Cragin, M. 2009. "Constructing data curation profiles." *The International Journal of Digital Curation* 4, no. 3: 93–103.

108. Wong, W.; Stelmaszewska, H.; Barn, B.; Bhimani, N. and Barn, S. 2009. "JISC user behaviour observational study: User behaviour in resource discovery." *Final report.* http://www.jisc.ac.uk/publications/programmerelated/2010/ubirdfinalreport.aspx.

109. Yep, J. and Shulman, J. 2014. "Analyzing the Library's Twitter Network: Using NodeXL to Visualize Impact." *College and Research Library News* 75, no. 4: 177–186.

110. Zickuhr, K.; Rainie, L. and Purcell, K. 2013. "Library services in the digital age." *Washington, DC: Pew Research Center's Internet & American Life Project.* http://libraries.pewinternet.org/files/legacy-pdf/PIP_Library%20services_Report.pdf.

111. Zimmerman, A.S. 2008. "New knowledge from old data: The role of standards in the sharing and reuse of ecological data." *Science, Technology & Human Values* 33, no. 5: 631–652. Doi:10.1177/0162243907306704.

2

What is Enough? Satisficing Information Needs

Chandra Prabha, Ph.D.
OCLC Research

Lynn Silipigni Connaway, Ph.D.
OCLC Research

Lawrence Olszewski, Ph.D.
OCLC

Lillie R. Jenkins, Ph.D.
OCLC

A reprint of:

Prabha, Chandra, Lynn Silipigni Connaway, Lawrence J. Olszewski, and Lillie R. Jenkins. 2007. "What is Enough? Satisficing Information Needs." *Journal of Documentation*. 63 (1). http://dx.doi.org/10.1108/00220410710723894

© 2007 OCLC Online Computer Library Center, Inc.

INTRODUCTION

The current information environment is rich, characterized by a proliferation of information sources and providers, a multiplicity of methods for accessing information, and a redundancy of content from multiple sources. In this "overloaded" information environment, many information users tend to experience a sense of information inadequacy and anxiety. How do individuals navigate this complex landscape of information? Furthermore, how do individuals assess the information they find as being enough to satisfy their specific need? In this complex information environment, understanding how individuals choose to satisfy their information needs takes on new urgency. Insight into information seeking can be gained by understanding how users seek information sources and how they choose content to meet their needs. Yet the library and information science literature has neglected to study how individuals decide what and how much information is enough to meet their needs or goals.

Research on information-seeking and -searching behavior has paid ample attention to sources of information sources used. The process of seeking and searching for information also has received considerable attention from researchers, resulting in several models, many of which are centered on information seeking and searching in academic or professional settings. Though the models delineate the processes, they have not shed much light upon how users recognize what or how much information is enough to accomplish their objectives.

The present article extends the information-seeking, -searching, and -gathering process to include how and when individuals stop looking for information, given a goal or a task that creates the need for information. Individuals are motivated to seek information to satisfy their needs (Wilson, 2005). Given the information glut, how do individuals manage information in such a way as to provide a sufficient answer? This, in essence, is what is meant by satisficing. Satisficing, as defined by Herbert Simon (1955), may be applied to library and information science as an information competency whereby individuals assess how much information is good enough to satisfy their information need. Scholars from different fields have drawn on the satisficing concept to reflect on the "contrast between choosing what is satisfactory and choosing what is best" (Byron, 2004, p. 1).

To amplify this central thesis relating satisficing to search-stopping behavior, this article presents examples of satisficing information needs in relation to the academic tasks that create a need for information in the first place. Role theory and rational choice theory provide a framework for understanding why users decide to stop looking for more information when searching for information to meet their needs.

Role and rational choice theories in human information behavior

Both role theory and rational choice theory are attempts to explain human behavior. Role theory explains individuals' preferences by situating their search for information in a social context within a social system (Mead, 1934; Marks and MacDermid, 1996). Rational choice theory, on the other hand, addresses how individuals decide how much effort is needed to find information in order to accomplish their objectives.

ROLE THEORY

The term role has its origin in theatre as a part played by an actor, which was written on a roll of paper (Biddle and Thomas, 1966). The term began to be used in a technical sense in the 1930s when social scientists recognized that social life is akin to theatre where actors play their "predictable" roles (Biddle and Thomas, 1966). More cogently, role theory explains that: "When people occupy social positions their behavior is determined mainly by what is expected of that position rather than by their own individual characteristics" (Abercrombie et al., 1994, p. 360). George Herbert Mead (1863-1931), Ralph Linton (1893-1953), and Jacob Moreno (1889-1974) contributed to the development of role theory (Borgatta and Montgomery, 2000). Each attempted to explain behavior from their distinct disciplinary perspectives. Mead, who approached it from a philosophical perspective, viewed roles as coping strategies that individuals learn as they interact in society. Linton, who studied from an anthropological angle, distinguished status from position in playing a role. Moreno, who studied from the viewpoint of a psychologist, saw roles as habits and tactics that individuals learn. In effect, "Roles provide behavioral guidelines, prescriptions or boundaries in the form of expectations" (The Gale Group, 2001). Role theory acknowledges the particularity of the situation including personal motivations, perceptions of information needs and priorities for information seeking (Mead, 1934; Blumer and Morrione, 2004).

Including the information-seekers' social role helps to understand how individuals seek information in different roles. However, role theory does not explain individual differences seen among those playing the same role. Rational choice theory, on the other hand, is useful in this pursuit because it addresses how individual incentives and intentions influence the information choices users make.

RATIONAL CHOICE THEORY

The origin of rational choice theory has been traced back to logic, mathematics and statistics, although much of it developed in economics (Green, 2002). Rational choice theory is based on the premise that complex social behavior can be understood in terms of elementary individual actions because individual action is the elementary unit of social life. Rational choice theory posits that individuals choose or prefer what is best to achieve their objectives or pursue their interests, acting in their self-interest (Green, 2002). Stated another way, "When faced with several courses of action, people usually do what they believe is likely to have the best overall outcome" (Scott, 2000).

Rational choice theory does not specify that all individuals work toward (or even desire) similar goals, nor do they assess costs and benefits similarly. Rather, actors assess "costs" and "benefits" according to their own "preferences, values or utilities" (Friedman and Hechter, 1988, p. 202). In other words, individuals "act with the express purpose of attaining ends that are consistent with their hierarchy of preferences." Rational choice theory has been adopted by several fields including anthropology, political science, psychology, consumer behaviorism, and sociology.

Sociologists use rational choice theory to explain human behavior in terms of individuals' goals and motivations (Green, 2002). In its purest form, rational choice theory assumes that it is possible to know and evaluate all of the possible choices. According to this theory, individuals compare the expected benefits they derive from taking various courses of action in pursuit of their objectives and then choose one that promises to maximize the benefits relative to the effort or cost required. In economics, individual actions that are based on individual preferences are defined as rational if they can consistently compare expected benefits from all of the alternative courses of actions. In other words, individuals make a cost-benefit analysis prior to selecting the optimal course of action to achieve a desired goal (Wikipedia, 2006).

In many real-life situations, individuals may not have at their disposal the full range of all possible choices with which to assess and compare the benefits of each choice in relation to the effort or cost; therefore, the premise of rational choice theory has been challenged and debated widely by scholars. Simon (1955) proposed the concept of satisficing, recognizing that in many situations it is neither possible to know the entire spectrum of options, nor is it possible to compare the benefits each may offer. In practice, satisficing translates into a judgment that the information is good enough to satisfy a need even though the full cost-benefit analysis was not performed.

Satisficing

Simon defines satisficing as a decision-making process "through which an individual decides when an alternative approach or solution is sufficient to meet the individuals' desired goals rather than pursue the perfect approach" (Simon, 1971, p. 71). When individuals satisfice, they compare the benefits of obtaining "more information" against the additional cost and effort of continuing to search (Schmid, 2004). In fact, in many organizations, "problems are considered resolved when a good enough solution has been found, that is the manager satisfices as she looks for a course of action that is satisfactory" (Choo, 1998, p. 49). Theoretically, decision makers consider all potential alternatives until the optimal solution emerges (Stroh et al., 2002). However, such an exhaustive analysis would require additional time and expenditure which information seekers must weigh against the likelihood that they will find additional information of sufficient value to offset the cost of continued searching. The consequences of putting time and effort into finding optimal solutions can be costly; therefore, "decision makers must be willing to forgo the best solution in favor of one that is acceptable" (Stroh et al., 2002, p. 94). In so doing, information seekers "...satisfice...and choose the one [solution] that produces an outcome that is 'good enough'" (Stroh et al., 2002, p. 94).

The foregoing examples suggest that users may satisfice their need for information based on what they are able to find and thus stop looking for more information. Users may also stop looking for information prematurely if the information systems are difficult or unusable.

The very abundance of information makes it crucial for information seekers to decide what information is enough to meet their objectives. This paper examines the theoretical concepts—role theory, rational choice, and satisficing—by attempting to explain the parameters within which users navigate the complex information-rich environment and determine what and how much information will meet their needs.

Previous studies and models on information seeking and searching

STUDIES

The information-seeking and -searching research that explicitly addresses the topic of "what is good enough" is scant, though several studies make oblique references to the stopping stage, or to the shifting of directions for want of adequate information. Kraft and Lee (1979, p. 50) propose three stopping rules:

1. The satiation rule, "where the scan is terminated only when the user becomes satiated by finding all the desired number of relevant documents";

2. The disgust rule, which "allows the scan to be terminated only when the user becomes disgusted by having to examine too many irrelevant documents"; and

3. The combination rule, "which allows the user to be seen as stopping the scan if he/she is satiated by finding the desired number of relevant documents or disgusted by having to examine too many irrelevant documents, whichever comes first."

The stopping rules suggested by these authors imply an emotional or affective response to the nature of the retrieved documents or their surrogates and do not address the influence of role and rational choice theories and the concept of satisficing on information-seeking behavior.

Dalton and Charnigo (2004, p. 414) found that "several [historians] mentioned that they had called a halt to research when they felt they had enough to write, even if other sources promised to yield additional information. Some had tailored their research topics to minimize travel." This study illustrates how historians satisfice their search for information in the context of research. In another study of historians, Duff and Johnson (2002) note that time and money are important constraints on how much information historians can gather, which illustrates how Stroh et al. (2002) define "acceptable." Lack of sufficient time and money clearly leads the historians in this study to settle or satisfice when they believe they have enough information to meet their objective.

Barrett (2005, p. 326) observes that "undergraduates employ a 'coping strategy' in their search for information, often seeking to find 'enough' information to fulfill assignment requirements with the 'least cost in terms of time or social effort.'" This comment once again exemplifies how undergraduates (information seekers in a different role) satisfice their need for information. Barrett's study of the information-seeking behavior of undergraduate students excludes how graduate students satisfice.

Some attention has been given to the topic of how the situation influences users' decisions to determine what information is good enough (i.e., appropriate). Leckie et al. (1996, p. 185) found that when:

> [...] confronted with too much unevaluated information, engineers will often select sources based on authors they already know and have used, and lawyers will tend to use their notes from other cases, as well as familiar digests, citators, and other ready reference sources... It is often important that the information be obtained immediately or within an acceptable period of time. Its usefulness and impact will decrease if it is obtained either too early or too late.

Furthermore, they note that "the cost involved with accessing a particular source will also affect whether a professional decides to use it. The importance of the need, time factor, and monies available will determine how much effort and expense a professional will spend, seeking information from any given source" (Leckie et al., 1996, p. 185). Although lawyers, as a professional group, fall outside the academic community, this example illustrates a practice of satisficing behavior. Meho and Tibbo (2003, p. 585) come to the following conclusion about the "ending stage" of research:

> The ending stage marks the end of the research cycle of a project. Although it is not discussed in this paper, an ending stage was assumed as all interview questions were geared toward discussing the entire research cycle of a project.

More importantly, they suggest that when researchers cannot find relevant information, they "try to use alternative sources or methods" (Meho and Tibbo, 2003, p. 585). In other words, Meho and Tibbo (2003, p. 585) report that these scientists are satisficing by "searching for new information...or continu[ing] working with whatever information had been obtained." However, they do not directly address the ending stage or the factors leading to it.

A very extensive analysis of "what is good enough" is undertaken by Zach (2005, p. 31), who found that senior arts administrators:

> [...] may reach the point of making the decision to complete the information-seeking process several times during the course of exploring an issue; they may then cycle through some or all of the steps one or more times before attaining the desired level of comfort with the results of the process. Sometimes it may be that additional information is necessary to provide greater clarity or understanding of the issue, but often it is that the administrator simply wants more time to process the input before taking the final step.

No administrator in the study applied predetermined criteria to make the decision to move forward to the next phase. The decision was made when the administrators felt satisfied with the inputs available to them or the decision was forced by external time constraints. Sometimes the two primary factors—comfort and time—were in conflict with each other, in which case they often resorted to satisficing. Administrators also agreed that the type of task or decision influenced when they would stop the exploration process. However, the essential element of the decision to move on was the belief that they had enough information to complete the task or make the decision, even if they knew that more information might be available.

MODELS

Information-related actions begin with the recognition of the need for finding information to address a situation or solve a problem, and end when the individuals resolve the situation or abandon the pursuit. Understanding how individuals satisfice their need for information may be viewed as recognizing how much effort individuals are willing to invest in finding information, in relation to the trade-offs of information quality, time constraints for achieving an objective, solving a problem, or addressing a situation. Satisficing the need for information is an integral component of the larger body of literature on information-seeking and -searching models.

Library and information science research has identified several models for information-seeking and -searching behavior. A benchmark model, proposed by Taylor (1968), suggests that librarians consider users' objectives and motivations in providing answers information seekers will accept. Taylor's model recognizes that individuals evaluate information in relation to the objectives that create their need for information. Krikelas (1983, p. 13) suggests "that the characteristic of the problem may be a more critical indicator of potential behavior than various personal or work characteristics." In other words, the nature of the problem may indicate how much or what information is needed to satisfice.

Krikelas also discusses Voigt's (1961) model, which describes three types of information needs identified by scientists. The scientist's first type of information need is to keep current in relevant fields of study. The second need is the scientist's need for "some specific piece of information" (Voigt, 1961, p. 21). The third type of information need, which occurs with the least frequency, is the need for an exhaustive search—the need to find all of the existing relevant information on a specific subject or topic, as in the case of a dissertation topic (Voigt, 1961). The exhaustive search is the type that provides the scientist with enough information to determine that the search process can stop. The three types of needs—monitoring, finding specific data, and searching exhaustively—require varying amounts of search effort. By connecting the information need to the information problem, Krikelas, like Taylor, acknowledges that individuals decide how much information is needed in relation to the nature of the problem.

Marchionini (1995) observes that the determination of when to stop looking for information may depend on external functions like setting/context/situation or a search system or on internal functions like motivation, task-domain knowledge, and information-seeking ability. In other words, all or some of these factors may influence the decision about how much information is enough. Foster (2004), like Marchionini, remarks that both external and internal contexts serve to frame information needs, thereby framing the conditions under which those needs become satisfied. He discovers that users' knowledge that they had "enough" information emerged as an iterative process of questioning whether they had acquired sufficient material to meet the present information need.

Wilson (2005) generalizes a theoretical model of a continuing information-seeking cycle which recognizes the episodic nature of information seeking. Although this model focuses on the information-seeking process, it does not explicitly explore the conclusion stage; therefore, the factors that individuals employ in deciding when to stop information seeking are not identified.

Kuhlthau (2005) depicts the information-search process as a sequential set of intellectual stages: becoming aware of the lack of knowledge or understanding (initiation), identifying a problem area or topic (selection), exploring the problem (exploration), defining the problem (formulation), collecting relevant information (collection), and explaining what the person learned (presentation). This model does not address the effort required to transition through the various information-seeking stages.

Ellis (1989) proposes a behavioral model based on the analysis of a detailed description of information-seeking activities by social scientists. In this model, the decision of whether the information found is sufficient to meet a user's needs is dependent upon chasing and evaluating references as well as systemically identifying content that is of interest to the user. Ellis characterizes six different types of information activities: starting, chaining, browsing, differentiating, monitoring and extracting. He emphasizes the information-seeking activities, rather than the nature of the problems or criteria used for determining when to stop the information search process. In a subsequent article, Ellis (1997) observes that even in the final stages of writing, individuals may continue the search for information in an attempt to answer unresolved questions or to look for new literature.

In Dervin et al.'s (2003) sense-making approach, ending an information-seeking episode involves the act of making sense of the situation or resolving the problem with information gathered for that purpose. After finding that information, the information seeker will most likely end the search episode, determining that enough information has been found. Dervin uses the term "outcome" to denote the information-seeking objective. Accomplishing that objective implies the conclusion of the information-seeking episode. Since this model emphasizes the importance of the situation in seeking information and recognizes the episodic nature of information seeking, it does not explicitly address the factors associated with stopping behavior, although sense-making recognizes that given the incomplete nature of reality, the information-seeking process is only ever partially fulfilled. In that sense, satisficing is a key element in Dervin's sense-making approach.

Findings of research on satisficing of academic information needs

In an attempt to identify how and why academic users satisfice their information needs, a major research project utilized online surveys and telephone, focus group and semi-structured interviews (IMLS, 2003). In Phase III of the study, a random sample of seventy-eight academic users participated in focus group interviews to identify how and why they get information. A total of eight focus group interviews were conducted in spring 2005. The median number of participants per focus group was ten and focus group participants included 31 faculty, 19 graduate students, and 28 undergraduate students. The students and faculty were interviewed in separate groups because the students may have felt uncomfortable freely expressing their opinions in the presence of faculty.

The participants were asked to recollect academic tasks that led them to perform thorough searches. Participants then were asked what made them decide that the information they had was enough while engaged in doing thorough searches. In other words, what criteria did the participants employ to stop looking for information, i.e., to satisfice? Another question asked participants to think of a time when they were in a situation where they needed answers or solutions and they did a quick search for the information, without a thorough evaluation of its credibility, even though they knew there were other sources available and decided not to use them.

RESPONSES TO ENDING THOROUGH SEARCHES

Some of the criteria that the participants mentioned may be viewed as quantitative, as exemplified by the student who stopped searching for information once he had acquired the required number of journal sources for an assignment. Other criteria mentioned by participants are qualitative, as exemplified by the remark that when the same information is repeated in several sources, the search is terminated.

The criteria students and faculty use for stopping the information search are shown in the lists below. The academic tasks or situations that prompted the information search are also shown in order to provide a context for the criteria students and faculty mentioned.

Undergraduate and graduate students

Undergraduate and graduate students discussed writing research reports or preparing presentations as examples of academic tasks. Responses of undergraduate and graduate students were combined (see below).

Situations creating the need to look for information (meeting assignment requirements):

- Writing research reports; and
- Preparing presentations.

Criteria used for stopping the information search (fulfilling assignment requirements):

1. Quantitative criteria:
   - Required number of citations was gathered;
   - Required number of pages was reached;
   - All the research questions were answered; and
   - Time available for preparing.

2. Qualitative criteria:
   - Accuracy of information;
   - Same information repeated in several sources;
   - Sufficient information was gathered; and
   - Concept understood.

QUANTITATIVE CRITERIA

Some students concluded their search as soon they had collected the required number of sources. One graduate student said, "We had to research a certain topic, and we had to have ten sources, and they all had to be journal sources or peer-reviewed sources." Another student said that as soon as he collected enough information to write the number of pages for the report, he stopped the search. This student said, "I don't feel the need to expound on the subject beyond the number of required pages." Another student said that when he found all the information he was trying to research and all the questions had been answered, he stopped looking for information. For many students, the amount of time available for doing the assignment and the relative reward (the value being in terms of the final grade in the course) influenced when they stopped looking for more information.

QUALITATIVE CRITERIA

A graduate student who was looking for the temperature that the Chinese used for making ceramics 500 years ago kept looking for that information until she found the answer in a book. She was then convinced of the accuracy of the information and purchased the title. Some students said that they knew that "it was time to stop looking for information" when a great deal of the information was repeated in several sources. "After I've read everything in the article for like the third time through, I'll just quit. I am like, I have enough," remarked one undergraduate student. Some students stop looking for information once they judge that they have sufficient information to write the assigned report, or when they understand the concept well enough to articulate their thoughts in a report.

Faculty

Faculty referred to both teaching and scholarly or research needs as prompting them to perform thorough searches. As shown below, faculty mentioned preparing lectures to deliver to students, preparing and delivering presentations for classes, and designing and conducting workshops as situations creating the need to look for information.

Situations creating the need to look for information (meeting teaching needs):

- Preparing lectures and presentations;
- Delivering lectures and presentations;
- Designing and conducting workshops;
- Meeting scholarly and research needs; and
- Writing journal articles, books and grant proposals.

Criteria used for stopping the information search (fulfilling teaching needs):

1. Quantitative criteria:

    — Time available for: preparing lectures and presentations; delivering lectures
    — And presentations; and designing and conducting workshops; and
    — Fulfilling scholarly and research needs.

2. Qualitative criteria:
   — Every possible synonym and every combination were searched;
   — Representative sample of research was identified;
   — Current or cutting-edge research was found;
   — Same information was repeated;
   — Exhaustive collection of information sources was discovered;
   — Colleagues' feedback was addressed;
   — Journal reviewers' comments were addressed; and
   — Publisher's requirements were met.

QUANTITATIVE CRITERIA

Deadlines dictated how much time faculty invested in finding information sources. One criterion —amount of time available—was mentioned frequently by many faculty members as affecting their decision to stop looking for information. "Usually if there is a deadline and then I turn it in ..." said one faculty member. Another faculty member who had recently written a grant proposal said that if an article he wanted was not easily available, he did not include it in the bibliography.

Faculty distinguished between the time available for delivering a lecture or a presentation and the time available for preparing it. Limited by time constraints, one faculty member stopped searching once he had enough information to produce a presentation for class lectures. Faculty were likely to spend more time looking for information to prepare for a two-hour seminar as opposed to a 50-minute classroom lecture.

QUALITATIVE CRITERIA

Some faculty stopped their searches when the topic had been searched "using every possible synonym and in every combination." Others stated that as long as "they represent research legitimately, sampling was okay." However, the representative sample must include information that is current, cutting-edge, or unique to the topic. Other faculty said that when they saw the same information repeated in several sources, they stopped looking further. Occasionally, they found an exhaustive collection of material on their topic in one location. For example, a music faculty member who was looking for information to write a biography found about fifty boxes of valuable material at the Library of Congress. Since the material covered the entire life of the individual of interest, the faculty member decided at that point that he could stop looking for information.

A few participants sought comments on their manuscripts, including bibliographies from their colleagues who are also experts in that field. Once the comments from colleagues were addressed, they submitted the manuscripts to the journal publishers. A few faculty members said they consider the search completed once they address journal reviewers' suggestions or publishers' requirements. Faculty seem to apply qualitative criteria for stopping their search for information when fulfilling scholarly or research tasks such as writing journal articles, books or grant proposals.

In summary, the conditions that lead students and faculty to stop looking for more information are both qualitative and quantitative in nature:

1. Quantitative criteria for stopping:

   — Requirements are met;
   — Time constraints are limited; and
   — Coverage of material for publication is verified by colleagues or reviewers.

2. Qualitative criteria for stopping:

   — Trustworthy information was located;
   — A representative sample of sources was gathered;
   — Current information was located;
   — Cutting-edge material was located;
   — Exhaustive search was performed; and
   — Exhaustive collection of information sources was discovered.

RESPONSES TO QUICK SEARCHES

An overwhelming number of participants went to the Internet for quick answers. Of these, a good number preferred Google to search the Internet. They gave a number of specific reasons for choosing the Internet. Participants valued the Internet for finding information quickly and conveniently. They valued the opportunity the Internet affords for familiarizing themselves with topics about which they know little. Human sources of information (such as parents or friends) are a common information source for undergraduate students. The objectives of the situations or problems that led them to find information quickly rarely called for a formal or systematic approach to searching.

Role and rational choice theories in human information behavior

As noted, the objective of the research was to discover how users decide when to stop looking for more information. Role and rational choice theories and the concept of satisficing, a derivative of the rational choice theory, were introduced to help place information-seeking behavior in a larger social context. Student responses are separated from faculty responses.

UNDERGRADUATE AND GRADUATE STUDENTS

Undergraduate and graduate students tend to view any assignment that the instructor described as a "research report" as requiring a thorough search for information. Whenever the research report had specific requirements such as the number of citations to journal literature, a required number of pages, or the time allotted for class presentations, fulfilling specific requirements took precedence over doing a "thorough" search. Some students were indeed aware that they could search endlessly and explore the topic in great depth but chose not to do so; instead they satisficed their information needs by remaining within the boundaries of what was required for the assignment.

For students, the relative reward (the value being in terms of a final grade) was a key factor in deciding the amount of time to invest in assignments and clearly suggests the operation of rational choice theory. The quantitative and qualitative criteria students employ indicate that they are acting rationally in choosing to stop looking for more information.

FACULTY

Faculty responses can be placed in two groups, qualitative and quantitative, based upon the information-seeking task chosen. The amount of time they spent searching for information tended to depend on the amount of time they had at their disposal when it came to giving lectures, making presentations, or conducting workshops. However, faculty occasionally mentioned that the time available was a factor in stopping to look for information when they were pursuing their research and scholarly endeavors such as writing journal articles or books.

Faculty are acting rationally in juggling the amount of time they allocate to prepare for class lectures or presentations. When pursuing scholarly endeavors, such as publishing an article, they are acting rationally in not concluding their information search until they receive feedback from colleagues or reviewers. The larger objective is to publish the article, and thus they will invest whatever effort is needed to accomplish that goal.

These faculty members employ several criteria to decide how much information is enough for their purpose. Some of the criteria are qualitative, or intrinsic, judgments, such as the credibility of the source of information; other criteria are quantitative, or extrinsic, assessments such as time constraints. Based upon their responses in the focus group interviews, faculty indicate that they make rational decisions in determining when to stop their search for more information.

Discussion and conclusions

Studies of information seeking and searching make oblique inferences to satisficing in the context of disengaging from the information-seeking process. Previous studies mention several factors utilized by individuals when determining when to stop looking for information. These factors include the:

- Users' objectives or motivations for wanting the information;
- Characteristics of the information need;
- External variables such as setting, context, and situation;
- Internal variables such as motivation and searching skills; and
- Phase of the project (ending phase).

Role theory, rational choice theory, and satisficing are introduced to determine how these concepts can contribute to a deeper understanding of human information behavior. The Institute of Museum and Library Services (IMLS) study "Sense-making the information confluence" (IMLS, 2003), which asked students and faculty explicitly how they decide how much information is enough, reveals that the participants' approaches to information sources and strategies, and the amount of time and effort they devote to searching, correspond directly to the perceived importance of their objectives. Although these findings support previous research and theories, they are not generalizable because of the small sample size. However, these results are important since the study directly asks users to explain their information-searching behaviors in the current information environment and their responses substantiate information behavior theories and findings from previous studies.

Undergraduate and graduate students tend to stop looking for information when they find the required number of sources for an assignment. This behavior supports the theory of Kraft and Lee (1979) that individuals find the desired number of documents and then stop. This also supports Barrett's (2005) findings that undergraduate students seek to find enough information to fulfill course requirements.

Faculty as well as undergraduate and graduate students indicate that time constraints influence when they stop looking for information. This finding corroborates the results of the study of historians' information-seeking behavior by Duff and Johnson (2002) and Dalton and Charnigo (2004). They report that historians stop their information-gathering process because of time and financial constraints. Dalton and Charnigo (2004) also state that some historians develop research topics based on the proximity of primary sources, a factor influenced by the limitations of time and money.

Zach's (2005) study indicates that art administrators stop looking for information when they feel comfortable that they can complete the task, even if they think that additional information may be available. The comments by all participants in the focus group interviews support this type of satisficing information-seeking behavior.

All the participants in the focus group interviews said that the first place they look for information is the Internet, closely followed by human sources. The rationale for this behavior is the immediacy and convenience of acquiring the information. Leckie et al. (1996, p. 185) report that engineers and lawyers say it is very important to obtain information immediately or "its usefulness...will decrease if it is obtained either too early or too late." With the ubiquitous accessibility of Internet search engines, cell phones, and text and instant messaging, immediate access to information is the expected norm.

Role theory helps to explain why students and faculty practice different search behaviors. The students' criteria for stopping an information search are influenced by the requirements of their class assignments. Faculty's criteria for stopping an information search are based on publication requirements and deadlines and the amount of time available for preparing and delivering lectures and presenting papers. Time constraints are an overwhelming factor for faculty in deciding how much effort they are willing to invest in satisfying their information needs.

In describing their information seeking and searching, participants mentioned their rationale for choosing specific strategies and sources. The situational contexts of the participants' information-seeking experiences affect every stage of their search—from the choice of their first source (Google in many cases, or human resources such as family, friends, and colleagues)—to ongoing strategies (depth of search, value judgments on resource authority, browsing and searching) and then decisions on how much information is enough.

Implications for library and information science practice and research

In order for libraries to stay relevant, their systems need to emulate Internet search engines. Such features as simplified searching and the collocation of all types of information (e.g., books, journals, articles, web pages, etc.) facilitate users' search experience which obviates the need to understand the complexity of library systems. Both OCLC (De Rosa et al., 2005) and Williams (2006) indicate that users want their library systems to be as easy to use as Google.

The findings of the focus group interviews also indicate that libraries need to promote the library resources that are available to users. Both the OCLC report (De Rosa et al., 2005) and many of the focus group interview participants (IMLS, 2003) state that they were unaware of the full-text sources available through library-hosted databases. Those who are aware of them tend to find them difficult to use because of the need to know specific subject coverage of databases, a knowledge that is often difficult to comprehend when doing interdisciplinary research. In addition, participants indicate that the inconsistent search protocols of library web sites and online catalogs discourage effective use.

A vast amount of human computer interaction (HCI) research attempts to understand the search process. HCI addresses how users conceptualize searching and how the design of systems impacts users' satisficing their information needs.

The findings from Phase III of the research project (IMLS, 2003) broaden the scope of earlier user research, which tends to focus more on the process of information seeking and searching. This research often portrays users' information-seeking behaviors as static and habitual. Satisficing, an idea introduced as early as 1955 (Simon, 1955), helps to explain how individuals make information choices. Schmidtz (2004, p. 30) views satisficing as a "humanly rational strategy."

REFERENCES

Abercrombie, N., Hill, S. and Turner, B. 1994. *The Penguin Dictionary of Sociology.* 3rd ed., New York: Penguin Group USA.

Barrett, A. 2005. "The Information-Seeking Habits of Graduate Student Researchers in the Humanities", *Journal of Academic Librarianship* 31, no. 4: 324–31.

Biddle, B.J. and Thomas, E.J. 1966. *Role Theory: Concepts and Research.* New York: Wiley.

Blumer, H. and Morrione, T.J. 2004. *George Herbert Mead and Human Conduct.* Walnut Creek, CA: AltaMira Press.

Borgatta, E.F. and Montgomery, R.J.V. (Eds). 2000. *Encyclopedia of Sociology.* New York: Macmillan Reference USA.

Byron, M. 2004. *Satisficing and Maximizing: Moral Theorists on Practical Reason.* Cambridge: Cambridge University Press.

Choo, C.W. 1998. *The Knowing Organization: How Organizations Use Information to Construct Meaning, Create Knowledge, and Make Decisions.* New York: Oxford University Press.

Dalton, M.S. and Charnigo, L. 2004. "Historians and Their Information Sources." *College and Research Libraries* 65, no. 5: 400–25.

De Rosa, C., Cantrell, J., Cellentani, D., Hawk, J., Jenkins, L.R. and Wilson, A. 2005. *Perceptions of Libraries and Information Resources: A Report to the OCLC Membership. OCLC,* Dublin, OH.

Dervin, B., Foreman-Wernet, L. and Lauterbach, E. (Eds). 2003. *Sense-Making Methodology Reader: Selected Writings of Brenda Dervin.* Cresskill, NJ: Hampton Press.

Duff, W.M. and Johnson, C.A. 2002. "Accidentally Found on Purpose: Information-Seeking Behavior of Historians in Archives." *Library Quarterly* 72, no. 4: 472–96.

Ellis, D. 1989. "A Behavioural Model for Information Retrieval System Design." *Journal of Information Science* 15, no. 4: 237–47.

Ellis, D. 1997. "Modelling the Information Seeking Patterns of Engineers and Research Scientists in an Industrial Environment." *Journal of Documentation* 53, no. 4: 384–403.

Foster, A. 2004. "A Nonlinear Model of Information-Seeking Behavior." *Journal of the American Society for Information Science and Technology* 55, no. 3: 228–37.

Friedman, D. and Hechter, M. 1988. "The Contribution of Rational Choice Theory to Macrosociological Research." *Sociological Theory* 6, no. 2: 201–18.

(The) Gale Group 2006. *Role Theory: Foundations, Extensions, and Applications.* The Gale Group: Chandler, AZ. http://cultures.families.com/role-theory-foundationsextensions-applications-eos (accessed 19 June 2006) (inaccessible 26 October 2015).

Green, S.L. 2006. Rational Choice Theory: An Overview, Baylor University: Waco, TX. http://business.baylor.edu/steve_green/green1.doc (accessed 25 June 2006).

IMLS. 2006. "Sense-Making the Information Confluence: the Whys and Hows of College and University User Satisficing of Information Needs." Funded by the Institute of Museum and Library Services, The Ohio State University, and OCLC Online Computer Library Center, Inc., http://imlsosuoclcproject.jcomm.ohio-state.edu/ (accessed 28 June 2006) (inaccessible 26 October 2015).

Kraft, D.H. and Lee, T. 1979. "Stopping Rules and Their Effect on Expected Search Length." *Information Processing & Management* 15, no. 1: 47–58.

Krikelas, J. 1983. "Information-Seeking Behavior: Patterns and Concepts." *Drexel Library Quarterly* 19, no. 2: 5–20.

Kuhlthau, C.C. 2005. "Kuhlthau's Information Search Process." Fisher, K.E., Erdelez, S. and McKechnie, L. (Eds.) *Theories of Information Behavior.* Medford, NJ: Information Today, p. 230–4.

Leckie, G.J., Pettigrew, K.E. and Sylvain, C. 1996. "Modeling the Information Seeking of Professionals: a General Model Derived from Research on Engineers, Health Care Professionals, and Lawyers." *Library Quarterly* 66, no. 2: 161–93.

Marchionini, G. 1995. Information Seeking in Electronic Environments, Cambridge University Press: Cambridge.

Marks, S.R. and MacDermid, S.M. 1996. "Multiple roles and the self: a theory of role balance." *Journal of Marriage and the Family* 58, no. 2: 417–32.

Mead, G.H. 1934. *Mind, Self & Society: From the Standpoint of a Social Behaviorist.* Chicago: University of Chicago Press.

Meho, L.I. and Tibbo, H.R. 2003. "Modeling the Information-Seeking Behavior of Social Scientists: Ellis's Study Revisited." *Journal of the American Society for Information Science and Technology* 54, no. 6: 570–87.

Schmid, A.A. 2004. *Conflict and Cooperation: Institutional and Behavioral Economics.* Malden, MA: Blackwell.

Schmidtz, D. 2004. "Satisficing as a Humanly Rational Strategy." Byron, M (Ed.). *Satisficing and Maximizing: Moral Theorists on Practical Reason.* New York: Cambridge University Press, p. 30–58.

Scott, J. 2006. *Rational Choice Theory.* University of Essex: Colchester. http://privatewww.essex.ac.uk/ , scottj/socscot7.htm (accessed 20 June 2006) (inaccessible 26 October 2015).

> Alternative URL http://www.soc.iastate.edu/sapp/soc401rationalchoice.pdf (accessed 26 October 2015).

Simon, H. 1955. "A Behavioral Model of Rational Choice." *Quarterly Journal of Economics* 69, no. 1: 99–118.

Simon, H. 1971. "Designing Organizations for an Information-Rich World." in Greenberger, M. (Ed.). *Computers, Communications and the Public Interest.* Baltimore, MD: Johns Hopkins University Press, p. 37–72.

Stroh, L.K., Northcraft, G.B. and Neale, M.A. 2002. *Organizational Behavior: A Management Challenge.* 3rd ed., Lawrence Erlbaum: Mahwah, NJ.

Taylor, R.S. 1968. "Question-Negotiation and Information Seeking in Libraries." *College and Research Libraries* 29, no. 3: 178–94.

Voigt, M.J. 1961. *Scientists' Approaches to Information.* Chicago: American Library Association.

Wikipedia 2006. "Rational Choice Theory." *The Free Encyclopedia.* http://en.wikipedia.org/w/index.php?title=Rational_choice_theory (accessed 7 May 2006).

Williams, L. 2006. "Making 'E' Visible." *Library Journal* 23. http://www.libraryjournal.com/article/CA6341888.html (accessed 23 June 2006) (inaccessible 26 October 2015)

> Alternative URL http://lj.libraryjournal.com/2006/06/ljarchives/making-e-visible/ (accessed October 2015).

Wilson, T.D. 2005. "Evolution in Information Behavior Modeling: Wilson's Model." Fisher, K.E., Erdelez, S. and McKechnie, L. (Eds.). *Theories of Information Behavior.* Information Today: Medford, NJ, p. 31–6.

Zach, L. 2005. "When is 'Enough' Enough? Modeling the Information-Seeking and Stopping Behavior of Senior Arts Administrators." *American Society for Information Science and Technology* 56, no. 1: 23–35.

3

"Screenagers" and Live Chat Reference: Living Up to the Promise

Marie L. Radford, Ph.D.
Rutgers, The State University of New Jersey

Lynn Silipigni Connaway, Ph.D.
OCLC Research

A reprint of:

Radford, Marie L., and Lynn Silipigni Connaway. 2007. "'Screenagers' and Live Chat Reference: Living Up to the Promise." *Scan.* 26 (1).

© 2007 State of New South Wales through the Department of Education and Communities.

Note: This article is one of the outcomes from the project Seeking Synchronicity: Evaluating Virtual Reference Services from User, Non-User, and Librarian Perspectives. It is funded by the Institute of Museum and Library Services, Rutgers, the State University of New Jersey, and OCLC Online Computer Library Center. The grant website is: http://www.oclc.org/research/projects/synchronicity/. The authors would like to thank Jocelyn DeAngelis Williams, Patrick Confer, Stephanie Kip, Julie Strange, Timothy Dickey, Susanna Sabolcsi-Boros, Mary Anne Reilly, and Vickie Kozo for their help with this project.

INTRODUCTION

Much scholarly and popular literature focuses on the Millennial Generation, born from 1979–1994 (Sweeney, 2006), also called Net Generation, Digital Generation, or Echo Boomers (Sweeney, 2006; Oblinger & Oblinger, 2005, 2006; Hallam & Partridge, 2006). This generation is second in size to the Baby Boomers (born 1946–1964) and will eventually outnumber Boomers, perhaps as early as 2010 (Sweeney, 2006, p. 2). Millennials have "behaviors and characteristics that distinguish them in degree or kind from previous generations *at the same age*" (emphasis in original, p. 1). Their communication and information-seeking behaviors are distinctly different from older cohorts and radically different from Baby Boomers. Millennials prefer electronic interfaces that offer more choice/selectivity; flexibility/convenience; and personalization/customization options, and demonstrate a penchant for experiential learning, impatience, a results-oriented approach to communication and searching tasks; and an aptitude for multi-tasking (Sweeney, 2006).

Twelve- to 18-year-old Millennials are referred to here as "screenagers" because of their affinity for electronic communication via computer, phone, television, etc. screens (see Rushkoff, 1996). Agosto and Hughes-Hassell (2005) found: "when these teenagers have information needs, they turn to telephones, televisions, computers, and radios before turning to print resources such as newspapers, books, and magazines. In fact, books and magazines, still staples of many public and school libraries, were listed at the bottom of their list of resources" (p. 161). Screenagers are at home in instant messaging and chat environments to a degree unmatched by preceding generations, and exhibit Millennial characteristics to a greater degree than the older group (19–27 year olds).

Responding to user demand and technological trends, an increasing number of libraries provide Web-based virtual reference services (VRS) as alternatives to traditional face-to-face (FtF) reference. VRS include asynchronous (e.g., e-mail), and synchronous (e.g., instant messaging/chat) formats. Information seekers increasingly turn to VRS for anonymity, convenience, (Tenopir, 2004), and extended hours (Ruppel & Fagan, 2002). Yet Braun (2002) noted that libraries have been slow to adopt instant messaging or chat that screenagers find more appealing than e-mail.

Literature review

The proliferation of VRS underscores the need to understand the behavior of users and providers, examine participant satisfaction, explore the needs of specific populations, and promote successful interactions. Interpersonal aspects have been shown to be critical to clients' perceptions of successful FtF reference interactions (Radford, 1993, 1998, 1999; Dewdney & Ross, 1994) and in virtual environments (Radford, 2006a; Walter & Mediavilla, 2005). VR encounters produce a complete transcript of each interaction, allowing researchers to conduct content analyses of the dialogue that may be too difficult and/or obtrusive to attempt during FtF encounters.

Much VRS research involves evaluations of task-related dimensions such as accuracy (see Arnold & Kaske, 2005, Foley, 2002; Gross & McClure, 2001; Kaske & Arnold, 2002; Sloan, 2004; and White, Abels, & Kaske, 2003). More investigators are turning their attention to the interpersonal characteristics of VRS (see Carter & Janes, 2002; Janes & Mon, 2004; Mon, 2006; Nilsen, 2004; Radford, 2003, 2006a, 2006c; and Walter & Mediavilla, 2005).

Millennials and libraries

Millennials have unique approaches to communication and information-seeking that influence their perception and use of libraries. They have "grown up with computers and video games ... accustomed to multimedia environments: figuring things out for themselves without consulting manuals; working in groups; and multitasking" (Lippincott, 2005, p.13.2). Sweeney (2006) believes: "While some in the older generations may adapt quickly, they will always be immigrants and will never be as competent, resourceful, or 'natural' as the Millennial 'natives' born into this new culture" (p. 1). Older generations tend to search the web to complete a given task, but Millennials see the "web as their information universe ... [and] prefer the global searching of Google to more sophisticated but more time-consuming searching provided by the library" (Lippincott, 2005, p. 13.3, see Schacter, Chung, & Dorr, 1998). They want easy access to full-text documents and become impatient with complex searching that yields citations or abstracts and "want not just speedy answers, but full gratification of their information requests on the spot" (p. 13.13, see Connaway and Prabha, Forthcoming).

Millennials make limited use of libraries and view librarians in negative terms. Radford (2006c) found that librarians who reprimand adolescents for chat behaviors (such as flaming) can provoke or exacerbate rude behavior, and provides recommendations for promoting positive encounters. Research with urban teens found: "participants conveyed negative attitudes toward libraries and librarians and reported frustration with ... aspects of library service such as strict rules, unpleasant staff, lack of culturally relevant materials, dreary physical spaces, and limited access to technology" (Agosto & Hughes-Hassell, 2005, p. 161).

Walther and Mediavilla (2005) believe VRS will appeal to Millennials who are frequent users of IM and social networking sites such as MySpace.com® (Hempel, 2005). Further, Millennials "were not competent participants in the text-oriented discourse environment created by reference librarians. When teens go online with their friends, spelling is less important than rapid response, and capital letters and punctuation are nonexistent. The aim is to connect. Content is almost irrelevant. Indeed when teens go online with their friends, the medium is the message" (Walter & Mediavilla, 2005, p. 12, see also Fagan & Desai, 2003, and Janes, 2002). Walther and Mediavilla (2005) believe that: "Unfortunately, the librarians we studied seem to have grafted inferior versions of the communication styles and protocols of face-to-face reference onto some rather clunky software" (p. 14). They conclude that VRS has not yet lived up to its promise for young people.

Theoretical perspective and research questions

This research builds on the work of Watzlawick, Beavin and Jackson (1967), as applied by Radford to FtF (1993, 1999) and chat (2006a, 2006c) reference encounters. Watzlawick et. al, (1967) proposed that all messages have two dimensions: content (information) aspects and relational (affect, interpersonal) aspects. Research questions derived from gaps in the literature and application of the Watzlawick et al. (1967) perspective are:

- What are teenager's communication and information-seeking preferences?
- What relational dimensions are present in chat reference?
- What are the differences in the relational dimensions of teenaged VRS users, other users and librarians?
- What critical factors influence decisions to use VRS?
- How is the lack of nonverbal cues compensated for in VRS?
- How does VRS users' satisfaction with FtF reference compare to VRS?

Method

Data were collected from three focus groups and from analysis of a random sample of 431 VRS transcripts from an international service provider. Procedures for data collection, selecting participants, data analysis, and a report of results are given below.

FOCUS GROUP INTERVIEWS

Three focus groups were conducted with young Millennials (screenagers), in three Northeastern states, one each from rural, suburban, and urban areas who were regular library users, but had not used VRS. Participants were recruited by librarians from one school and two public libraries in collaboration with public school teachers. Two (rural and urban) groups were held at public libraries, one (suburban) at a public high school. The suburban high school participants were from a history class. The urban and rural participants were recruited by public librarians.

Of the 33 total participants, 18 (55%)[1] were female and 15 (45%) male. Ethnic composition was: 21 (64%) Caucasian, 6 (18%) African-American, and 6 (18%) Hispanic/Latino. Thirty-one (94%) participants were in high school and 2 (6%) were in junior high, with ages from 12–18. Participants signed informed consent forms and parental signatures were also obtained for those under 18.

The transcripts were audio taped and transcribed verbatim. Names were removed for confidentiality. The transcripts were qualitatively analyzed and common themes were identified for each question (see appendix A for focus group questions).

Focus group results and discussion

PREFERENCE FOR INDEPENDENT INFORMATION-SEEKING

Several common themes emerged across all three groups. These screenagers prefer to use Google, other search engines, browse the web, ask friends, or find information themselves, rather than ask a librarian for help (see also Agosto & Hughes-Hassell, 2005, 2006). Urban and rural teens trusted Google results above advice from librarians (see also Schacter, Chung & Dorr, 1998). A rural teen voiced the majority opinion: "I wouldn't really trust my librarian. I trust Google." Another rural teen said: "I find something on Google and there's enough information on it and it seems logical, I'll just go with it." Another usually used Google results without verification, but would check for research papers: "Especially if it's something like you're doing a paper in class and you already know the subject pretty well and all you're looking for are sources to validate what you, you're putting like your argument on paper. You validate your argument. I really don't double check it. I'm like well 'this is what I'm trying to say. This is the source I'm going to use.' But if it's like a research paper, I'll double check my sources a couple of times just to make sure it's the right information."

Google is seen as easier and more convenient than library subscription-based databases. Suburban teens alone trusted results from databases (such as SIRS or Galenet) above Google or web surfing. They had been taught to use these resources in English class and have easy access to them through their school library's website. They agreed, however, that Google would be used to gather background information in beginning research projects. Suburban teens had also been taught to evaluate web content. One urban student said: "What I've seen lately is that you can have a page that's perfectly structured and everything, but yet it can be inaccurate with, um, information … Some pages like that are biased like towards one thing. So you have to make sure you look at everything on the page." Many teens trusted their ability to evaluate web resources above that of the librarian, although others understand that librarians know where to find quality information. Valenza (2006) notes that adolescents have an "apparent lack of concern for their ability to discern the quality of their sources … students spend little time evaluating what they have on the screen, apparently not able to distinguish wheat from chaff" (p. 19) and asserts that "People, teens included, stop their searching at good enough" and frequently choose to "satisfice," following "a path of minimum effort" (p. 20, emphasis in original, see also Prabha, Connaway, Olszewski, and Jenkins, Forthcoming).

PREFERENCE FOR FTF INTERACTION

Unexpectedly, the majority prefer FtF interactions with the librarian to mediated communication when they choose to ask for help. Participants had established strong relationships with their public (urban) and school (suburban) librarians. One suburban teen noted: "Yeah. I think it's easier to have her right there because you can get her feedback on the articles. Like she'll pull up a few and then she'll tell you like what she thinks; it's scholarly or like what she thinks. Then if you're 'This isn't right for me,' she can help you find what you actually need." Another suburban teen agreed: "As long as you're having conversation with someone else at least you can build a relationship. That's just something that you can't get through a computer typing in stuff." Both rural and urban screenagers reported that they were more likely to ask their public librarians for reader's advisory help than for school-related information.

Although the majority carried cell phones, they had never used their phones to call a librarian for homework help and were largely unaware that their library had a phone reference service. One urban female was unaware of the library's web page. None of the teens would ever email a librarian.

LIBRARIAN STEREOTYPES

Although they valued the interpersonal relationships with their librarians, the urban and rural groups held negative stereotypes. This excerpt from the urban group reveals that the adult reference librarians were viewed negatively.

> Lisa:[2] Yeah, like if they're not helpful, they'll point me in the direction and say "Oh ... (talk-over)
>
> Joe: Yeah. Sometimes, sometimes I've asked them like where's a certain book and they'll be like, they'll just point at a random shelf ... And then, and then I look and there's like three shelves next to each other and I'm like "Which one is it?" So, it's like you have to go and look at every book to see if the book is there.
>
> Sarah: And you get embarrassed; you don't want to ask them again once you've already asked them ... (talk-over)
>
> Joe: ... It's like they close their eyes and they're like that "That one right there." (laughs)
>
> Multiple Participants: (laughter)
>
> Sarah: And then cause you've already asked them, you don't want to feel like you're pestering them too much so you don't go and ask them again. It's like, it's like, you don't want to go "So which shelf are you pointing at?" Because, I mean, once they do their famous point, it's just like ... (laughs)
>
> Multiple Participants: (laughter)
>
> Sarah: ... you don't want to go near them again. That's it. So, you'd rather try your luck in searching it out yourself or going on the computer.
>
> Ed: I have actually, uh, left the library and came back another day for the book. Because they would do **the** point and then, ... (talk-over).

It is especially poignant that Ed "actually, uh, left the library and came back another day for the book" rather than interact with the librarian a second time to clarify directions. Sarah refers to "their famous point" evoking one of the components of the librarian stereotype (see Radford & Radford, 1997). Clearly, screenagers choose to avoid possible embarrassing situations (see Goffman, 1967).

A rural teen was concerned about approaching a school librarian after an orientation session: "they spend like the first forty-five minutes of that first day explaining everything that you've heard for like four years and you know how to do it and you're just like 'Can I go and do this? I know what I'm doing.' And I'm like, if you go ahead they'll yell at you and it's just like, uh, it drives you crazy." An urban teen voiced a stereotypical view that librarians: "go and use books and just do more traditional librarian kind of thing." One rural teen described his school librarian as mean and the school library atmosphere as unwelcoming: "Aaaah, if it's necessary, I'll go. But if not, I'd rather stay away from it."

REASONS FOR NOT USING VRS

Several reasons emerged to explain why participants had not tried VRS, although nearly all of the participants were avid IM users, except for the urban students who use email (see also Agosto & Hughes-Hassell, 2005). Participants used IM for socializing, not for serious pursuits like homework help. One reason teens did not use VRS was that they were unaware that these services existed—even though two of the locations had free statewide VRS available 24/7. Some feared that chat librarians either would not understand, ignore, or would not care about their information needs. One rural teen said:

"Plus I think the IMing kind of gives it a cold feeling to it like, you know. They really don't care. They're just doing their job. When you can actually sit and talk to someone face-to-face you kind of can see if they care or not, you know. If they don't care, you're like 'Well, you're not going to help me very much anyway' and you can move on. But the IM, you can keep trying to ask the same person the same question like over and over. And if they don't care, they're just going to keep ignoring you."

Participants had little confidence in the multi-tasking or technical abilities of the librarians. One rural teen said: "A librarian's trying to do like 15 of those conversations at once they're going to mix up replies, mix up the ... what and it, I just don't think it'd be a very applicable ..."

Reflecting Millennial impatience, a suburban teen thought VRS would be time consuming: "I don't really want to take the time actually to type out, like explaining what I'm doing, what I need it for, what type of sources I need." Others felt that asking difficult, e.g., high-level math and science, questions would prove too complex for VRS librarians.

PRIVACY CONCERNS

Participants had serious privacy and security concerns that stem, in part, from, widespread media attention to Internet predators. Already warned to avoid disclosing personal information in chat rooms, teens are reluctant to engage with VRS librarians since they may possibly be dangerous strangers or cyber stalkers. One urban screenager said; "I don't usually like to talk to like people I don't know on the Internet." A rural participant said: "I'm not going to go get tutored on the Internet by somebody who I personally don't know who might be some psycho serial killer out there when I could get personal help from my home and people in my community."

Factors influencing future use

When asked what would encourage them to try VRS, some said a trusted librarian, teacher, or friend's recommendation—or better marketing and publicity by service providers—might help. One rural student said: "I like going to people I know. I would probably try it as a last desperate resort ... I'd feel a little creeped out talking to some random person about it but okay, I'd give it a shot." Others felt that if they could choose a trusted librarian, or one wanting to develop a positive relationship they would try VRS.

Chat transcripts—data collection and analysis

Six hundred chat reference transcripts were randomly selected from a population of approximately 479,673 from OCLC's QuestionPoint[3] service over eighteen months (July 2004 to November 2006). Four hundred ninety-two transcripts were analyzed for this paper; 431 of these were deemed usable after eliminating system tests or technical problems. Transcripts were first coded for educational level through user self-identification or inference. The five education level categories were: Primary School Student (grades K–5), Secondary School Student (screenagers, grades 6–12,), College Student (undergraduate/graduate), Adult (not in college), and Unknown. Self-identified cases revealed their year/grade level in school or age, or were tagged in the XML data for grade level. When such information was not expressly stated, cues in transcripts were used to infer education level, such as context or subject of questions. When education level was ambiguous (e.g., when an assignment could be for an advanced high school class or an introductory college class) the educational level was coded "unknown."

To check coding reliability, a second coder reviewed education levels for 86 (20%) of 431 transcripts. There was 92% agreement initially, but all but one disagreement was resolved after discussion for 99% final agreement.

Once educational level had been coded, all transcripts were stripped of identifying information (e.g., name, email address, IP address, telephone number). The "cleansed" transcripts were then coded using Radford's Relational Communication Category Scheme to identify type and frequency of interpersonal communication. Qualitative analysis involved repeated reading, identification, comparison, and categorization of issues, patterns, and themes following the constant comparative method (Glaser & Strauss, 1967; Lincoln & Guba, 1985). The category scheme and coding method was applied in a manner used in previous studies (see Radford, 1993, 1999, 2006a) and was further expanded and refined during transcript coding for this project.[4] The theoretical perspectives of Watzlawick, Beavin, and Jackson (1967) and Goffman (1972, 1956) provide frameworks for category development focusing attention on content (task) versus relational (interpersonal) aspects of communication. See appendix B for the Radford Relational Communication Category Scheme.

Chat transcript analysis—results and discussion

In the 431 usable transcripts, 22 (5%)[5] users self-identified; an additional 72 (17%) users were inferred to be screenagers (secondary students) for a total of 94 (22%). The remaining users were classified into: primary school students, college students, adult (not in college) and unknown. Results for the 94 (22%) screenagers were compared to results for 150 (35%) users with identifiably different education levels. The educational level of the remaining 187 (43%) could not be determined.

Many interpersonal dynamics present in FtF reference interactions were found to be present in VR. As seen in the Radford Category Scheme, facilitators that assist in relationship development and barriers that impede relationship development were identified in the transcripts. See Appendices C and D for examples of transcripts with Relational Facilitators and Barriers.

table 1 defines Facilitators and Sub-Themes used to classify the data. Greeting Rituals establish contact with a "Hi" or "Hello" in response to a (usually) canned script sent by the system, e.g., "Hello and welcome to Ask-A-Librarian. I am reading your question now." Similarly, Closing Rituals refer to exchanges during which the user may thank the librarian and/or add a farewell such as "good bye" and are met with similar response/script from the librarian such as "Thank you for using Ask-a-Librarian. Please return if you need additional information." Users and librarians demonstrate deference by employing polite expressions, apologies, and repair strategies when mistakes are made. Rapport Building consists of conversational give and take, self-disclosure, inclusive language (i.e., let's or we), use of informal language, and other strategies common in FtF dialogue. Nonverbal communication is rerepresented by use of emoticons [e.g., ;)] spelling of nonverbal behavior (i.e., ha ha), phrase abbreviations (i.e., LOL for Laughing Out Loud), use of all caps (i.e., FLAMING), and other rapidly evolving text-based techniques.

TABLE 1 RELATIONAL FACILITATORS—THEMES AND DEFINITIONS[6]

Major theme	Definition
Relational facilitators	Interpersonal aspects having a positive impact on the librarian-client interaction and enhancing communication (Radford, 1993, 1999, 2006a).
Sub-theme	**Definition**
Greeting ritual	Hello message, marking the beginning of an interpersonal interaction by exchanging "salutations" (see Goffman, 1972, p. 76).
Rapport building	Aspects of the interaction that "involve[s] conversation encouraging give and take, establishment of mutual understanding, and development of relationships" (Radford, 1999, p. 25).
Deference	Showing courtesy and respect. Regularly conveying one's appreciation and confirming the relationship between participants (Goffman, 1956).
Rerepresentation of nonverbal cues	Use of text characters or characteristics to compensate for nonverbal cues not present in chat (see also Walther & D'Addario, 2001).
Closing ritual	A goodbye message signaling the end of interpersonal encounters, "some form of farewell display performed during leave-taking" (Goffman, 1972, p. 79).

Differences in facilitators—screenagers compared to others

The process of comparing counts and averages of occurrences for the Facilitators found in Screenagers' transcripts revealed interesting differences. Screenager transcripts had lower numbers/averages in a number of categories (see table 2).

TABLE 2 RELATIONAL FACILITATORS—LOWER NUMBERS/PERCENTAGES FOR SCREENAGERS

Category	Number occurrences screenagers (n=94)	Number occurrences others (n= 150)
Thanks	88 (.94%)	193 (1.29%)
Self disclosure	53 (.56%)	136 (.91%)
Seeking reassurance	51 (.6%)	106 (.71%)
Agreement to try suggestion	47 (.5%)	111 (.74%)
Closing ritual	34 (.36%)	79 (.53%)
Admitting lack of knowledge	9 (.10%)	32 (.21%)
Encouraging remarks	1 (.01%)	8 (.05%)

Teens typically have low levels of self-disclosure and are reluctant to admit lack of knowledge or agree to advice, so these results are not unexpected (Radford, 2006b). They engage in fewer closing rituals, since they are generally impatient and may suddenly leave the chat session. However, they say "thanks" at nearly the rate of those at other educational levels, demonstrating better manners than usually attributed to teens. Screenagers are also enthusiastic (Sweeney, 2006), so it is also not surprising that they express their gratitude.

Screenager transcripts had higher numbers/averages in some Facilitator categories (see table 3). Teens favor typing shortcuts and alternative spellings, having embraced the keystroke-conserving tactics of Instant Messaging and text messaging, as seen prominently here (see Carter, 2003; Zlinko 2006). It is therefore not surprising that Millennials frequently use alternate spellings, lower case, and alpha-numeric shortcuts such as "ne1" (anyone).

TABLE 3 RELATIONAL FACILITATORS—HIGHER NUMBERS AND PERCENTAGES FOR SCREENAGERS

Category	Number occurrences screenagers (n=94)	Number occurrences others (n= 150)
Alternate spellings	34 (.36%)	22 (.15%)
Punctuation/repeat punctuation	27 (.29%)	33 (.22%)
Lower case	22 (.23%)	26 (.17%)
Slang	11 (.12%)	3 (.02%)
Self-correction	10 (.11%)	6 (.04%)
Enthusiasm	9 (.10%)	10 (.07%)
Explanation for abrupt ending	6 (.06%)	3 (.02%)
Alpha-numeric shortcuts	3 (.03%)	0

TABLE 4 RELATIONAL BARRIERS[7]

Major theme	Definition
Relational barriers	Interpersonal aspects of the chat conversation that have a negative impact on the librarian-client interaction and that impede communication (see also Radford, 1993, 1999, 2006a).
Sub-theme	**Definition**
Relational disconnect/ failure to build rapport	Failing to encourage give and take, establish mutual understanding, and engage in relationship development (see Radford, 1999, p. 25).
Closing problems	Ending the chat interaction without a closing ritual or exchange of farewell or goodbye (see Goffman, 1972).
Negative closure	Strategies "that library staff uses to end the reference transaction, apart from providing a helpful answer" (Ross & Dewdney, 1998, p. 154).

table 4 defines Barriers and Sub-Themes that emerged from the data. Screenager transcripts had higher numbers/averages in four barrier categories (see table 5). Abrupt Endings come with the "cyberterritory" in chat, but the "disappearing user" is puzzling for librarians who wonder if technical problems occured, or if the user has left the computer. Millennials, known for their multi-tasking (Sweeney, 2006), may have other chat windows open, get involved in a phone conversation, or abruptly transfer their focus to other tasks. Millennials are also impatient, so again this result is not unexpected (Sweeney, 2006). The number of users who were rude/insulting or goofing around was low, reflecting findings from analysis of a statewide VRS (Radford, 2006a) that may be viewed as surprising since many librarians believe that teens are often rude in VRS encounters.

TABLE 5 RELATIONAL BARRIERS—HIGHER NUMBERS AND PERCENTAGES FOR SCREENAGERS

Category	Number occurrences screenagers (n=94)	Number occurrences others (n= 150)
Abrupt endings	41 (.44%) (41 transcripts)	47 (.31%) (47 transcripts)
Impatience	12 (.13%) (8 transcripts)	4 (.03%) (3 transcripts)
Goofing around	8 (.09) (4 transcripts)	8 (.05) (1 transcript)
Rude or insulting	3 (.03) (3 transcripts)	0 (0 transcripts)

Implications of focus group and transcript analysis

These results have many implications for school librarians working with young Millennials. Teen's stereotypical images of librarians and fear of being reprimanded or embarrassed suggest that librarians need to be more aware that teens may be hesitant to ask questions. Results suggest that teens should be encouraged, treated gently, and invited to ask for follow-up help. Librarians might consider accompanying teens to shelves to locate materials and checking with them often during the information seeking process. Teens clearly value FtF interaction, so librarians may want to take extra time to get to know students, create positive relationships, and use constructive feedback techniques (e.g., catch them being good).

Since Millennials like collaborative work, ample group space ought to be designated wherever possible. Teens' preference for independent information seeking needs to be accepted and respected. However, they require guidance in becoming savvy searchers and evaluating resources. Teens are impatient so instruction on efficient use of search engines and library databases could be promoted as time saving in the long run.

Librarians could do much to allay teens' fear of using VRS. Teens reveal that they would try VRS if encouraged by trusted librarians. Demos of VRS could be given along with discussion of what types of questions and chat behaviors are appropriate (see Radford, Barnes, & Barr, 2006, for user guidelines). Techniques to avoid dangerous chat situations could be offered. Results also suggest that students should be encouraged to enter library phone numbers into their cell phones for quick ready reference or verification questions.

School librarians are urged to try VRS with their students or join/promote a local consortium since these results indicate that screenagers will respond positively to these services if encouraged to do so and treated with respect as users. This research suggests that the above strategies would increase teen use of FtF as well as VR library services.

Conclusion

Results clearly indicate that screenagers have different communication and information behaviors than those of previous generations. The teens' traditional views of librarians carry over into their decision-making process for choosing VRS. They do not think of chat as a possible venue for homework help, worry about chat conversations with strangers, and have been told to avoid potentially dangerous situations online, so they need to be reassured by trusted adults or friends before they will try VRS.

Focus group interviews reveal that relational dimensions are critically important to adolescents who are experiencing a period of rapid emotional as well as physical development (see also Kuhlthau, 2004). Valenza (2006) notes that a blend of FtF and electronic services may be best: "For today's learners, libraries can be exciting hybrid experiences of face-to-face lessons learned, reinforced with effective online supports" (p. 23).

Walter and Mediavilla (2005) recommend involving teenagers in developing and evaluating VRS services. "It would be interesting to see what would happen if the designers of such online reference services followed the principles of good young adult library practice and involved the teens as active participants in both the planning and the delivery of the services. At the moment, teens are from Neptune, librarians are from Pluto. Better services would result if they could meet somewhere closer together in cyberspace" (p. 14).

This research project is reaching out to young Millennials to learn more about their communication and information-seeking behaviors. One goal is to gain a greater understanding of their preferences and needs to ensure that virtual and FtF library services are effective and responsive. VRS offers a promising avenue to reach young Millennials if they are encouraged and welcomed by librarians. Future relevance and sustainability of library services may hang in the balance in this Google-dominated information environment if VRS does not live up to this promise.

NOTES

1. Percentages are rounded to the nearest whole number for demographic data.

2. Participants' names have been changed to protect anonymity. Participant comments appear verbatim. Interviewer comments to call upon next speaker have been removed to heighten readability.

3. The international VRS provider, OCLC Online Computer Library Center's QuestionPoint, is supported by a global network. It has been developed by OCLC and the Library of Congress and has recently merged with 24/7 Reference developed by the Metropolitan Cooperative Library System in Southern California. QuestionPoint is used in more than 1,000 libraries in twenty countries; 24/7 serves approximately 500 libraries (http://www.oclc.org/questionpoint).

4. QSR NVivo 7 (QSR International 2003–2006) software was used in data analysis and coding of the chat transcripts. NVivo enables the researchers to effectively sort large amounts of qualitative data into themes and provides numerous report options for data reduction and representation.

5. Percentages are rounded to the nearest whole number for demographic data.

6. An earlier version of this table was published in Radford (2006a, p.1049).

7. An earlier version of this table was published in Radford (2006a, p.1053).

REFERENCES

Agosto, D.E., & Hughes-Hassell, S. 2005. "People, places, and questions: An investigation of the everyday life information-seeking behaviors of urban young adults." *Library and Information Science Research* 27: 141–163.

Agosto, D. E., & Hughes-Hassell, S. 2006. "Toward a model of the everyday life information needs of urban teenagers, part 1: Theoretical model." *Journal of the American Society for Information Science and Technology* 57, no. 10: 1394–1403.

Arnold, J. & Kaske, N. 2005. "Evaluating the quality of a chat service." *portal: Libraries and the Academy* 5, no. 2: 177–193.

Braun, L. W. 2002. *Teens.library: Developing Internet services for young adults.* Chicago: American Library Association.

Carter, D. S. & Janes, J. 2002. "Unobtrusive data analysis of digital reference questions and service at the Internet Public Library: An exploratory study." *Library Trends* 49, no. 2: 251–265.

Carter, K. A. 2003. "Type me how you feel: Quasi-nonverbal cues in computer-mediated communication." *ETC: A Review of General Semantics* 60, no. 1: 29–39.

Connaway, L.S. & Prabha, C. Forthcoming. "Identifying serials user's needs: Preliminary analysis of focus group and semi-structured interviews at colleges and universities." *Serials Librarian.*

Dewdney, P. & Ross, C. S. 1994. "Flying a light aircraft: Reference service evaluation from the user's viewpoint." *RQ.* 34, no. 2: 217–230.

Fagan, J. C. & Desai, C. M. 2003. "Communication strategies for instant messaging and chat reference services." B. Katz (Ed.). *Digital Reference Services*, p. 121–156. Binghamton, NY: Haworth Information Press.

Foley, M. 2002. "Instant messaging reference in an academic library: A case study." *College and Research Libraries* 63, no. 1: 36–45.

Gerhardt, P. 2004, 7 September. "Homework problems? Help is a click away." *Washington Post,* p. C08.

Glaser, B. G. & Strauss, A. L. (1967). *The discovery of grounded theory: Strategies for qualitative research.* Hawthorne, New York: Aldine de Gruyter.

Goffman, E. 1959. *The presentation of self in everyday life.* Garden City, NY: Doubleday Anchor.

Goffman, E. 1967. *Interaction ritual, essays on face-to-face behavior.* Garden City, NY: Doubleday.

Gross, M. & McClure, C. 2001. "Assessing quality in digital reference services: Overview of key literature on digital reference." Information Use Management and Policy Institute, Florida State University. http://dlis.dos.state.fl.us/bld/Research_Office/VRDphaseII.LitReview.doc (accessed 3 November 2006) (inaccessible 26 October 2015).

Hallam, G. & Partridge, H. 2006. "Evidence based library and information practice: Whose responsibility is it anyway?" Evidence Based Library and Information Practice 2006 *1, no. 3.* http://ejournals.library.ualberta.ca/index.php/EBLIP/article/view/107/145 (accessed 3 November)

Hempel, J. 2005. "The Myspace generation: They live online. They buy online. They play online. Their power is growing." *Business Week,* 12 December, p. 86.

Janes, J. 2002. "Live reference: Too much too fast?" *NetConnect,* Fall, p. 12–14.

Janes, J. & Mon, L. 2004. "The thank you study: User satisfaction with digital reference." Presented at the ALISE Conference, San Diego, CA, 6–9 January 2004.

Kaske, N., & Arnold, J. 2002. "An unobtrusive evaluation of online real time library reference services." American Library Association, Annual Conference, Atlanta, GA, 15 June 2002. http://www.lib.umd.edu/groups /digref/kaskearnoldunobtrusive.html (accessed 3 November 2006) (inaccessible 26 October 2015).

Kuhlthau, C. C. 2004. Seeking meaning: *A process approach to library and information services,* (2nd Ed.). Westport, CT: Libraries Unlimited.

Lincoln, Y. & Guba, E. 1985. *Naturalistic inquiry.* Newbury Park, CA: Sage.

Lippincott, J. 2005. "Net Generation students and libraries." D. G. Oblinger, and J. L. Oblinger, (Eds.), *Educating the Net Generation.* EDUCAUSE. http://www.educause.edu/content.asp?PAGE_ID=5989&bhcp=1 (accessed 3 November 2006) (inaccessible 26 October 2015).

>   Alternative URL https://net.educause.edu/ir/library/pdf/pub7101m.pdf
>   (accessed October 2015).

Metz, C., Clyman, J., & Todd, M. 2003. "IM everywhere." *PC Magazine,* 11 November, 22 no. 20: 128–136.

Mon, L. 2006. *User perspectives on satisfaction with digital reference services.* Unpublished Doctoral Dissertation, University of Washington.

Nilsen, K. 2004. "The library visit study: User experiences at the virtual reference desk." *Information Research* 9, no. 2. Paper 171. http://InformationR.net/ir/9-2/paper171.html (accessed 3 November 2006)

Oblinger, D.G. & Oblinger, J. L. 2005. (Eds.), *Educating the Net Generation.* EDUCAUSE. http://www.educause.edu/content.asp?PAGE_ID=5989&bhcp=1 (accessed 3 November 2006) (inaccessible 26 October 2015).

>   Alternative URL http://www.educause.edu/research-and-publications/books/educating-net-generation (accessed 26 October 2015).

Oblinger, D.G. & Oblinger, J. L. 2006. "Is it age or IT: First steps toward understanding the Net Generation." *CSLA Journal,* Spring, 29, no. 2: 8–16.

Prabha, C., Connaway, L.S., Olszewski, L. & Jenkins, L. Forthcoming. "What is enough? Satisficing information needs." *Journal of Documentation.*

QSR NVivo 7. [Computer Software]. 2003–2006. Doncaster, Australia: QSR International Pty Ltd. http://www.qsrinternational.com/.

Radford, M. L. June, 2006. "Encountering virtual users: A qualitative investigation of interpersonal communication in chat reference." *Journal of the American Society for Information Science and Technology* 57, no. 8: 1046–1059.

Radford, M. L. 2006. "The critical incident technique and the qualitative evaluation of the Connecting Libraries and Schools Project." *Library Trends* 54, no. 1: 46–64.

Radford, M. L. 2006. "Investigating interpersonal communication in chat reference: Dealing with impatient users and rude encounters." R. David Lankes, Eileen Abels, Marilyn White and Saira N. Haque. (Eds.) *The Virtual Reference Desk: Creating a Reference Future,* p. 23–46. New York: Neal-Schuman Publishers.

Radford, M. L. 2003. *In synch? Evaluating chat reference transcripts.* Presented at the Virtual Reference Desk 5th Annual Digital Reference Conference, San Antonio, TX, 17–18 November 2003.

Radford, M. L. 1999. "The reference encounter: Interpersonal communication in the academic library." Chicago: ACRL, A Division of the American Library Association.

Radford, M. L. 1998. "Approach or avoidance? The role of nonverbal communication in the academic library user's decision to initiate a reference encounter." *Library Trends,* Spring, 46, no. 4: 699–717.

Radford, M. L. 1993. "Relational aspects of reference interactions: A qualitative investigation of the perceptions of users and librarians in the academic library." Unpublished doctoral dissertation, Rutgers, The State University of New Jersey. DAI A54/07, 2368.

Radford, M. L., Barnes, S. B., & Barr, L. 2006. *Web Research: Selecting, Evaluating, and Citing.* (2nd ed.). Boston, MA: Allyn and Bacon Publishers.

Radford, M. L. & Radford, G. P. 1997. "Power, knowledge, and fear: Feminism, Foucault and the stereotype of the female librarian." *The Library Quarterly,* July, 67, no. 3: 250–266.

Rezabek, L.L. & Cochenour, J.J. 1998. "Visual cues in computer-mediated communication: Supplementing text with emoticons." *Journal of Visual Literacy* 18: 201–215.

Rice, R. E., & Love, G. 1987. "Electronic Emotion: Socio-emotional content in a computer-mediated communication network." *Communication Research* 14, no. 1: 85–108.

Ross, C. S., & Dewdney, P. 1998. "Negative closure: Strategies and counter-strategies in the reference transaction." *RUSQ,* winter, 38, no. 2: 151–163.

Ruppel, M. & Fagan, J.C. 2002. "Instant messaging reference: Users' evaluation of library chat." *Reference Services Review* 30, no. 3: 183–197. http://www.lib.siu.edu/~jfagan/papers/imref.html (accessed 3 November 2006) (inaccessible 26 October 2015).

Rushkoff, D. 1996. *Playing the future: What we can learn from digital kids.* New York: Harper Collins.

Schacter, J., Chung, G. & Dorr, A. 1998. "Children's Internet searching on complex problems: Performance and process analyses." *Journal of the American Society for Information Science,* July, 49, no. 9: 840–849.

Sloan, B., ed. 2004. Digital reference services: bibliography. http://alexia.lis.uiuc.edu/~b-sloan/digiref.html (accessed 3 November 2006) (inaccessible 26 October 2015).

Sweeney, R. 2006. Millennial behaviors and demographics. http://www.library.njit.edu/staff-folders/sweeney/Millennials/Millennial-Behaviors-August-14-2006.doc (accessed 3 November 2006) (inaccessible 26 October 2015).

Tenopir, C. November 2004. "Rethinking virtual reference." *Library Journal* 129, no. 18: 34.

Valenza, J. K. 2006. "They might be gurus." *Teacher Librarian* 34, no. 1: 18–26.

Watzlawick, P., Beavin, J. & Jackson, D.D. 1967. *Pragmatics of human communication.* NY: Norton.

Walther, J. B. 1992. "Interpersonal effects in computer-mediated interaction: A relational perspective." *Communication Research* 19, no. 1: 52–90.

Walther, J.B. 1994. "Anticipated ongoing interaction versus channel effects on relational communication in computer-mediated interaction." *Human Communication Research* 20: 473–501.

Walther, J.B., & D'Addario, K. P. 2001. "The impacts of emoticons on message interpretation in computer-mediated communication." *Social Science Computer Review* 19, no. 3: 342–347.

Walter, V.A. & Mediavilla, C. 2005. "Teens are from Neptune, librarians are from Pluto: An analysis of online reference transactions." *Library Trends* 54, no. 2: 209–227.

Zlinko, C. 9 October 2006. "Don't say it, type it." *San Francisco Chronicle.* http://www.columbusdispatch.com/emailme/emailme.php?story=dispatch/2006/10/09/20061009-F1-00.html (inaccessible 26 October 2015).

APPENDIX A—FOCUS GROUP QUESTIONS FOR NON-USERS OF VIRTUAL REFERENCE SERVICES (AGES 12–18)

1. When you are stuck in a homework assignment and need information, what do you do when you need help?

2. When you need help with homework and decide to get help from a librarian, what do you do?
   — [PROBES: do you usually go to the library, email a librarian, or call the library on the phone? How do you decide what kind of help to try?]

3. Do you know that you can ask librarians questions or for help using email or IM (instant messaging)? If yes, why haven't you tried them?

4. Would you like to try "IM"ing or chatting with a librarian for help? What would make you interested in trying email or IM to get help from librarians?

5. What have you heard about getting librarian help or getting library resources on the Web from your friends or teachers?

APPENDIX B—RADFORD RELATIONAL COMMUNICATION CODING SCHEME

FACILITATORS

- Greeting Ritual
- Deference
  — Agreement to Try What is Suggested or To Wait
  — Apology
  — Asking for Other to Be Patient
  — Expressions of Enthusiasm
  — Suggesting Strategy or Explanation in a Tentative Way
  — Polite Expressions
  — Praise, Admiration
  — Self-Deprecating Remarks
  — Thanks
- Rapport Building
  — Familiarity
  — Humor
  — Informal Language
  — Alternate Spelling, Abbreviated Single Words
  — Slang Expressions
  — Interjections
  — Offering Confirmation
  — Approval
  — Empathy
  — Inclusion
  — Offering Reassurance
  — Encouraging Remarks, Praise
  — Enthusiastic Remarks
  — Repair Self Correction
  — Seeking Reassurance, Confirmation Self Disclosure
  — Self Disclosure
  — Admitting Lack of Knowledge
  — Explaining Search Strategy
  — Explaining Technical Problems
  — Offer Personal Opinion Advice, Value Judgment
  — Rerepresentation of Nonverbal Cues
  — ALL CAPS
  — Alpha-Numeric Shortcuts
  — Asterisk for Emphasis
  — Ellipsis
  — Emoticons
  — Lower Case
  — Phrase Abbreviations
  — Spells Nonverbal Behaviors
  — Punctuation or Repeated Punctuation
- Closing Ritual
  — Explanation Abrupt Ending
  — Invites to Return If Necessary
  — Makes Sure User Has No More Questions
  — Offers to Continue Searching & E-Mail Answer

BARRIERS

- Negative Closure
  - Abrupt Ending
  - Disclaimer
  - Failure to Refer
  - Ignoring Cues that User Wants More Help
  - Premature or Attempted Closing
  - Premature Referral
  - Sends To Google

- Relational Disconnect Failure to Build Rapport
  - Condescending
  - Derisive Use of Spelling NV Behaviors
  - Disconfirming
  - Failing to Offer Reassurance
  - Failure or Refusal to Provide Info
  - Goofing Around
  - Ignoring Humor
  - Ignoring Self-Disclosure
  - Impatience
  - Inappropriate Script or Inappropriate Response
  - Inappropriate Language
  - Jargon, No Explanation
  - Lack of Attention or Ignoring Question
  - Limits Time
  - Mirrors Rude Behavior
  - Mistakes
  - Misunderstands Question
  - Reprimanding
  - Robotic Answer
  - Rude or Insulting

APPENDIX C—SAMPLE TRANSCRIPT WITH RELATIONAL FACILITATORS

"Mathematics in the Islamic empire"

(Note: U=User, L=Librarian)

1	U	i need a good website about the accomplishments of mathrmatics during the islamic empire
2	L	[A librarian will be with you in about a minute.]
3	L	[A librarian has joined the session.]
4	L	[You have been conferenced with MD]
5	L	(Name) welcome to (service name) I'm looking at your question right now; it will be just a moment.
6	L	Hi (name) - sorry about the delay there. This is (name), a librarian in Baltimore County...
7	U	ok
8	L	Okay, we should be able to find something on that topic. Math and Islam. Just a minute or two while I search. Please let me know if there's anything specific in this area that you're looking for, okay?
9	U	i don;t care about the delay i have plenty of time
10	L	Thanks for understanding. We just had a very busy spell on the service and I just finished up another call. Let's see... searching now.
11	U	i just need any certan mathematicians or the accomplishments of mathematics during the islamic Empire
12	L	Okay, to start I'm going to send you an article linked from the Math Forum:
13	L	[Page sent]
14	L	It should show on your screen in just a few seconds. Are you able to see it? the title is Arabic mathematics : forgotten brilliance?
15	U	thank you very much

16	L	Great - glad you can see it! There was one other article - did you want me to send it to you, or are you okay with just this one?
17	U	yes plaese
18	L	Okay, just a sec.
19	L	[Page sent]
20	U	i spelled please wrong
21	L	The title of this 2nd page I just sent was, "The Arabic numeral system"
22	U	thank you
23	L	No problem on the spelling. :) Typing this fast it's giong to happen.
24	L	*going*
25	L	Okay, what do you think? Will these answer your questions?
26	U	yes thank you
27	L	Great! Please do write us back if you need anything else.
28	L	Thank you for using name service! If you have any further questions, please contact us again. If you provided an e-mail address, you should receive a full transcript in a few minutes. You may click the "End Call" button now.
29	U	i am doing a history reseach project and i am having trouble finding things
30	U	[patron - has disconnected]
31	U	i am doing a history reseach project and i am having trouble finding things
32	L	Oh, well if you need any more detailed info, the subscription databases available through the Harford County home page should help. Let me know if you'd like any assisitance in that area.
33	L	[Thank you for using (service name!) If you have any further questions, please contact us again. If you provided an e-mail address, you should receive a full transcript in a few minutes. You may click the "End Call" button now.]
34		Note to staff: COMP [user has closed this session]

DISCUSSION OF RELATIONAL FACILITATORS IN "MATHEMATICS IN THE ISLAMIC EMPIRE" TRANSCRIPT

The above example of a positive interaction demonstrates a positive interaction between a librarian and user, with many examples of relational facilitators. Deference, for example, is shown by the librarian in several places. Immediately as the librarian greets the user, an apology is offered for the delay in responding to the user's query (line 6). Later in the transcript, the librarian thanks the user for being patient (line 10) and shares enthusiastic comments with the user (line 16). Another excellent example that highlights a relational facilitator in action is where the librarian reassures the user after a mistake in typing is noted (lines 20 and 23) and crowns the reassurance with a smiley face emoticon. The user demonstrates deference in return by in repeated use of polite expressions and thanks (lines 15, 17, 22, & 26). In line 25 the librarian is again deferential to the user in seeking feedback and approval. The librarian shows kindness, encouragement (line 23) and enthusiasm (line 27) to the user, all of which are relational facilitators which build rapport Lastly, even after the user logs off the librarian continues the positive interaction by inviting the user to return to use the service if further help is needed (lines 32 & 33).

APPENDIX D—SAMPLE TRANSCRIPT WITH RELATIONAL BARRIERS

"Physics"

(Note: U=User, L=Librarian)

1	U	Physics
2	L	[Please hold for the next available librarian. If you would like a transcript of this session emailed to you, please type your full email address now.]
3	L	[A librarian has joined the session.]
4	U	when you drive forward in a bumper car at high speed and then you slam into the car in front of you, you find yourself thrown forward in your car. Which way is ur car accelerating?
5	L	thank you for holding I was working with another patron.
6	L	Is this a homework question.
7	L	I'm not an expert on driving so I really can't answer that.
8	U	can u find a website or something
9	L	I'm not sure what you are asking.
10	U	when you drive forward in a bumper car at high speed and then you slam into the car in front of you, you find yourself thrown forward in your car. Which way is ur car accelerating?
11	U	....
12	U	hello?
13	L	Is this a homework a homework assignment. what subject is it.
14	L	I really don't understand how I can answer that for you.
15	U	can i hav another librarian
16	L	The information you gave you me does not help me find any resources to help you.

17	L	What do you mean by which way is your car accerlaerating. Are you sure thats what your assignment asks.
18	U	yes
19	L	What subject is this question from?
20	U	physics
21	L	Okay just one moment.
22	L	[Page sent]
23	L	This is one site that may help.
24	L	[Page sent]
25	L	[Page sent - LeapStart Learning Table. Learning Starts Here!]
26	L	this is another site that youmay try forhelp.
27	L	When we disconnect youwill have these links in a transcript.
28	L	[Page sent]
29	L	This site looks to be very helpful.
30	L	[Page sent - The Physics Classroom]
31	L	[Page sent - The Physics Classroom]
32	L	[Page sent - The Physics Classroom]
33	U	this isn't helpful
34	L	Well I really don't have any other resources that can assit you.
35	L	[Page sent - The Physics Classroom]
36	L	I cannot answer the question for you, I don't have the physics knowledge.
37	L	Maybe you will need to ask your instructor for a clear understanding.
38	L	[Page sent - The Physics Classroom]
39	U	do u kno ne1 who does
40	L	[Page sent - The Physics Classroom]

41	U	Sorry I do not.
42	U	ok
43	L	I have a few patron that I ned to assist.
44	U	ok bye
45	L	[Thank you for using (service name)! If you have any further questions, please contact us again.]
46		Note to staff: COMP [user has closed this session]

DISCUSSION OF RELATIONAL BARRIERS IN "PHYSICS" TRANSCRIPT

The above transcript demonstrates a negative interaction between a librarian and user with multiple examples of relational barriers. The user initiates the chat session by providing the subject area for the inquiry: "Physics." However, this primary piece of information is not attended to by the librarian who twice later asks the user to disclose this information again (see lines 13 and 20). While the librarian could have asked probing questions or performed a query negotiation at any moment during this encounter, no attempt was made to clarify the user's question other than asking about the subject and asking if this is a homework assignment (lines 6 and 13). Other examples of relational barriers include several occasions when the librarian avoids assisting the user and offers disclaimers (see lines 7, 34 and 36) including lack of subject knowledge. It becomes evident that the user is dissatisfied with the assistance from this particular librarian when he/she asks if another librarian can assist (line 15) and again when the user provides feedback that the web resources pushed to his/her desktop are not helpful (line 33). The librarian uses a negative closure strategy in attempting to refer user back to their teacher (line 37). In line 39 when the user asks if the librarian knows anyone (ne1) else who can help, the user is asking for a referral, but the librarian refuses to provide one (line 41). As a final rebuff, the librarian provides an excuse to leave and limits the time by saying he/she had other patrons to assist (line 43).

Sense-Making and Synchronicity: Information-Seeking Behaviors of Millennials and Baby Boomers

Lynn Silipigni Connaway, Ph.D.
OCLC Research

Marie L. Radford, Ph.D.
Rutgers, The State University of New Jersey

Timothy J. Dickey, Ph.D.
OCLC Research

Jocelyn DeAngelis Williams
Rutgers, The State University of New Jersey

Patrick Confer
OCLC Research

A reprint of:

Connaway, Lynn Silipigni, Marie L. Radford, Timothy J. Dickey, Jocelyn DeAngelis Williams, and Patrick Confer. 2008. "Sense-making and Synchronicity: Information-seeking Behaviors of Millennials and Baby Boomers." *Libri*. 58, no. 2: 123–135. http://dx.doi.org/10.1515/libr.2008.014

Reproduced with permission of K.G./SAUR VERLAG GMBH.

The content of this paper is based on a presentation at the international conference "i3: Information: Interactions and Impact," organized by the Robert Gordon University's Department of Information Management, and held in Aberdeen, Scotland, 25–28 June 2007.

This paper is one of the outcomes from two projects:

- "Sense-Making the Information Confluence: The Whys and Hows of College and University User Satisficing of Information Needs." Funded by the Institute of Museum and Library Services, Ohio State University, and OCLC Online Computer Library Center, Inc.

- "Seeking Synchronicity: Evaluating Virtual Reference Services from User, Non-User, and Librarian Perspectives." Funded by IMLS, Rutgers University, and OCLC, Online Computer Library Center, Inc. Marie L. Radford and Lynn Silipigni Connaway, Co-Principal Investigators. URL: http://www.oclc.org/research/projects/synchronicity/default.htm

INTRODUCTION AND PROBLEM DOMAIN

In an era of staggering changes to the global information environment, library and information science faces numerous challenges. The current digital landscape demands that library practice both becomes more intensely user-centered in all of its systems and services, and simultaneously return to its core philosophies in the face of cyberspace's limitless information sources and unregulated chaos. The accessibility and immediate delivery of full-text content on the Internet adds another dimension to users' expectations and experiences in information delivery.

Libraries are vying for information seekers' attention in the digital environment. Previously information resources were scarce; therefore people's attention centered on the library where numerous resources were organized, stored, and made accessible. Now information is abundant on the Internet and the information seekers' attention to library sources has become scarce (Prabha, et al. 2007; Harley, et al. 2006; OCLC 2006; "HotTopics: 2006 User Update" 2006). Traditionally, library-centered processes, systems, and services have required users to build and adapt their workflow around them. Librarians now must build systems and services around the users' workflow and habits. LIS professionals desiring to make changes have found it difficult to change libraries as quickly as other technology-based information providers because library systems and the services constructed around them have been in place (and deeply ingrained) for centuries. Libraries also must serve various constituencies with differing information-seeking habits and needs.

To remain relevant in this environment, libraries must provide services that match the information-seeking habits of a new generation, the Millennials, who "... *think and process information fundamentally differently from their predecessors*" (Prensky 2001a, np), along with those of one of their largest constituencies—the Baby Boomers. These two groups display different characteristics and information needs, presenting a dichotomy for library service and system development.

Two research projects, "Sense-making the Information Confluence: The Whys and Hows of College and University User Satisficing of Information Needs" (Dervin, Connaway and Prabha 2003) and "Seeking Synchronicity: Evaluating Virtual Reference Services from User, Non-User, and Librarian Perspectives" (Radford and Connaway 2005), studied the habits and needs of information seekers to identify patterns and characteristics for discovering and accessing information. Both studies include multi-method research designs to identify how and why individuals seek and use information. This discussion focuses on the information-seeking habits of Millennials and Baby Boomers, reporting the portions of the project findings relating to focus group and semi-structured interviews and Virtual Reference Services (VRS) transcript analyses phases for each project.

Study population

BABY BOOMERS

After World War II ended in 1945, and there was an exponential increase in births in the United States stretching between 1946 and 1964 (Krohn 2004; Dempsey 2007). Those born within this period are referred to as the "Baby Boom Generation" (Gillon 2004). Boomers are the largest growing generational demographic, representing over 25% of the US population (Kahlert 2000). As life expectancies increase, this statistic is likely to increase. Boomers are often divided into two cohorts. According to Campbell (2005), older Boomers are born between 1946 and 1956 and younger Boomers were born between 1956 and 1964. (For an in-depth discussion of the two cohorts, see Schuman and Scott 1989.)

During the 1950s, the US experienced prosperity and great economic growth, while the 1960s reflected times of social upheaval and cultural change (Gillon 2004). Although difficult to generalize, Boomers growing up in the 1950s and 1960s display certain characteristics which may be attributed to the social, cultural, and political environments experienced during their development (Campbell 2005). Overall, Boomers are better educated, more technology literate and economically more advantaged than any generation before them (Williamson, et al. 2006). Described as optimists and believers in the American Dream, they are self-absorbed, strive to be the center of attention, and tend towards a desire for self-gratification. Work is very important to them and they have a team orientation, while longing for personal and spiritual growth. Boomers are concerned with their health and believe "aging is optional" (Grossman 2000). Key characteristics are the desire to stay young, keeping their minds busy and maintaining mental agility, to remain active in the workforce longer, and to be in touch with technology (Dempsey 2007).

Boomers are heralding a shift in how previous generations approached work and technology. Older individuals are populating the workforce at an increasing rate, exposing them to technology which becomes integrated into daily life. Boomers have different requirements for information, as they read more and use public libraries more than previous generations (Joseph 2006). "The majority (56% of those currently ages 50–64 years, the early Boomers) have Internet access, have used computers and the Internet in their work lives, and report that they would miss the Internet if they could no longer use it" (Willis 2006, p. 44). During a six-year period (2000–2006) there was an increase from 13% to 43% of older individuals having Internet access and actively using it (Willis 2006). For Boomers, information-seeking and e-mail are the most prominent uses for computers and the Internet (Willis 2006).

Increasingly, Boomers engage with technology in libraries. They have high expectations for public libraries to provide the latest and best resources (Kahlert 2000). Their interests and habits bring new demands for information and technology: "… as the World Wide Web increasingly became a central resource for information, Boomer doggedness would shape the culture of that medium as well, turning it into an investigative tool for any citizen or consumer seeking the truth about the policies and products they were asked to consume." (Steinhorn 2006, p. 202). Although Boomers and Millennials demonstrate different behaviors and characteristics, they do share some similarities.

THE "MILLENNIAL" GENERATION

Born between 1979 and 2000, the "Millennial" generation (Howe and Strauss 2000) has also been called: "Net Generation," "Generation Y," or "Echo Boomers." The 76 million Millennials may constitute the most-studied generation in history. The defining characteristic of the Millennial mindset is that they are "digital natives" (Prensky 2001a), growing up immersed in technologies which for them are invisible and taken for granted, "like the air" (Tapscott 1998, p. 39). Far surpassing the general public, 20% of Millennials began using computers between the ages of 5 and 8, 72% check e-mail at least once a day, and 78% browse the Web for fun (Jones and Madden 2002). Technology surrounds them and dominates their socialization: "over 10,000 hours playing video games, over 200,000 e-mails and instant messages sent and received; over 10,000 hours talking on digital cell phones; over 200,000 hours watching TV ... —all before the kids leave college" (Prensky 2001b, p.1; see also Hempel 2005; Junco 2005; Gibbons 2007). Some specific generational features pertinent to libraries and information-seeking include the following:

Immediacy. According to Sweeney (2006), "Millennials, by their own admission, have no tolerance for delays" (p. 3). They respond quickly to communications from others, expect the same in return (Oblinger and Oblinger 2005), and seek information sources that are convenient (Van Scoyoc and Cason 2006).

Collaboration. Highly team-oriented, Millennials' relational patterns tend to be non-hierarchical and they can operate as an organism, "a single networked whole" (Rushkoff 1996). This especially applies to their online communication styles, which have evolved around instant messaging (IM) and chat rooms (Walter and Mediavilla 2005).

Experiential learning. Preferring to learn actively and by discovery (Oblinger and Oblinger 2005), their lifelong navigation of the Internet may give Millennials greater critical thinking skills and judgment (Tapscott 1998).

Visual orientation. Millennials work and learn well in a visual environment and process visual information efficiently (Rushkoff 1996). This can lead to difficulties in interactions with current library systems (Lippincott 2005).

Multitasking. Often charged with having shorter attention spans than previous generations, Millennials also seem to have developed a broader "attention *range*" to diverse inputs (Rushkoff 1996, p. 50–51). Their minds leap about in the manner of hypertext (Prensky 2001).

Results orientation. Millennials are practical, caring deeply about concrete results, grades, and achievements (Sweeney 2006).

Confidence. Millennials have positive outlooks, and feel high levels of "self-efficacy" in the information search process (Fields 2006; Fallows 2005). 70% of incoming college students rate themselves highly in "learning effectively," although approximately one third will not continue to the second year (Indiana University 2006; Ishler 2005, p. 29). While older generations go to the Web for specific tasks, Millennials are comfortable both on and offline (Lippincott, 2005 p. 13.3).

Researchers have begun delineating the information behaviors specific to Millennial teenagers. Rushkoff (1996) described the non-linearity of the thinking patterns of those he terms "children of chaos," coining the term "screenagers" to describe those who grew up surrounded by television and computers (p. 3). Julien (1999; 2004) studied the information-seeking behaviors of teenagers, concluding that many did not know where to look for information amid a plethora of sources, and desired emotional support during the process. Agosto and Hughes-Hassell (2006a; 2006b) found that the everyday life information needs of urban teenagers tended to mirror those of more advantaged, non-minority groups. One aspect of teens' information behaviors that seems certain is their preferences *against* traditional libraries (Agosto and Hughes-Hassell 2005; Edwards and Poston-Anderson 1996) and for digital libraries, which are increasingly important to them (Valenza, 2007).

Theoretical frameworks

Sociological and communication theories are the premise for the phases of the two studies discussed in this paper.

STUDY 1: SENSE-MAKING THE INFORMATION CONFLUENCE

The analysis of academics' information-seeking behaviors is based on sociological theory. Herbert Simon (1955, 1957), whose major area of research was organizational behavior, specifically decision-making and problem solving, believed that people do not have the capacity or cognitive ability to make optimal decisions. Instead, they make the best decisions possible within cognitive boundaries, referred to as bounded rationality (Simon 1957). Simon further suggests that individuals assess the amount of effort they will expend on gathering information to solve a problem; settling for "good enough," satisficing, instead of pursuing the optimal solution. Simon's term satisficing, a combination of the words satisfy and suffice, suggests that individuals settle for what can be accomplished within pre-determined or imposed parameters. Satisficing is a component of rational choice theory, which also provides a framework for describing information-seeking behaviors.

Rational choice theory describes a purposive action whereby individuals judge the costs and benefits of achieving a desired goal (Allingham 1999; Cook and Levi 1990; Coleman and Fararo 1992). Humans, as rational actors, are capable of recognizing and desiring a certain outcome, and of taking action to achieve it. This suggests that information seekers rationally evaluate the benefits of information's usefulness and credibility, versus the costs in time and effort to find and access it.

Role theory offers a person-in-context framework within the information-seeking situation which situates behaviors in the context of a social system (Mead 1934; Marks 1996). Abercrombie, et al. (1994, p. 360) state, "When people occupy social positions their behavior is determined mainly by what is expected of that position rather than by their own individual characteristics." Thus the roles of information-seekers in the academic environment influence the expectations for performance and outcomes. For example, faculty would be expected to look for information differently than undergraduate students. Faculty members are considered researchers and experts in their disciplines, while undergraduate students are novices and protégés, roles that place them differently within the organizational structure of the academy (Blumer, 2004; Biddle, 1979; Mead, 1934; Marks, 1996; Marks, 1977).

STUDY 2: SEEKING SYNCHRONICITY

The Seeking Synchronicity study drew from two heuristically rich theoretical frameworks, those of Goffman (1967) and Watzlawick, Beavin, and Jackson (1967). Human conversation can be analyzed in various ways, and according to Goffman (1967), interactions are comprised of civility rituals and conventions. The analysis of interpersonal communication in VRS transcripts parallels analysis of face-to-face (FtF) relational dynamics. As each VRS session generates an artifact, a complete transcript of the conversation, it is possible to capture relational aspects along with the query clarification and information exchange. Goffman draws attention to the idea that in FtF, as well as in computer-mediated communication (CMC), each person's goal and obligation is to uphold the other's "face" as well as their own. He defines "face" as the "positive social value a person effectively claims for himself by the line others assume he has taken during a particular contact" (1967, p.5) and used the term "face-work" to refer to the strategies people use in conversation to protect one another's positive social value.

In VRS transcripts, the cyber "face" of the librarian and user are observable in their adherence to or neglect of interpersonal rituals, including greetings, closings, and politeness conventions of deference, such as using "please" or "thanks" as appropriate (Goffman 1956, 1972; see also Chelton 1997). Chat text can be closely analyzed to gain insight into the dynamics of this goal-directed interaction as participants engage in the creation and maintenance of face during the encounter. The relational analysis of the chat transcripts draws on Goffman's framework to identify chat behaviors which can be classified as positive or negative face-work and builds on previous research (Radford 2006a).

Watzlawick, Beavin, and Jackson's (1967) relational theory informs the development of the themes and coding categories for the Seeking Synchronicity study. Their seminal work *Pragmatics of Human Communication* (1967) posits the dual nature of human communication in which all messages have two dimensions, content (information) and relational (affect, interpersonal) aspects. Relational theory formed the basis of numerous studies, including exploring communication in virtual environments (e.g., Walther 1996). This theory has been applied by Radford (1993, 1999) to FtF reference encounters and to developing a classification scheme for interpersonal aspects of VRS interactions (Radford 2006a, 2006b). The research questions addressed in this study derive from the gaps uncovered in the literature and application of the Watzlawick et al. (1967) and Goffman (1967) perspectives. These research questions are:

- What relational dimensions are present in chat reference transcripts?
- What is the relationship between content and relational dimensions in determining the quality of chat reference encounters?
- What are the critical factors that influence the decision to select and use virtual reference services (VRS)? Why do non-users opt to use other means?
- Are there differences in the relational dimensions/patterns of teen-aged VRS users, other users and librarians? If so, what are they?
- How do VRS users and librarians compensate for lack of nonverbal cues in chat reference?

Results and discussion of the two studies

STUDY 1: SENSE-MAKING THE INFORMATION CONFLUENCE

A three-year project (Dervin, Connaway, and Prabha 2003; Prabha et al. 2007; Connaway 2007) investigated the information-seeking behaviors and satisficing (Simon 1955, 1979) of faculty and graduate and undergraduate students from a sample of forty-four colleges and universities within a Midwestern region in the U.S. Seventy-eight randomly selected participants completed sense-making focus group interviews and a subset (N=15) of the focus group interview participants were selected for individual semi-structured interviews. The research's premise was to illuminate the information-seeking "hows" (activities and practices moment-to-moment) and "whys" (choices and changing criteria for evaluation), with emphasis on the richest possible context per episode. The findings may be parsed among the generations, by comparing results from undergraduate students (principally Millennials), graduate students (majority of older Millennials), and faculty (largely Boomers).

FOCUS GROUP AND SEMI-STRUCTURED INTERVIEW RESULTS AND DISCUSSION

Undergraduate students (Millennials) tend to seek academic and personal information based on speed and convenience. When describing their information behaviors, they overwhelmingly cited Google as a first choice, with human sources (parents and friends) second. Many of the undergraduate students mentioned asking parents for information in academic situations, specifically their fathers. This correlates with the "helicopter parents" phenomenon identified in the behaviors of undergraduate students at the University of Rochester (Carlson 2007; Gibbons 2007) and discussion of the interactions of Baby Boomer parents with college-age children (Lum 2006; Lipka 2005). Library sources, if mentioned, tended to be via electronic mediation and students may have been unaware they were library sources. Finding library OPACs difficult to navigate, some use Amazon.com as a discovery tool, and *then* go the library site. They do consider the authority of electronic sources, but seem to make many choices based on convenience (cost/benefit), concluding a search when minimum assignment requirements are met.

Graduate students, who overlap between the generations but are principally older Millennials, reveal somewhat different information behaviors for academic situations. Google remains high on their source list for quick searches, followed by human sources, but human sources included academic superiors and friends. They, too, value the Internet for convenience and currency, and access library sources electronically. Their research techniques, however, tend to be more sophisticated and exhaustive, including citation searching, interlibrary loans, and library databases. They may stop searching for information when reaching assignment limits, but also consider the impossibility of truly exhausting topics. Some of the graduate students mentioned parents as sources for personal information-seeking situations. One of the graduate students stated, "… I just go ask my dad, and he'll tell me how to put in a fence, you know? So why sort through all this material when he'll just tell me."

Generally older and more experienced, faculty members reveal yet another stratification in information-seeking patterns. Faculty admitted that they use Google for quick searches, but even there it came in second, behind personal libraries. Their human sources tended to be colleagues or other experts. They cited ease of locating information on the Internet (including access to library sources like databases and electronic journals), but praised the physical library collection, and specified the criteria of trustworthiness and authority that they apply to non-library sources. Not only were their information-seeking processes more sophisticated, they tend to continue searching until completely saturated with information on a topic.

STUDY 2: SEEKING SYNCHRONICITY

Seeking Synchronicity has studied the needs, behaviors, and impressions of librarians, users, and non-users of VRS. Results from the first two phases (focus group interviews and transcript analysis) of a four-phase project are presented here. (See Radford and Connaway 2005 for a detailed description of the project phases.) Phase one involves focus group interviews with users, non-users and librarians to explore their experiences with VRS, as well as to discover non-users' reasons for not using VRS and factors that might prompt future use. Phase two examines VRS transcripts to reveal multiple aspects of the interactions, including the nature of interpersonal communication.

FOCUS GROUP INTERVIEW RESULTS

Focus group interviews with eighteen Screenager and five graduate student non-users reveal a number of information-seeking patterns and concerns about VRS. Screenager non-users prefer to find information independently, asserting: "I wouldn't really trust my librarian. I trust Google" (Radford and Connaway 2007). Participants said some librarians help by only pointing toward resources, evoking negative librarian stereotypes (Radford and Radford 1997). However, Screenagers value the interpersonal communication of FtF interactions with librarians over "cold" VRS environments. Disinclined to use VRS, they feared encounters with Internet stalkers or "psycho-killers" masquerading as librarians. Also, they are skeptical of the speed and convenience of the service, the accuracy of information obtained in VRS, and the librarian's ability to answer difficult questions.

Graduate student non-users prefer FtF interactions, preferring a personal relationship with librarians. They favor Internet tools for information seeking, including Google and library Web pages. They are reluctant to use VRS because their questions are complex, question the reliability of VRS information, and worry about being logged into chat rooms. They fear appearing stupid or being negatively judged by the librarian (Swope and Katzer 1972). Additionally, the graduate students worry that professors may see their transcripts and make negative judgments. One admitted: "With Internet or computer-mediated things, I always worry that they are being saved … if the Department would get a report about what questions [I asked]."

All non-user groups would try VRS if it were recommended by a trusted librarian, colleague or friend or if there were expanded marketing/promotion. Screenager non-users said that the ability to choose a trusted librarian could influence future VRS usage. Graduate student non-users would use VRS if they became confident in its use, efficiency, and speed. One wondered: "Yeah, the utility of it. How useful is it? If it like they went there and it took twenty minutes and I didn't even get my question answered. I'd be like, 'I'm not going to do that.'"

Focus group interviews with nine VRS users (a mixture of Millennials and older generations including Boomers) also revealed information-seeking patterns. They value convenience and appreciate saving a trip to the library by using VRS. The collaborative nature of VRS is appreciated as noted: "It's helpful to have another person looking for you so you get twice as much information—which is quicker." Users like access to a knowledgeable professional who can guide their information search and enjoy chat's pleasant interpersonal environment and anonymity. VRS transcripts increased the utility of the service for the users who, reflecting Millennial preferences, also applaud immediacy and opportunities to multi-task. There is no consensus on the utility of VRS, however, as some users discuss their preference, like Screenager non-users, for independent information-seeking.

Users also report concerns about VRS. It can seem like just another search engine, with librarians entering search terms exactly as expressed by users. Others find that question responses seem generic, prompting them to wonder if the librarian is paying attention, or is a robot. Users express distrust in information received though VRS, and value FtF interactions for reliable information. Users want accessibility improvements such as larger and movable chat windows and automatic Web-links, but disliked the prospect of Voice Over Internet Protocol, believing it to be "completely unnecessary." Like the Screenager non-users, users are concerned with the abilities and subject expertise of VRS librarians and fear overwhelming them.

TRANSCRIPT ANALYSIS RESULTS

The study included an in-depth analysis of a sample of 850 transcripts randomly selected from over 500,000+ sessions from the QuestionPoint VRS. For this article, 492 transcripts were analyzed, and 431 were deemed usable after discarding system tests, major technical problems, and sessions without a discernable question. Following the theories of Goffman (1967) and Watzlawick, et. al (1967) discussed above, each usable transcript was coded for relational/interpersonal communication themes (Radford and Connaway 2007 for complete relational coding scheme; see also Radford 2006a) facilitated through use of QSR NVivo 7 (QSR International 2003–2006) qualitative analysis software. The three coders had an intercoder reliability rating of 93% after differences were discussed and resolved.

Transcripts were also coded into one of five educational/age levels: Primary School Student (K–5), Secondary School Student (6–12), College Student, Adult (not in college), and Unknown. For this article, the Millennial group was formed by combining Secondary School Student with College Student groups. Coding was based on the self-identified or inferred education/age level of the VRS user. In self-identified cases, the user mentioned their year/grade or age, or the transcripts had grade level tags in the XML data. Other candidates for self-identification included users who referred to children, discussed college assignments, or indicated education level during login. When such information was unavailable, cues such as context, nature of the query, or use of slang and abbreviations in transcripts were used to infer education/age level. Evidence included user's mentioning adult responsibilities, such as real estate ownership, questions about school or college level assignments, or the use of slang, spelling, and abbreviation patterns associated with younger users. Of the 431 users, 189 (44%) were coded as Millennials, and 48 (11%) as Adults with the remainder being Primary School or Unknown. The two coders had an intercoder reliability rating of 99% after differences were discussed and resolved.

RELATIONAL FACILITATORS

Relational Facilitators are the interpersonal aspects of the chat conversation that have a positive impact on the librarian-client interaction and that enhance communication (Radford 2006a, Radford 1993, 1999). As shown in table 1, below, Millennials have lower percentages than Adults for using polite expressions and for expressing gratitude. Chat conventions for Millennials are informal and may result in fewer politeness rituals. Millennials tend to avoid self disclosure to adults and are less likely to give personal information or opinions than Adults who may be more self-confident (Sweeney 2006).

Millennials appear to seek reassurance less often than Adults (OCLC 2006; Sweeney 2006) and the findings reflect this confidence (see table 1). This reduced need for reassurance also demonstrates the Millennials' comfort with chat as a medium for communication, just as the Adults' greater need for reassurance may indicate uneasiness with chat. The lower percentages of closing rituals for Millennials are reflected in higher percentages of Abrupt Endings (see table 3) and below discussion.

TABLE 1 LOWER AVERAGES RELATIONAL FACILITATORS, MILLENNIAL VS. ADULT

Facilitator category	Number per transcript Millennials (n=189)	Number per transcript adults (n=48)
Thanks	113 (60%)	34 (71%)
Self-disclosure	86 (46%)	30 (63%)
Facilitator category	Number per occurrence Millennials (n=189)	Number per occurrence adults (n=48)
Seeking reassurance	108 (57%)	38 (79%)
Closing ritual	83 (44%)	25 (52%)
Polite expressions	55 (29%)	17 (35%)

(n=237 transcripts)

As seen in table 2, below, Millennials are more likely than Adults to agree to suggestions made by librarians and to admit their lack of knowledge. This finding is surprising in light of previous research which found a reticence on the part of young Millennials to accept advice or disclose lack of knowledge (Radford and Connaway 2007). Here the Millennial category includes both younger and older segments. College students, whose typical reference questions focus on how to use databases or find articles, may be more willing to admit they lack knowledge or to go along with librarians' suggestions.

Millennials are more likely to engage in greeting rituals with VRS librarians, demonstrating their tendency to make connections through online communication and their use of chat for socializing. Adults may see the conversation as more businesslike than social and may not be as prone to engage in politeness rituals at the start of VRS interactions. Similarly, Millennials use more interjections, slang, and lower case which are transferred from social chat or reflect text messaging conventions (Radford and Connaway 2007).

TABLE 2 HIGHER AVERAGES RELATIONAL FACILITATORS, MILLENNIAL VS. ADULT

Facilitator category	Number per occurrence Millennials (n=189)	Number per occurrence adults (n=48)
Agree to suggestion	132 (70%)	22 (46%)
Lower case	36 (19%)	5 (10%)
Greeting ritual	36 (19%)	5 (10%)
Admit lack knowledge	36 (19%)	3 (6%)
Interjections	36 (19%)	3 (6%)
Slang	14 (7%)	0

(n=237 transcripts)

RELATIONAL BARRIERS

Relational Barriers are interpersonal aspects of the chat conversation that have a negative impact on the librarian-client interaction and that impede communication (Radford 2006a; see also Radford 1993, 1999). As seen in table 3, Millennials have higher averages than Adults for abrupt endings, impatience, and for being rude/insulting. The Millennials' propensity to forgo closing rituals and sign off abruptly reflects their comfort with the evanescence of the relationship formed with VRS librarians and their impatience. Additionally, abrupt signoff could be an indication of multi-tasking activities (Radford and Connaway 2007; Sweeney 2006). The higher percentages of impatience and rude/insulting categories confirm research findings for Millennial characteristics, including adolescent irreverence in anonymous environments (Radford and Connaway 2007, Radford 2006b, Sweeney 2006).

TABLE 3 HIGHER AVERAGES RELATIONAL BARRIERS, MILLENNIAL VS. ADULT

Barrier category	Number per transcript Millennials (n=189)	Number per transcript adults (n=48)
Abrupt endings	72 (38%)	15 (31%)
Impatience	9 (5%)	1 (2%)
Rude or insulting	3 (2%)	0

(n=237 transcripts)

As shown above, transcripts have much to reveal regarding interpersonal dimensions of VRS and differences between the generations in communication style and preferences.

FINDINGS COMMON TO BOTH STUDIES

Both the Seeking Synchronicity and Sense-Making studies included graduate students as participants in the research. There are common behaviors demonstrated by these older Millennials and the Screenagers. The Screenagers perceived that asking a follow-up question was "pestering" the librarian, a finding echoed in the older MIllennials. In focus group interviews with doctoral students, these participants expressed fear that they would be perceived as "bothering" the librarian if they were to approach to ask a question. While Screenagers cited "embarrassment" as a deterrent from seeking help from a librarian, the graduate students were concerned of "looking stupid" by asking the librarian for assistance.

Both studies indicate that Screenagers and older Millennials consistently identify Google as one of the first sources they use for quick searches and they value the Internet for its convenience and currency. Human sources are also consistently named, but the older Millennials mentioned friends and professors while the Screenagers mentioned parents more frequently. The older Millennials tend to use electronic mediation to access library sources and tend to stop searching for information when they meet the requirements of an assignment. As one graduate student stated, "I obviously turn to electronics first, then library second … because it's convenient. But if I want more in-depth info, then I go to the library."

Conclusion and implications

SENSE-MAKING THE INFORMATION CONFLUENCE

When asked to describe the ideal information system, Millennials suggested that the library catalog be more like an Internet search engine or Amazon.com. They also wanted the library to provide space for them to socialize and work in groups and suggested 24/7 access to a librarian via telephone, such as a 'lifeline" (referring to the television program, Who Wants to be a Millionaire?) Older Millennials were most interested in expediency, desiring roaming librarians, drive-up book drops, library delivery of print materials to their campus addresses, and a coffee house-like environment. The faculty (the majority were Baby Boomers) wanted a less intimidating library with better signage, and a book store like environment.

SEEKING SYNCHRONICITY STUDY

Preliminary results of the Seeking Synchronicity study make it readily apparent that Screenagers have different communication and information behaviors in the chat reference environment than those of previous generations (see also Agosto and Hughes-Hassell 2005, 2006) and librarians. Comparison of patterns of interpersonal communication styles reveals differences in relational dimensions for adolescents who are experiencing a period of rapid emotional as well as physical development (see also Kuhlthau 2004). Valenza (2006) notes that a blend of FtF and electronic services may be best for young people. Walter and Mediavilla (2005) recommend involving teens in the development and evaluation of VRS to ensure that their preferences and needs are considered. To effectively meet the needs of Millennial youth, librarians must develop a range of services that are customizable and flexible, incorporate regular feedback, provide trusted guidance, include the opportunity for social and interactive learning, be visual and kinesthetic, and feature communication that is real, raw, relevant and relational (Partridge and Hallam 2006). This project has endeavored to gain a greater understanding of Millennial needs and behaviors to ensure that virtual and traditional library services are responsive to their preferences. The stakes are high for maintaining relevance and sustainability of reference services to today's young users in recognition of their rapidly changing, My Space-, Google-, and Wikipedia-dependent information environment.

Implications for libraries

Findings from the phases of these two studies imply that libraries need to include traditional print and audiovisual sources, as well as electronic. The library website should be updated often to include current information, personalized online services, and interactive capabilities (Storey 2005). Librarians need to create different areas for different user needs. Millennials want social areas that also provide "multiple streams of information" (Storey 2005, 10). Boomers want more quiet spaces that resemble the bookstore environment with access to refreshments, comfortable seating, and good lighting. Above all, both Millennials and Boomers demand attention and want librarians to be available to them as guides and assistants, but not as gatekeepers. As more information about the characteristics and behaviors of the Boomer and Millennial generations becomes available, librarians can develop services and systems that meet the needs of both. Contemporary users are becoming increasingly disenchanted with traditional library services and systems. Business as usual will please neither the large Millennial or Boomer populations who are inquisitive, savvy, demanding, and increasingly independent information seekers.

Future research

SENSE-MAKING THE INFORMATION CONFLUENCE

Focus group and semi-structured interviews were preceded by large scale online survey and telephone interviews. The analysis of the results of the surveys and telephone interviews can be compared to similar studies of academics' information-seeking behaviors. These comparison and analyses can be used to develop information-seeking models that can be used for future study of information-seeking behaviors as well as for the development of library systems and services.

SEEKING SYNCHRONICITY STUDY

The chat transcript analysis findings reported for the Seeking Synchronicity project are preliminary results from the initial year of a two year study. Transcript analysis has continued with a goal of analyzing a total of 800+ chat sessions. Also, nearing completion are two further data collection phases involving 600 Web-based surveys (200 with each participant group of users, non-users, and librarians) and 300 phone interviews (100 with each group). The Web-based surveys and phone interviews are in progress, building on preliminary results and probing more deeply into user/librarian preferences for modes of communication and on issues of satisfaction. Following the conclusion of data analysis, results will be compared to those from other related studies and a theoretical model will be constructed encompassing content and relational dimensions in the VRS environment.

REFERENCES

Abercrombie, N., S. Hill, and B. Turner. 1994. *The Penguin dictionary of sociology.* 3rd ed. New York: Penguin.

Agosto, DE., and S. Hughes-Hassell. 2005. "People, places, and questions: An investigation of the everyday life information-seeking behaviors of urban young adults." *Library and Information Science Research* 27, no. 2: 141–163.

_____. 2006. "Toward a model of the everyday life information needs of urban teenagers, part 1: Theoretical model." *JASIS&T* 57, no. 10: 1394–1403.

_____. 2006. "Toward a model of the everyday life information needs of urban teenagers, part 2: Empirical model. *JASIS&T* 57, no. 11: 1418–1426.

Allingham, M. 1999. *Rational choice.* New York: St Martin's Press.

Biddle, BJ. 1979. *Role theory: Expectations, identities and behaviors.* New York: Academic Press.

Blumer, H., and TJ. Morrione. 2004. *George Herbert Mead and human conduct.* Walnut Creek: AltaMira Press.

Campbell, K. 2005. "The many faces of the baby boomers." *The Christian Science Monitor* 26. January. http://www.csmonitor.com/2005/0126/p15s02-lihc.html (accessed 14 September 2007).

Carlson, S. 2007. "An anthropologist in the library: The University of Rochester takes a look at students in the stacks." *The Chronicle of Higher Education,* 53, no. 50. http://chronicle.com/weekly/v53/i5050a02601.htm (accessed 14 September 2007) (inaccessible 26 October 2015).

Chelton, MK. 1997. "The 'overdue kid:' A face-to-face library service encounter as ritual interaction." *Library and Information Science Research* 19, no. 4: 387–399.

Coleman, JS., and TJ. Fararo, (Eds.). 1992. *Rational choice theory: Advocacy and critique.* Newbury Park: Sage Publications.

Connaway, LS. 2007. "Mountains, valleys, and pathways: Serials users' needs and steps to meet them. Part I: Preliminary analysis of focus group and semi-structured interviews at colleges and universities." *Serials Librarian* 52, no. 1/2: 223–236.

Cook, KS. and M. Levi, (Eds.). 1990. *The limits of rationality.* Chicago: University of Chicago Press.

Dempsey, B. 2007. "What boomers want." *Library Journal* 132, no. 12: 36–39.

Dervin, B., LS. Connaway, and C. Prabha. 2003. "Sense-making the information confluence: The whys and hows of college and university user satisficing of information needs." http://imlsosuoclcproject.jcomm.ohio-state.edu (accessed 7 September 2007) (inaccessible 26 October 2015).

Edwards, S., and B. Poston-Anderson. 1996. "Information, future time perspectives, and young adolescent girls: Concerns about education and jobs." *Library & Information Science Research* 18, no. 3: 207–233.

Fallows, D. 2005. "Search engine users: Internet searchers are confident, satisfied, and trusting-but they are also unaware and naïve." *Pew Internet and American Life Project.* http://www.pewinternet.org/pdfs/PIP_Searchengine_users.pdf (accessed 12 September 2007) (inaccessible 26 October 2015).

    Alternative URL http://www.pewinternet.org/files/old-media//Files/Reports/2005/PIP_Searchengine_users.pdf.pdf (accessed 26 October 2015).

Fields, AM. 2006. "Self-efficacy and the first-year university student's authority of knowledge: An exploratory study." *Journal of Academic Librarianship* 31: 539–545.

Gibbons, S. 2007. *The academic library and the Net Gen student: Making the connections.* Chicago: American Library Association.

Gillon, S. 2004. *Boomer nation: The largest and richest generation ever and how it changed America.* New York: Free Press.

Goffman, E. 1956. "The nature of deference and demeanor." *American Anthropologist* 58, no. 3: 475–499.

    _____. 1967. *The interaction ritual, essays on face-to-face behavior.* Garden City: Doubleday.

    _____. 1972. *Relations in public: Microstudies of the public order.* New York: Basic Book.

Grossman, T. 2000. *The Baby Boomers' guide to living forever.* Golden, CO: Hubristic Press.

Harley, D., J. Henke, S. Lawrence, I. Miller, I. Perciali, D. Nasatir, C. Kaskiris, and C. Bautista. 2006. *Use and users of digital resources: A focus on undergraduate education in the humanities and social sciences.* http://digitalresourcestudy.berkeley.edu/report/digitalresourcestudy_final_report.pdf (accessed 29 July 2007) (inaccessible 26 October 2015).

Hempel, J. 2005. "The Myspace generation: They live online. They buy online. They play online. Their power is growing." *Business Week:* 12 December, 86.

"HotTopics: 2006 user update: How information providers can keep pace with user demands for time-saving solutions." *Outsell Now* 2 (26 May). http://now.outsellinc.com/now/ (accessed 29 July 2007) (inaccessible 26 October 2015).

Howe, N., and W. Strauss. 2000. *Millennials rising: The next great generation.* New York: Random House.

Indiana University, Center for Postsecondary Research. 2006. NSSE: *National survey of student engagement.* Bloomington, IN: Indiana University Press.

Ishler, JLC. 2005. "Today's first-year students." ML. Upcraft, JN. Gardner, BO. Barefoot, and Associates (Eds.). *Challenging and supporting the first-year student A handbook for improving the first year of college.* San Francisco, CA: Jossey-Bass, p. 15–26.

Jones, S., and M. Madden. 2002. "The Internet goes to college: How students are living in the future with today's technology." *Pew Internet and American Life Project.* http://www.pewinternet.org/pdfs/PIP_College_Report.pdf (accessed 4 September 2007) (inaccessible 26 October 2015).

Joseph, M. 2006. "Active, engaged, valued: Older people and public libraries in New South Wales." *Aplis* 19, no. 3: 113–117.

Julien, HE. 1999. "Barriers to adolescents' information seeking for career decision making." *JASIS&T* 50, no. 1: 38–48.

_____. 2004. "Adolescent decision-making for careers: An exploration of information behavior." MK. Chelton and C. Cool, (Eds.). *Youth information-seeking behavior: Theories, models, and issues.* Lanham, MD: Scarecrow Press, p. 321–352.

Junco, R. 2005. "Technology and today's first-year students." ML. Upcraft, JN. Gardner, BO. Barefoot, and Associates (Eds.). *Challenging and supporting the first-year student: A handbook for improving the first year of college.* San Francisco, CA: Jossey-Bass, p. 221–239.

Kahlert, M. 2000. "The impact of the baby boomers on public libraries: Myth and reality." *Australian Public Libraries and Information Services* 13, no. 1: 25–40.

Krohn, FB. 2004. "A generational approach to using emoticons as nonverbal communication." *Journal of Technical Writing and Communication* 34, no. 4: 321–328.

Kuhlthau, CC. 2004. *Seeking meaning: A process approach to library and information services,* 2nd Ed. Westport, CT: Libraries Unlimited.

Lipka, S. 2005. "State Legislators as Co-Pilots: Some 'Helicopter Parents' Play Politics to Protect Their Children's Interests on Campuses." *Chronicle of Higher Education* 52, no. 17: A22–A23.

Lippincott, JK. 2005. "Net generation students and libraries." DC. Oblinger and JL. Oblinger, (Eds.). *Educating the Net Generation.* Boulder, CO: EDUCAUSE: p. 13.1–13.15.
http://www.educause.edu/content.asp?PAGE_ID=5989andbhcp=1
(accessed 4 September 2007) (inaccessible 26 October 2015).

    Alternative URL https://net.educause.edu/ir/library/pdf/PUB7101M.pdf
    (accessed 26 October 2015).

Lum, L. 2006. "Handling 'Helicopter Parents.'" *Diverse: Issues in Higher Education* 23, no. 20: 40–43.

Marks, SR. 1977. "Multiple roles and role strain: Some notes on human energy, time, and commitment." *American Sociological Review* 42: 921–936.

_____ and SM. MacDermid. 1996. "Multiple roles and the self: A theory of role balance." *Journal of Marriage and the Family* 58, no. 2: 417–432.

Mead, GH. 1934. *Mind, self & society: From the standpoint of a social behaviorist.* Chicago: University of Chicago Press.

Oblinger, DG. and JL. Oblinger (Eds.). 2005. *Educating the Net Generation* (EDUCAUSE). http://www.educause.edu/content.asp?PAGE_ID=5989&bhcp=1 (accessed 21 January 2007) (inaccessible 26 October 2015).

> Alternative URL https://net.educause.edu/ir/library/pdf/PUB7101M.pdf. (accessed 26 October 2015).

OCLC Online Computer Library Center, Inc. 2006. *College students' perceptions of libraries and information resources: A report to the OCLC membership.* OCLC: Dublin, Ohio. http://www.oclc.org/reports/pdfs/studentperceptions.pdf (accessed 12 September 2007).

Partridge, H., and G. Hallam. 2006. "Educating the Millennial generation for evidence based information practice." *Library Hi Tech* 24, no. 3: 400–419.

Prabha, C., LS. Connaway, L. Olszewski, and LR. Jenkins. 2007. "What is enough? Satisficing information needs." *Journal of Documentation* 63, no. 1: 74–89.

Prensky, M. 2001. "Digital natives, digital immigrants." *On the Horizon* 9, no. 5. http://www.marcprensky.com/writing (accessed 4 September 2007) (inaccessible 26 October 2015)

> Alternative URL http://marcprensky.com/articles-in-publications/ (accessed 26 October 2015).

_____. 2001. "Do they really think differently?" *On the Horizon* 9, no. 6. http://www.marcprensky.com/writing (accessed 4 September 2007) (inaccessible 26 October 2015)

> Alternative URL http://marcprensky.com/articles-in-publications/ (accessed 26 October 2015).

QSR NVivo 7. (Computer Software). 2003–2006. Doncaster, Australia: QSR International Pty Ltd. http://www.qsrinternational.com/ (accessed 14 Sept. 2007).

Radford, ML. 1993. *Relational aspects of reference interactions: A qualitative investigation of the perceptions of users and librarians in the academic library.* Ph.D. dissertation. Rutgers University.

_____. 1999. *The reference encounter: Interpersonal communication in the academic library.* Chicago: American Library Association.

_____. 2006. "Encountering virtual users: A qualitative investigation of interpersonal communication in chat reference." *JASIS&T* 57, 8: 1046–1059.

_____. 2006. "Investigating interpersonal communication in chat reference: Dealing with impatient users and rude encounters." RD. Lankes, E. Abels, M. White and SN. Haque (Eds.). *The Virtual Reference Desk: Creating a Reference Future.* New York: Neal-Schuman Publishers, p. 23–46.

_____, and LS. Connaway. 2005. "Seeking synchronicity: Evaluating virtual reference services from user, non-user, and librarian perspectives." Proposal for a research project, submitted 1 February 2005, to the National Leadership Grants for Libraries program of the Institute of Museum and Library Services (IMLS). http://www.oclc.org/research/projects/synchronicity/proposal.pdf (accessed 21 January 2007).

_____, and LS. Connaway. 2007. "Screenagers and live chat reference: Living up to the promise." *Scan* 26, no. 1: 31–39.

_____, and GP. Radford. 1997. "Power, knowledge, and fear: Feminism, Foucault and the stereotype of the female librarian." *The Library Quarterly* 67, no. 3: 250–266.

Rushkoff, D. 1996. *Playing the future: How kids' culture can teach us to thrive in an age of chaos.* New York: HarperCollins.

Schuman, H., and J. Scott. 1989. "Generations and collective memories." *American Psychological Review* 54: 359–81.

Simon, HA. 1955. "A behavioral model of rational choice." *Quarterly Journal of Economics* 69, no. 1: 99–118.

_____. 1957. "A behavioral model of rational choice." In *Models of man: Social and rational.* New York: John Wiley & Sons.

_____. 1979. *Models of thought.* Yale University Press: New Haven, CT.

Steinhorn, L. 2006. *The Greater Generation: In Defense of the Baby Boom Legacy.* New York: Tomas Dunn Books.

Storey, T. 2005. "The Big Bang!" *OCLC Newsletter* 267: 7–12.

Sweeney, R. 2006. *Millennial behaviors and demographics.* http://library1.njit.edu/staff-folders/sweeney/Millennials/Article-Millennial-Behaviors.doc (accessed 4 September 2007) (inaccessible 26 October 2015).

Swope, MJ., and J. Katzer. 1972. "The Silent Majority: Why don't they ask questions?" *Reference Quarterly* 12: 161–166.

Tapscott, D. 1998. *Growing up digital: The rise of the Net Generation.* New York: McGraw-Hill.

Valenza, JK. 2006. "They might be gurus." *Teacher Librarian* 34, no. 1: 18–26.

_____. 2007. "It'd be really dumb not to use it: Virtual libraries and high school students' information seeking and use, a focus group investigation." MK. Chelton and C. Cool (Eds.). *Youth information-seeking behavior II: Theories, models, and issues.* Lanham, MD: Scarecrow Press, p. 292–317.

Van Scoyoc, AM., and C. Cason. 2006. "The electronic academic library: Undergraduate research behavior in a library without books." *Portal: Libraries and the Academy* 6, p. 47–58.

Walter, VA., and C. Mediavilla. 2005. "Teens are from Neptune, librarians are from Pluto: An analysis of online reference transactions." *Library Trends* 54, no. 2: 209–227.

Walther, JB. 1996. "Computer-mediated communication: Impersonal, interpersonal and hyperpersonal interaction." *Communication Research* 23, no. 1: 3–43.

Watzlawick, P., J. Beavin, and DD. Jackson. 1967. *Pragmatics of human communication.* New York: Norton.

Williamson, K., M. Bannister, L. Makin, G. Johanson, D. Schauder, and J. Sullivan. 2006. "Wanting it now: Baby Boomers and the public library of the future." *Australian Library Journal* 55, no. 1: 54–72.

Willis, SL. 2006. "Technology and learning in current and future generations of elders." *Generations* 2006, p. 44–48.

5

The Digital Information Seeker: Report of Findings from Selected OCLC, RIN and JISC User Behaviour Projects

Lynn Silipigni Connaway, Ph.D.
OCLC Research

Timothy J. Dickey, Ph.D.
OCLC Research

A reprint of:

Connaway, Lynn Silipigni, and Timothy J. Dickey. 2010. *The Digital Information Seeker: Report of Findings from Selected OCLC, RIN, and JISC User Behaviour Projects*. [Bristol, England]: HEFCE. http://www.jisc.ac.uk/media/documents/publications/reports/2010/digitalinformationseekerreport.pdf

© 2010 HEFCE

This work is licensed under a Creative Commons Attribution-NonCommercial-NoDerivs 2.0 UK: England & Wales

http://creativecommons.org/licenses/by-nc-nd/2.0/uk

EXECUTIVE SUMMARY

Introduction

There are numerous user studies published in the literature and available on the web. There are studies that specifically address the behaviours of scholars while others identify the behaviours of the general public. Some studies address the information-seeking behaviours of scholars within specific disciplines while others identify the behaviours of scholars of multiple disciplines. There are studies that only address undergraduate, graduate, or post graduate students or compare these individual groups' information-seeking behaviours to those of scholars. Still other studies address the behaviors of young adults (Screenagers (Rushkoff 1996) and Millennials).

In the interest of analyzing and synthesizing several user behaviour studies conducted in the US and the UK, twelve studies were identified. These twelve selected studies were commissioned and/or supported by non-profit organizations and government agencies; therefore, they have little dependence upon the outcomes of the studies. The studies were reviewed by two researchers who analyzed the findings, compared their analyses, and identified the overlapping and contradictory findings. This report is not intended to be the definitive work on user behaviour studies, but rather to provide a synthesized document to make it easier for information professionals to better understand the information-seeking behaviours of the libraries' intended users and to review the issues associated with the development of information services and systems that will best meet these users' needs.

The twelve studies included in this report are listed in chronological order:

- *Perceptions of libraries and information resources* (OCLC, December 2005), http://www.oclc.org/us/en/reports/2005perceptions.htm
- *College students' perceptions of libraries and information resources* (OCLC, April 2006), http://www.oclc.org/us/en/reports/perceptionscollege.htm
- *Sense-making the information confluence: The whys and hows of college and university user satisficing of information needs* (IMLS/Ohio State University/OCLC, July 2006), http://www.oclc.org/research/projects/imls/default.htm
- *Researchers and discovery services: Behaviour, perceptions and needs* (RIN, November 2006), http://www.rin.ac.uk/our-work/using-and-accessing-information-resources/researchers-and-discoveryservices-behaviour-perc
- *Researchers' use of academic libraries and their services* (RIN/CURL, April 2007), http://www.rin.ac.uk/our-work/using-and-accessing-information-resources/researchers-use-academiclibraries-and-their-serv

- *Information behaviour of the researcher of the future* (CIBER/UCL, commissioned by BL and JISC, January 2008), http://www.jisc.ac.uk/media/documents/programmemes/reppres/gg_final_keynote_11012008.pdf
- *Seeking synchronicity: Evaluating virtual reference services from user, non-user and librarian perspectives* (OCLC/ IMLS/ Rutgers, June 2008), http://www.oclc.org/research/projects/synchronicity/default.htm
- *Online catalogs: What users and librarians want* (OCLC. March 2009), http://www.oclc.org/us/en/reports/onlinecatalogs/default.htm
- *E-journals: Their use, value and impact* (RIN, April 2009), http://www.rin.ac.uk/our-work/communicatingand-disseminating-research/e-journals-their-use-value-and-impact
- *JISC national e-books observatory project: Key findings and recommendations* (JISC/UCL, November 2009), http://www.jiscebooksproject.org/
- *Students' use of research content in teaching and learning* (JISC, November 2009), http://www.jisc.ac.uk/media/documents/aboutus/workinggroups/studentsuseresearchcontent.pdf
- *User behaviour in resource discovery* (JISC, November 2009), http://www.jisc.ac.uk/whatwedo/programmes/inf11/userbehaviourbusandecon.aspx

A description of the key findings reported in each of the selected studies is included in this document. After this, the common findings of the studies as well as contradictory findings are discussed. The report ends with the identification of issues that librarians must address in order to meet the needs of diverse user groups. Some suggestions for further research and development are included.

Summaries of each of the selected studies included in this report

A brief summary of the findings of each study is provided to give the readers a basic overview and understanding of each study. URLs are included for each of the studies for those who are interested in more detailed and in-depth information about the studies.

Perceptions of libraries and information resources (De Rosa 2005) and *College students' perceptions of libraries and information resources* (De Rosa 2006) present two views of a global *online* survey of library use. The 2005 report includes both academic and non-academic users. The results reinforce the library's brand as one of "books" and the overwhelming nature of search engine use. Most users do trust library resources and information as much as they trust search engines. They do not think of the library for accessing electronic resources. The general population is using libraries and electronic resources of all kinds less often.

Sense-making the information confluence: The whys and hows of college and university user satisficing of information needs (Dervin et al. 2006; Connaway, Prabha, and Dickey 2006; Prabha, Connaway, and Dickey 2006) includes qualitative data from undergraduate, graduate student, and faculty perspectives on information-seeking and library systems. It offers a rich portrait of academic users' information behaviours, including their rational and contextual decisions, their valuation of familiarity, convenience, and currency, and nuances to their use of Google and other search engines; each section concludes with concrete recommendations to improve library systems.

Researchers and discovery services: Behaviour, perceptions and needs (Research Information Network 2006) reports on a lengthy qualitative study using telephone surveys of researchers and librarians in UK universities, followed by in-depth interviews and focus groups with postdoctoral researchers. The study indicates a "general satisfaction with the research discovery services available" (ibid, p. 6). The main frustration of researchers in the sciences and arts and humanities is accessing online journals, which is supported by librarians who report accessing online journals as a key problem. The most utilized resources are general search engines, internal library portals and catalogues, specialist search engines, and subject-specific gateways; researchers see the search as an integral part of the research process and have developed methods of searching to minimize any sort of information overload (ibid, p. 8).

Researchers' use of academic libraries and their services (Consortium of University Research Libraries, and Research Information Network 2007) utilizes quantitative data and "qualitative insights" (ibid, p. 2) from researchers and librarians to provide information about how researchers interact with academic library services in the UK. The majority of researchers has embraced digital content and uses digital aides to find information, creating a decrease in library visits. However, the respondents do believe librarians will play a key role in this new information environment, and in new types of information resources. Evidence illustrates the importance researchers place on direct access to all kinds of digital materials. *Information behaviour of the researcher of the future* (Centre for Information Behaviour and the Evaluation of Research 2008) attempts to recreate a longitudinal study from the literature together with some new primary data mining from the British Library and JISC web sites. The authors describe the project as a "virtual" longitudinal study ... refining many popularly-held notions of the information behaviours of the "Google generation." The findings state that although young people have "apparent facility with computers" and confidence in their own ability, these are actually masking their lack of information literacy skills and performance. It concludes with predictions that the information environment of 2017 will be that of "a unified web culture," e-book prominence, mass book digitization, and additional forms of publication.

Seeking synchronicity: Evaluating virtual reference services from user, non-user and librarian perspectives (Radford, and Connaway 2008) evaluates the practice, sustainability, and relevance of virtual reference services (VRS) to libraries, with several complementary data collection phases from librarian providers, and both users and non-users of VRS. Among the outcomes of the project are significant implications for librarians' best practices, data on user behaviour differences by age demographics, and empirical data on the "elusive" non-users of library services.

Online catalogs: What users and librarians want (Calhoun et al. 2009) includes end-user (both academic and the general public) focus group interviews, online pop-up surveys for WorldCat.org users, and a Web-based survey of librarians to compare librarian and user perspectives on metadata and interface needs in library systems. The report identifies differences between the two respondent groups, and reinforces users' desires for discovery-to-delivery seamless access and for enhanced catalogue content.

E-journals: Their use, value and impact (Research Information Network 2009) encompasses a deep log analysis of several months' usage of ScienceDirect and Oxford Journals in UK universities, in order to provide an analysis of how academic researchers in the UK have responded to the growing availability of e-journals. Data indicate that e-journals are a critical component to research institutions in the UK and prove to have a good return on investment.

JISC national e-books observatory project: Key findings and recommendations (JISC, and UCL 2009) combines data from a deep log analysis report, a user survey report, focus group interviews, and print and circulation data reports for e-book usage at UK universities. It aims to find current attitudes towards e-books held by students and staff, and to evaluate JISC e-book usage. Overall, "e-books are now part of the academic mainstream" (ibid, p. 5) and "libraries ... are a key player in the emerging market for e-books at present. Age and gender are also important predictors of e-book take-up" (ibid, p. 6). Most e-books are discovered through the library catalogue and links on the library web pages.

Students' use of research content in teaching and learning (Hampton-Reeves et al. 2009) reports on a survey of undergraduates at three UK universities, with follow-up focus group interviews based upon the initial data. The students generally prefer keyword searches in a large number of tools, but do distinguish between more traditional sources of research information (journals, library catalogues) and the potential pitfalls of the Internet.

User behaviour in resource discovery (JISC 2009) uses qualitative data gathered in focus group and indepth user interviews to "identify, understand and compare the information-seeking" behaviour of students and researchers in the business and economics disciplines who are "using subscribed and free resource discovery systems available" in three UK institutions (ibid, p. 17). The "poor usability, high complexity, and lack of integration" of many resources "acts as a barrier to information search and retrieval" (ibid, p. 6). That level of difficulty keeps the user from being able to concentrate on the actual content of the material. Additionally, information literacy skills were found to be lacking. Even though users may be able to use a search engine or other resource, they did not necessarily know how to get quality information from it.

Common findings

These studies allow us to draw several broad conclusions about the state of user studies. Evidence produced by multiple studies is limited by the common problem that some studies have small sample sizes and purposive samples. However, this meta-analysis combines both quantitative and qualitative studies. Both have strengths and weaknesses and are complementary. The qualitative, exploratory studies provide rich data portraits of specific user groups while the large-scale quantitative studies confirm them. These rich data portraits combined with the large-scale quantitative analyses offer several common themes that were identified in the review of the twelve user behaviour studies.

Among the central findings are the following:

- **Disciplinary differences do exist** in researcher behaviours, both professional researchers and students.
- **E-journals are increasingly very important** to the process of research at all levels.
- The evidence provided by the results of the studies supports the centrality of Google and search engines.
  — Google is often used to **locate and access e-journal content.**
- At the same time, the entire **discovery-to-delivery** process needs to be supported by information systems, including increased access to resources.

— **Journal backfiles** are particularly problematic in terms of access.

The realities of the online environment observed above led several studies to some common conclusions about changing user behaviours:

- Regardless of age or experience, academic discipline, or context of the information need, **speed and convenience are important** to users.
    - Researchers particularly appreciate **desktop access to scholarly content.**
    - Users also appreciate the **convenience of electronic access over the physical library.**
- Users are beginning to desire **enhanced functionality in library systems.**
- They also desire **enhanced content** to assist them in evaluating resources.
- They seem generally **confident in their own ability** to use information discovery tools.
- However, it seems that **information literacy has not necessarily improved.**
    - **High-quality metadata is thus becoming even more important** for the discovery process.

In addition, some common findings regarding content and resources arise:

- **More digital content** of all kinds and formats is almost uniformly seen as better.
- People still tend to think of **libraries as collections of books.**
- Despite this, researchers also **value human resources** in their information-seeking.

In some cases, the studies reviewed included findings which seem to contradict one another, and for which evidence may be mixed:

- There is evidence for both broad and narrow **range of tools used for scholarly research.**
- There is evidence both in favour and against **formal training in electronic searching.**
- There are mixed conclusions on the question of whether **recommendations, provided by recommender systems, and social media** are having an impact on information seeking.

In a few cases, the above findings from the studies under review offered evidence that runs counter to popular perceptions of the current information scene.

- Many popular media claims about the "Google generation" may not be supported by all the evidence.
- In choosing among search engines, some evidence indicates that speed may not be the most important evaluative factor.
- The studies that addressed library OPACs provide little support for the advanced search options which are still popular in these systems.

Implications for libraries

A synthesis of findings from these major user studies points toward a number of implications for libraries. The implications below represent broad tendencies. The various user studies themselves do take into account differences in behaviour based on age and gender of the subjects, and context and situation of the information needs. Differences based on academic discipline have been a common finding throughout the user behaviour studies. The studies ask different questions of their subjects. In order to generalize findings and to present a valid portrait of user behaviours, it is necessary to conduct longitudinal studies of large populations.

Implications for libraries which are shared by multiple studies include the following:

- The library serves many constituencies, with *different needs and behaviours*.
- Library systems must do better at providing seamless access to resources.
- Librarians must increasingly consider a greater variety of digital formats and content.
  — More digital resources of all kinds are better.
- Library systems and content must be prepared for changing user behaviours.
- Library systems need to look and function more like search engines, i.e., Google and Yahoo, and Web services, i.e., Amazon.com, since these are familiar to users who are comfortable and confident in using them.
- High-quality metadata is becoming more important for discovery of appropriate resources.
- The library must advertise its brand, its value, and its resources better within the community.

This review concludes with suggestions for future research. The studies included in this meta analysis used both qualitative and quantitative research techniques, which complement each other. The large-scale online and interview surveys conducted in the quantitative studies, coupled with the rich data portraits provided by the qualitative studies, identify key issues which can be studied using more statistically generalizable methods. A large, random sample of specific demographic groups of information seekers should be identified in order to conduct a wide-ranging user behaviour study to identify how individuals engage in both the virtual and physical worlds to get information for different situations. Such an investigation would contribute to a better understanding of how individuals navigate in multiple information environments and could influence the design and integration of systems and services for devices and applications, as well as cloud computing. Such a study, undertaken at this pivotal moment in both library funding and explosion of information resources, could provide invaluable guidance for both libraries and the field of information science.

REFERENCES

Calhoun, Karen, et al. 2009. *Online Catalogs: What Users and Librarians Want: An OCLC Report.* Dublin, OH: OCLC. http://www.oclc.org/us/en/reports/onlinecatalogs/default.htm.

Centre for Information Behaviour and the Evaluation of Research. 2008. *Information Behaviour of the Researcher of the Future: A CIBER Briefing Paper.* London: CIBER. http://www.jisc.ac.uk/media/documents/programmemes/reppres/gg_final_keynote_11012008.pdf. (inaccessible 26 October 2015).

Connaway, Lynn Silipigni, Chandra Prabha, and Timothy J. Dickey. 2006. *Sense-making the Information Confluence: The Whys and Hows of College and University User Satisficing of Information Needs. Phase III: Focus Group Interview Study.* Report on National Leadership Grant LG-02-03-0062-03, to Institute of Museum and Library Services, Washington, D.C. Columbus, OH: School of Communication, The Ohio State University. http://imlsproject.comm.ohio-state.edu/imls_reports/PHASE_III/PH_III_report_list.html. (inaccessible 26 October 2015).

Consortium of University Research Libraries, and Research Information Network. 2007. *Researchers' Use of Academic Libraries and Their Services: A Report.* London: Research Information Network and Consortium of University Research Libraries (CURL). http://www.rin.ac.uk/our-work/using-and-accessing-information-resources/researchers-use-academic-libraries-and-their-serv.

De Rosa, Cathy. 2005. *Perceptions of Libraries and Information Resources: A Report to the OCLC Membership.* Dublin, OH: OCLC Online Computer Library Center. http://www.oclc.org/us/en/reports/2005perceptions.htm.

De Rosa, Cathy. 2006. *College Students' Perceptions of Libraries and Information Resources: A Report to the OCLC Membership.* Dublin, OH: OCLC Online Computer Library Center. http://www.oclc.org/us/en/reports/perceptionscollege.htm.

Dervin, Brenda, CarrieLynn D. Reinhard, Sarah K. Adamson, Tingting T. Lu, Noelle M. Karnolt, and Teena Berberick, eds. 2006. *Sense-making the Information Confluence: The Whys and Hows of College and University User Satisficing of Information Needs. Phase I: Project Overview, the Three-Field Dialogue Project, and State-of-the-Art Reviews.* Report on National Leadership Grant LG-02-03-0062-03, to Institute of Museum and Library Services, Washington, D.C. Columbus, OH: School of Communication, The Ohio State University. http://imlsproject.comm.ohio-state.edu/imls_reports/imls_PH_I_report_list.html. (inaccessible 26 October 2015).

Hampton-Reeves, Stuart, Claire Mashiter, Jonathan Westaway, Peter Lumsden, Helen Day, Helen Hewerston, and Anna Hart. 2009. *Students' Use of Research Content in Teaching and Learning: A Report of the Joint Information Systems Council (JISC).* http://www.jisc.ac.uk/media/documents/aboutus/workinggroups/studentsuseresearchcontent.pdf.

JISC and UCL. 2009. *JISC National e-Books Observatory Project: Key Findings and Recommendations: Final Report.* http://www.jiscebooksproject.org/reports/finalreport/.

Prabha, Chandra, Lynn Silipigni Connaway, and Timothy J. Dickey. 2006. *Sense-making the Information Confluence: The Whys and Hows of College and University User Satisficing of Information Needs. Phase IV: Semi-structured Interview Study.* Report on National Leadership Grant LG-02-03-0062-03, to Institute of Museum and Library Services, Washington, D.C. Columbus, OH: School of Communication, The Ohio State University. http://imlsproject.comm.ohio-state.edu/imls_reports/imls_PH_IV_report_list.html. (inaccessible 26 October 2015).

Radford, Marie L., and Lynn Silipigni Connaway. 2008. *Seeking Synchronicity: Evaluating Virtual Reference Services from User, Non-user, and Librarian Perspectives: IMLS Final Performance Report.* Report on Grant LG-06-05-0109-05, to Institute of Museum and Library Services, Washington, D.C. Dublin, OH: OCLC Online Computer Library Center. http://www.oclc.org/research/activities/synchronicity/reports/20080626-final.pdf.

Research Information Network. 2006. *Researchers and Discovery Services: Behaviour, Perceptions and Needs.* London: Research Information Network. http://www.rin.ac.uk/our-work/using-and-accessinginformation-resources/researchers-and-discovery-services-behaviour-perc. (inaccessible 26 October 2015).

> Alternative URL http://www.rin.ac.uk/our-work/using-and-accessing-information-resources/researchers-and-discovery-services-behaviour-perc (accessed 26 October 2015).

Research Information Network. 2009. *E-journals: Their Use, Value and Impact. London: Research Information Network.* http://www.rin.ac.uk/our-work/communicating-and-disseminating-research/ejournals-their-use-value-and-impact.

Rushkoff, Douglas. 1996. *Playing the Future: How Kid's Culture Can Teach Us to Thrive in an Age of Chaos.* New York: HarperCollins.

Wong, William, Hanna Stelmaszewska, Nazlin Bhimani, Sukhbinder Barn, and Balbir Barn. 2009. *User Behaviour in Resource Discovery: Final Report.* http://www.jisc.ac.uk/whatwedo/programmes/inf11/userbehaviourbusandecon.aspx. (inaccessible 26 October 2015).

6

"If it is too inconvenient I'm not going after it:" Convenience as a Critical Factor in Information-seeking Behaviors

Lynn Silipigni Connaway, Ph.D.
OCLC Research

Timothy J. Dickey, Ph.D.
OCLC Research

Marie L. Radford, Ph.D.
Rutgers, The State University of New Jersey

A reprint of:

Connaway, Lynn Silipigni, Timothy J. Dickey, and Marie L. Radford. 2011. "'If It Is Too Inconvenient I'm Not Going After It': Convenience as a Critical Factor in Information-seeking Behaviors." *Library & Information Science Research.* 33 no. 3: 179–190. http://dx.doi.org/10.1016/j.lisr.2010.12.002

© 2011 Elsevier, Inc. All rights reserved.

Background and literature review

It can be argued that in the not too distant past, resources were scarce and libraries were one of the only sources for trustworthy information. Users were obliged to conform to library practices and standards in order to successfully meet their information needs. Now users' attention is scarce and resources are abundant with the development of the Internet, web browsers and services (blogs, chat, social media sites, etc.) and easily accessed, abundant digitized content. This article provides an overview of findings from two multi-year grant-funded projects for which the authors were principal investigators that address the questions: Why do people choose one information source instead of another? and What factors contribute to their selection of information sources? Specifically, the emergence of the concept of "convenience" as a critical factor in information-seeking choices among a variety of different types of people, across a period of several years, and in a variety of contexts is explored below.

The ways people decide to get information often are dependent upon the context of the information need. Context can be an academic or work setting, such as a class, office, or factory, or a personal setting, such as a home or coffee shop. The literature suggests that individuals will consult different sources and will use different forms of communication to meet their information needs based upon the context and their individual situation. Context and situation are sometimes used interchangeably in the information science (IS) literature (see also Cool, 2001). Savolainen (2006) suggests that time is a significant context in information seeking. Prabha, Connaway, Olszewski, and Jenkins (2007) reported that time can affect the thoroughness of information seeking, the sources accessed, and the mode of inquiry context (including situation).

Librarians are finding that they must compete with other, often more convenient, familiar, and easy-to-use information sources. The user once built workflows around the library systems and services, but now, increasingly, the library must build its services around user workflows. In the current information environment, there is anecdotal evidence that people will sacrifice content for the convenience of accessing information sources. However, there has been little documented evidence to support this assumption. This paper provides evidence that convenience is a major factor for selecting information sources. *The American Heritage Dictionary of the English Language* (2000) defines convenience as "something that increases comfort or saves work." In terms of information seeking, aspects of convenience include familiarity with a resource, perceived ease-of-use, and physical proximity, though information-seeking studies to date have tended only to deal with convenience in passing. Bawden and Vilar (2006), for example, review the literature on the ease of use of the web and the difficulty of library systems, concluding that "Users believe that web search is fast and easy, providing immediate access to information and giving them what they want" (p. 349). In their IMLS-sponsored report on the use of libraries, museums, and the Internet, Griffiths and King (2008) state that, for adult users, "The Internet is not always chosen because it is considered the best source (74% of occurrences), but is nearly always chosen because it is convenient or easy to use (93%) and to a lesser degree is chosen because it does not cost much in time or money (69%)" (p. 38). Convenience/ease of use is one of four main reasons adults choose information sources; other reasons include being the "best" resource, not costing much, and providing trusted information (ibid, p. 36). The Idaho Commission for Libraries engaged a research group to carry out state-wide focus groups with "digital natives" (Prensky, 2001). The report (2007) states that both older and younger digital natives (12–25 years of age) agree that the "Internet is a convenient way to access information at or through libraries." Sites associated with libraries were well-viewed by digital natives, and the library was seen as having the role of providing information through other media such as the Internet, but that the Internet does not replace libraries (ibid, p. 47).

Lombardo and Condic (2001) investigate perceptions of and knowledge of online journal article databases by undergraduates. They found that users are not lazy when they rely on full-text articles; they are finding ways around the inconvenience of physically accessing print articles. Similarly, Agosto (2002) sees young people's choices to take the simplest approach to information gathering in terms of bounded rationality. Gross and Latham (2009), in reviewing undergraduate perceptions of information literacy find that their subjects tend to define information literacy as product (getting information and easy outcomes) rather than as a process of learning. Pullinger (1999) reports on research attempting to understand why users might opt to use online resources instead of the physical library; results indicated that the users find libraries frustrating, and they try to avoid going there. Problems cited in this study include limited hours, distance to the library, and the time that it takes for library research (p. 165). Fast and Campbell (2004) compare OPAC searching and web searching. Undergraduates and graduate students in their sample preferred using the web, with reasons including time and effort required. Students found web searching fast and easy; there is a simplicity that appeals (ibid, p. 143). Head and Eisenberg (2010) conducted focus group interviews and online surveys to identify "how and why students (enrolled at six different U.S. colleges) use *Wikipedia* during the course–related research process." The authors conclude that *"Wikipedia* meets the needs of college students because it offers a mixture of coverage, currency, convenience, and comprehensibility in a world where credibility is less of a given or an expectation from today's students." Antell and Engel (2006) survey university faculty and find that physical age as well as "scholarly age" (i.e., time since last diploma) can affect use of physical library space. A more recent study of academic researchers reinforced the current "convenience, speed, and interactivity of searching" within electronic environments (Niu, Hemminger, Lown, Adams, Brown, et al., 2010, p. 877). One of their minor themes focused on the convenience of the physical library. Younger scholarly users in this study identify somewhat more with physical libraries than expected.

Theoretical foundations and methodology

The present study investigates convenience as a constant theme in different information-seeking behaviors, by analyzing data from two multi-year IMLS-funded projects: *Sense-making the information confluence: The whys and hows of college and university user satisficing of information needs* (Sense-Making: Dervin, & Reinhard, 2006; Connaway, Prabha, & Dickey, 2006; Prabha, Connaway, & Dickey, 2006); and Seeking synchronicity: *Evaluating virtual reference services from user, non-user, and librarian perspectives* (Seeking Synchronicity: Radford & Connaway, 2008). Convenience was first explored as a factor in these data by Connaway, Radford, and Dickey (2008) and Connaway, Radford, Dickey, Williams, and Confer (2008). In the first study, data from non-users of virtual reference services revealed factors—prominently including convenience—in the information-seeking behaviors of the subjects; the second study compared data on the information behaviors of the "Millennial" generation and the "Baby Boomers." Both studies especially highlighted the Millennials' preference for Google and human sources for quick searches for information. A more focused examination of the data from the two projects for evidence of convenience-related findings informs the present study.

Convenience is a situational criterion in people's choices and actions during the informationseeking process. The concept can include their choice of an information source, their satisfaction with the source and its ease of use, and their time horizon in information seeking. The theoretical framework for this understanding is founded in the concepts of bounded rationality and rational choice theory, with Savolainen's (2006) concept of time as a context in information seeking, and gratification theory, informing the emphasis on the seekers' time horizons.

Much of rational choice theory developed in economics (Green, 2002); it posits that even the most complex social behavior may be viewed in terms of discrete and elementary individual actions. Individuals are seen as acting in their own self-interest in these individual actions—not necessarily acting towards achieving similar goals as other individuals, but according to their own "preferences, values or utilities" (Friedman & Hechter, 1998, p. 202). The theory has been applied to a number of disciplines in the social sciences, and recently emerged in information science (Prabha, Connaway, Olszewski, & Jenkins, 2007).

Similarly, gratification theory developed elsewhere in the social sciences, specifically in research about the social world of poor people. Chatman (1991) applied it to information-seeking behavior in this population. Specifically, she used the "prevailing finding ... that poor people seek immediate gratification because of behavioral characteristics not found in other classes. That is, because they are more inclined toward quick arousal, pleasure, or excitement, and they engage in activities that result in instantaneous pay-offs" (p. 442). The issue of her subjects' narrow time horizon is a major contextual factor in their approach to information seeking (see also Dervin, 1977, and Dervin & Vilan, 1986).

Additionally, Savolainen's (1995) work in the area of everyday-life information seeking (ELIS) emphasizes the importance of time as a contextual factor. He concludes one study by calling for more "conceptual studies clarifying the nature of temporal or more broadly, spatiotemporal factors as contextual qualifiers of information seeking" (Savolainen, 2006, p. 124). "Limited time horizons in everyday life tend to restrict information seeking" (p. 114), but the library and information science field lacks empirical studies of the phenomenon. Savolainen later (2008) reported on time and access-related factors in ELIS. Both "Availability and accessibility of information" and situational factors such as "lack of time" affected subjects' choice of information sources (Savolainen, 2008, p. 90–91). "Ease and speed of use" and "Quick to contact/access/convenient" were identified as major factors in similar studies (Julien & Michels, 2004; Fischer, Naumer, Durrance, Stromsky, & Christiansen, 2006).

Thus, aspects of convenience including choice of source, ease of access and use, and time factors can be central contextual limiters in information seeking. This centrality is borne out by the data from the two projects analyzed here, and have not changed over time: the first study (Sense-Making) data were collected in 2003, and are supported by data from the second study (Seeking Synchronicity) in 2007. The importance of convenience as a situational factor is relatively constant across demographic boundaries, as well—between the two studies, a wide variety of information behaviors were collected.

In the Sense-Making study, (Dervin, & Reinhard, 2006; Connaway et al., 2006; Prabha et al, 2006) investigators studied the information-seeking behaviors of faculty, undergraduates, and graduate students from a sample of forty-four colleges and universities within a Midwestern region in the U.S. during a period of three years. In Phase II of the research (Phase I had been exploratory, three hundred and seven randomly sampled subjects responded to an online survey and telephone interview follow-up regarding five situations of their information seeking, for a total N=1522 informants-in-situation; in Phase III, seventy-eight subjects completed sense-making focus group interviews, and a subset of fifteen focus group participants were randomly selected for individual semi-structured interviews in Phase IV. The research intended to illuminate the information-seeking "hows" (moment-to-moment activities and practices) and "whys" (rational choices and criteria for them), with emphasis on the richest possible context for each choice. Although the Sense-Making study only included academic respondents, they were also asked questions pertaining to their information-seeking behaviors in personal situations.

Prior analysis of these data included extensive coding of the survey responses according to sense-making concepts (Dervin et al., 2006), analysis of the focus group and interview data in terms of "satisficing" of information needs (Simon 1955, 1979; Prabha et al., 2007), and parsing the focus group and interview data by generation (Millennials and Baby Boomers, see Connaway et al., 2008). For the present study, all data were re-examined for respondents' use of terms such as "convenience," "convenient," "fast/easy/quick," or for indications that a specific rational choice saved them time in the process.

The Seeking Synchronicity project studied the needs, behaviors, and impressions of users, nonusers, and librarian providers of virtual reference services (VRS) (Radford & Connaway, 2008). The respondents for this study included both academics and the general public. Both user and non-user data will be included in this discussion. Phase I of the project incorporated eight exploratory focus group interviews; Phase II examined a random sample of actual VRS transcripts. In the third phase, members of each population (see table 1) responded to online surveys, which included both quantitative (comparisons and Likert scale questions) and qualitative (open-ended discussions about positive and negative experiences with reference services) data; in the fourth, telephone interviews were conducted with VRS users and non-users and results were transcribed and analyzed for themes emerging from the data. For the present study, a wide variety of quantitative and qualitative questions which evinced data on convenience ease of access and use, and time as a context in individual decisions were considered.

TABLE 1: SEEKING SYNCHRONICITY PHASE III—ONLINE SURVEYS AND PHASE IV—TELEPHONE INTERVIEWS, DEMOGRAPHICS OF VRS USERS AND NON-USERS

Data collection phases	Demographic breakdown
VRS users' online survey (N=137)	62% female 78% Caucasian 63% suburban 64% age 29+
VRS non-users' online survey (N=184)	68% female 72% Caucasian 58% suburban 33% 12–18; 33% 19–28; 33% 29+
VRS users' telephone interviews (N=76)	74% female 80% Caucasian 63% suburban 71% age 29+
VRS non-users' telephone interviews (N=107)	66% female 70% Caucasian 55% suburban 48% age 19–28

Findings

SENSE-MAKING PHASE II—ONLINE SURVEYS

Convenience, including issues of ease of access/use and time, permeates the data in each phase of both research projects about how different individuals make choices in their information seeking. In the second phase of the Sense-Making project, the final IMLS report states that, "Situation … was by far the best predictor across all information seeking and uses measures" (Dervin & Reinhard, 2006, p. ES-3); situation in this case includes questions of convenience such as information seeking late at night, or in a desperate need for quick answers. "Under some conditions, the idea of options of any kind is alien to users. They grab whatever is quickest and easiest. Under other conditions, they reach for more but have an acute awareness of the exigencies of life-facing." (ibid, p. ES-4) Even the analysis based on sense-making terminology notes that 74.5% of situations in these data were focused in the "present horizon" of time (ibid, p. ES-30).

The rather narrow terminology selected for assigning convenience codes ("convenience," "convenient," "easy," "quick," "fast," and various words for saving time) to the qualitative survey responses nevertheless resulted in a large number of results in which convenience was an issue in the respondents' own words. Out of a total N=307 respondents, 171 used one or more of these phrases, for a total number n=285 occurrences (see table 2). All three study populations—faculty, graduate students, and undergraduates—used convenience-phrases, though the use was most concentrated in the graduate student population. Convenience seemed to be more of an issue with these academic library users in research-related situations: (the second, fourth, and fifth questions on the survey, see appendix 1) than in more personal situations. Please see table 3 for a breakdown of the analysis of convenience language by situation.

TABLE 2: SENSE-MAKING PHASE II—ONLINE SURVEY RESPONDENTS USING CONVENIENCE PHRASES

Rank	# responding with convenience phrases
Faculty	36
Graduate student	76
Undergraduate student	59
TOTAL:	171

TABLE 3: SENSE-MAKING PHASE II—ONLINE SURVEY SITUATIONS ELICITING CONVENIENCE PHRASES

Survey question	# of convenience phrases
Q1: Troublesome situation in university life	39
Q2: Situation specifically involving research	83
Q3: Troublesome situation in life outside university	11
Q4: Situation in university life where you used electronic resources	88
Q5: Situation in life outside university where you used electronic resources	64
TOTAL:	285

When the survey questions or telephone follow-up delved into the information sources that respondents used in each situation, convenience most often appeared as a factor when they were using Internet search engines, electronic databases, or the college/university libraries. Far more often, their mentions of a source's convenience were in cases where they answered that the particular source helped their information search. At the same time, some of the times they claimed that the source hindered their information search, lack of convenience or time-saving was apparently part of the problem they experienced. These findings held across the three populations under study, though faculty were moderately more positive in their assessment of databases' convenience than the two types of student, who both favored search engines. See table 4 for an analysis of online survey data for convenient information sources, and table 5 for online survey data for convenient information sources by population.

TABLE 4: SENSE-MAKING PHASE II—ONLINE SURVEY CONVENIENT INFORMATION SOURCES

Information sources used (from a list provided in the survey)	Convenience phrases	Convenience phrases where source helped	Convenience phrases where source did not help
Internet search engine	56	52	4
Electronic databases	48	44	1
College or university libraries	17	12	5
Library catalogs	8	6	2
Own observations	6	5	1
Journal articles	6	4	2
Students, classmates	5	5	0
Public libraries	5	2	3
Newspapers	5	2	3
Government agencies	4	3	1
Personal web pages	3	3	0
Web diaries, blogs	3	3	0
Reference books	3	1	2
Professors, teachers	2	2	0
Family, friends	3	1	2
Museums	2	1	1
Internet chat rooms	3	2	0
Other non-fiction books	2	0	2
Co-workers, colleagues	1	1	0
Other professionals	1	1	1

TABLE 5: SENSE-MAKING PHASE II—ONLINE SURVEY TOP CONVENIENT INFORMATION SOURCES BY POPULATION.

Information sources used (from a list provided in the survey)	Convenience phrases	Convenience phrases where source helped	Convenience phrases where source did not help
Faculty			
Electronic databases	12	12	0
Search engines	10	9	1
Library catalogs	2	2	0
College, university libraries	0	0	0
Graduate students			
Search engines	31	31	0
Electronic databases	16	12	1
College, university libraries	5	4	1
Library catalogs	5	3	2
Undergraduates			
Search engines	15	12	3
Electronic databases	11	9	0
College, university libraries	8	5	3
Library catalogs 1	1	1	0

SENSE-MAKING PHASE III—FOCUS GROUP INTERVIEWS

Eight focus group interviews (two groups of graduate students and three each of undergraduates and faculty) were organized around four specific kinds of information-seeking situations, but since the participants otherwise had free rein in their responses, the data are less quantifiable (see appendix 2 for the complete focus group interview questions). However, regardless of academic rank, convenience still emerged as a major contributing factor in individual choices as to the selection of which information strategies or resources to use. This response was especially true for the first question in the focus group interviews: "Think of a time when you had a situation where you needed answers or solutions and you did a quick search and made do with it. You knew there were other sources but you decided not to use them. Please include sources such as friends, family, professors, colleagues, etc."

Participants in the nine focus group interviews centered their discussion of this question on different kinds of information sources, but made their decisions for a quick search based on the convenience of the source. Undergraduates tended to discuss only web-based sources in this instance, with a heavy reliance on Google in particular. Graduate students also cited Google as being quick and easy; one commented, "Google, I don't have to know, I go to one spot." (FG-6) A the same time, if they are unable to locate an Internet source for their quick search, they use the library as a convenient repository of information ("Even with the library, it's start with the imminent. I use the online resources. If I can avoid a physical trip to the library ... I'll avoid it." FG-6). Faculty most often cited their personal home or office library—an incredibly convenient source—as the most often-used place to find quick information, though many of them also spoke about Google or colleagues: "If I just have a quick thing, and I just want an answer, I will call a colleague that has some expertise. ... Instead of looking up all the different papers of all the different methods ... call them up. It's much faster." (FG-5)

Later in each focus group, the participants were asked, "Have there been times when you did not use a library (university/college, public, etc.) and used other source(s) instead?" In the case of this second question, the three academic groups did display somewhat different kinds of information behaviors, but convenience (including temporal contexts) again factored into their responses. Undergraduates offered specific criticisms of the library catalog as difficult to use in this instance, though they claimed they will use online reserves from the library—after the library closes, a clear convenience choice. They and graduate students both commented with some frequency on how easy the web is to use, especially in comparison to library systems: "I don't go into the [library] system unless I have to because there's like 15 logins, you have to get into the research databases. Then it takes you out of that to [the local consortium] ..." (FG-6) Graduate students in one focus group interview provided further data regarding their perceptions of the convenience of online books ("And plus they don't get overdue!" FG-8). Faculty again mentioned web searches as easy to use, though these searches often next lead them to the library for authoritative and credible information, an evaluation they make in spite of convenience factors.

The third question posed to each focus group participant was, "Think of an academic situation where you needed answers or solutions and you did a thorough search (you did not take the first answer that you found). Describe the situation." In response to this more thorough research question, undergraduates continue to cite Google and Amazon as frequent, easy-to-use and convenient sources. Use of library systems is mediated by considerations of convenience, such as the comment, "I use [the local union catalog], but I don't really need to come into a library, as long as I have a computer at home." One undergraduate cited the difficulty of the library OPAC, claiming the best process was to discover works on Amazon and paste them more conveniently into the OPAC to find the location of the item or into their work. Undergraduates' views were probed to determine when they considered they had "enough" information; quite often temporal considerations impacted their answers ("... time is a big factor for me, at least like if depending on how much time I have to do the project or how long I wait to start it depends on how thorough it will be and how much time I'll spend on it," FG-2; "I've always thought that the library was a good source if you have a few months to spend on a paper." FG-7). Once again graduate students indicated that some of their choices were influenced by considerations of convenience. Specifically, they credit e-books and interlibrary loans as time-saving services. Faculty, whose professional lives are bound up with the inconvenience of saturation research on topics, had little to offer the discussion of convenience on this question.

Finally, the participants were asked to imagine an ideal information system, created via a "magic wand." Several comments from each population speak to the convenience to which they would aspire. Ideas from undergraduates include the ability to use keyword searching in all books (a prophecy of Google Book Search?), a universal library catalog for all libraries, reference staff that conveniently rove about the library ("… where they have people who walk around and are there available to help you not always just confined behind a desk where you have to go up and they're like, well if you take a left after that bookcase then a right." FG-2), federated search in databases (speaking to both time saving and ease of use), and better hyperlinks. Graduate students desired better book and journal delivery systems, presumably for the convenience of receiving materials in their office ("But other times, it says you have to actually go get the article, and I do a lot of research under a lot of supervisors and stuff. So it's such a drag." FG-6). Faculty mention selective alerts for new information in their field, termed Selective Dissemination of Information (SDI) in information science; although the respondents did not use the term, they described the service ("… a constant perusing of what's available and if something is new that gets a hit, it's automatically directed to us whether we ask for it or not." FG-1), as well as virtual reference services available from their computer ("Something that I really liked about our website, was the ask a librarian icon." FG-9).

SENSE-MAKING PHASE IV—SEMI-STRUCTURED INTERVIEWS

The final phase of data collection in this project involved semi-structured interviews with a small subset of previous study participants: 5 undergraduates, 4 graduate students, and 6 faculty members. The interviews took place in "natural environments" such as an office, home, or dormitory. Since four of the five questions (see appendix 3) involved relatively intense academic work, convenience was not a major factor in many participants' discussion of their information seeking processes (see table 6). However, in the case of the fifth situation, "Now, please take me on a tour of your favorite website where you get answers to questions that interest you. … Help me understand what makes this site helpful when others are not. Show me, if you can, examples of non-helpful sites," convenience became much more germane to the respondents (N=13 for this question).

TABLE 6: SENSE-MAKING: PHASE IV—SEMI-STRUCTURED INTERVIEW RESPONDENTS CITING CONVENIENCE

Situation	Respondents citing convenience (N=15)	Times convenience is cited
Q1: Writing an academic paper, proposal, or class assignment	2	2
Q2: Work on a current paper, assignment, or scholarly task	4	5
Q3: Work on a current paper, assignment, or scholarly task using electronic resources	5	7
Q4: Repetitive situation in life requiring repeating seeking of electronic inputs	5	6
Q5: Tour of favorite website	9	15

Once again in these data, the respondents valued convenience both of place ("Mostly I use the Internet for things like this because it's convenient. Since I work at the computer all the time, it's right there so, you know, when I have a few extra minutes I'll just type in a search and find information and print it out if I need to") and of time ("I would do everything if not electronically, then somehow vacuum it to someone so they get it immediately."). Interestingly, one respondent even brought the concept of the convenience of books into this website-specific question: "I like to have the piles of books all around me so I can just grab from each place and start writing my paper or whatever I'm doing."

SEEKING SYNCHRONICITY PHASE III—ONLINE SURVEYS

Three years after the data were collected for the Sense-Making project, analysis of the Seeking Synchronicity research revealed a remarkably similar highlighting of convenience factors in information-seeking behaviors. The third phase of the Seeking Synchronicity project (online surveys) had a more narrow focus on librarian-provided reference services; two of the three populations under study were users of virtual reference services (VRS) and non-users of VRS (who were asked questions regarding their use of other modes of library reference service). Convenience, in terms of general ease of information seeking, of time issues, and of physical location, again was a major factor in both VRS users' and non-users' individual decisions and choices in their information seeking.

Convenience factors scored uniformly high among both users (N=137, see 7able 7) and non-users (N=184, see table 10). In many cases, the "frequent" users of VRS (N=59), defined for this purpose as respondents who reported using virtual reference 4-6 times or more, rated convenience even higher than less frequent users in their choice to use the service. Users (and especially frequent users) rated the chat medium as the "most efficient" of all reference modes, and rated the "convenience of my access" to VRS as excellent or very good. When asked to rate different factors which affect their decision to use VRS, 95% of users (100% of frequent users) cited convenience directly; needs for information late at night or on the weekend, at times when the subject could not get to a library, or when there was a "desperate need for quick answers" also rated highly in their choice. "Immediate answers" and "convenience" were among the most highly rated specific features valued in VRS. Finally, time issues play into the users' complaints with the service—a slow Internet connection or slow response time on the part of the library would tend to discourage them from using VRS, and many suggested faster software as a desirable improvement. See Table 7 for an analysis of convenience as a factor for VRS users.

TABLE 7: SEEKING SYNCHRONICITY PHASE III—ONLINE SURVEY VRS USER RESPONDENTS CITING CONVENIENCE AS A FACTOR IN INFORMATION SEEKING

VRS users:	All survey respondents N=137	Frequent VRS users N=59
Comparing users' experience among formats,		
2.2 The format that is most efficient is:	55% chat	66% chat
Comparing specific aspects of chat,		
3.5 The convenience of my access to reference help is:	85% excellent or very good	86% excellent or very good
What factors are important to you when choosing VRS?		
4.2 Chat reference is convenient:	95% very important or important	100% very important or important
4.15 I needed reference help late at night or on the weekend:	74% very important or important	78% very important or important
4.16 I had a desperate need for quick answers:	72% very important or important	78% very important or important
4.17 I could not get to the library:	73% very important or important	78% very important or important
What factors are important to you when choosing other formats?		
5.1 The library is convenient:	76% very important or important	81% very important or important
5.2 Other formats are convenient:	78% very important or important	80% very important or important
What specific features are important to you in VRS?		

VRS users:	All survey respondents N=137	Frequent VRS users N=59
6.1 Immediate answers:	89% very important or important	92% very important or important
6.2 Convenience:	97% very important or important	98% very important or important
What items might discourage you from using VRS?		
7.2 Slow Internet connection:	69% strongly agree or agree	64% strongly agree or agree
7.15 Slow response time:	57% strongly agree or agree	58% strongly agree or agree
What might improve your experience?		
8.4 Faster software:	87% very important or important	75% very important or important

The documented centrality of convenience in the information seeking of VRS users is sustained across most demographic categories, though a very small number of significant differences emerged. The data across three age groups—12–18, 19–28, and 29 and older—were subjected to ANOVA with a confidence level of $\alpha=.05$ (see table 8). The youngest cohort of respondents was more likely to express a "desperate need for quick answers" than the oldest group, and also more likely to request faster software. The middle cohort was more likely to be discouraged by a slow Internet connection. The 29+ age group was less likely to find VRS the most efficient format for reference help (55% awarded the honor to traditional face-to-face reference), but these differences by age categories were not statistically significant. Two survey questions elicited significant differences by respondent's location (e.g., rural, suburban, or urban, see table 9). Suburbanites were much less likely to rate chat as the most efficient format for reference services than respondents from urban areas, and less likely than urbanites to rate as highly the convenience of their access to reference help (in each case, the number of rural respondents was too low for significant results).

TABLE 8: SEEKING SYNCHRONICITY PHASE III—ONLINE SURVEY VRS USERS, AGE DIFFERENCES.

Question	12-18	19-28	29+
VRS users	**N=26**	**N=23**	**N=88**
Comparing experience among formats,			
2.2 The format that is most efficient is:	58% chat	56% chat	55% FtF; 39% chat
What factors are important to you when choosing VRS?			
4.16 I had a desperate need for quick answers:	92% very important or important	70% very important or important	66% very important or important
What items might discourage you from using VRS?			
7.2 Slow Internet connection:	52% strongly agree or agree	96% very important or important	64% very important or important
What might improve your experience?			
8.4 Faster software:	96% very important or important	70% very important or important	74% very important or important

No statistically significant differences α=.05

TABLE 9: SEEKING SYNCHRONICITY PHASE III—ONLINE SURVEY VRS USERS, GEOGRAPHICAL DIFFERENCES

Question	Rural	Suburban	Urban
VRS users	**N=13**	**N=85**	**N=38**
Comparing experience among formats,			
2.2 The format that is most efficient is:	69% chat	32% chat	(56% FtF) 68% chat
Comparing specific aspects of chat,			
3.5 The convenience of my access to reference help is:	92% excellent or very good	78% excellent or very good	97% excellent or very good

Significant differences α=.05

Likewise among the non-users of VRS (these individuals did use libraries, they just did not use VRS) surveyed, convenience emerged as a factor in choices in their library information seeking. When responding to a question about the convenience of their access to face-to-face reference services (FtF), almost half rated it excellent or very good (a much less enthusiastic endorsement than the 95% of VRS users who rated the convenience of VRS excellent or very good). However, when asked about the convenience of their preferred mode of obtaining reference assistance, a large majority cited the convenience of whichever specific mode was their preference. For those who prefer reference services by telephone or email, both physical and temporal convenience played a negative role in their choice not to use a library, and the fear that "Chat reference might not be offered at times I need the service" was a significant deterrent expressed as a reason these non-users had not tried VRS; see table 10 for an analysis of convenience as a factor for non-users of VRS. Demographic differences among these data were negligible.

TABLE 10: SEEKING SYNCHRONICITY PHASE III—ONLINE SURVEY VRS NON-USERS RESPONDENTS CITING CONVENIENCE AS A FACTOR IN INFORMATION SEEKING

VRS non-users:	N=184
Comparing specific aspects of FtF,	
3.5 The convenience of my access to reference help is:	45% excellent or very good
Reasons for not choosing chat:	
5.5 Chat reference might not be offered at times I need the service:	60% strongly agree or agree
Comparing specific features of other formats, (NB respondent pool then is divided by their preferred mode)	
I prefer: A. FtF B. telephone C. electronic formats	137 FtF/9 telephone/38 electronic formats
4.A1 The library is convenient (those preferring library):	84% very important or important
4.B1 The telephone is convenient (prefer telephone):	73% very important or important
4.C1 Electronic formats are convenient (prefer electronic):	91% very important or important
What might discourage you from using other formats?	
4.B9 The library is not convenient (prefer telephone):	57% strongly agree or agree
4.B10 The library is not open at convenient hours (prefer telephone):	59% strongly agree or agree
4.C16 The library is not convenient (prefer electronic):	67% strongly agree or agree
4.C17 The library is not open at convenient hours (prefer electronic):	70% strongly agree or agree

SEEKING SYNCHRONICITY PHASE IV—TELEPHONE INTERVIEWS

The majority of the transcript data from the Phase IV telephone interviews (see appendix 4 for the interview questions) were coded according to the principles of grounded theory, allowing the codes to emerge from the respondents' language. Thus, the overall percentages for the occurrence of any single data point will be smaller. Nevertheless, codes related to convenience, including physical and temporal convenience, emerged in response to several different interview questions for both the VRS users and non-users. (In the following discussion and tables, code names are as assigned by researchers to each set of transcripts as they emerged from the data.)

Convenience-related codes emerged from four questions in the telephone interviews with VRS users (see table 11). The most important question for users' thoughts about convenience was the question of whether the users would recommend VRS to others (they overwhelmingly would) and why (question 10). Fully a third of those interviewed made positive comments on the speed and efficiency of VRS, and 22% made some reference to its convenience, including availability after-hours, and getting answers in the online workflow. The same two aspects of their experience with VRS also emerged in their responses to a question probing for the kind of situation when chat is their first choice of mode for obtaining reference services (question 3); in this case specific aspects of convenience include after-hours need, online workflow, and being at a home or office.

One negative type of data emerged from a question asking VRS users how much time they might wait to get virtual answers from a subject specialist (question 9). Despite a majority of respondents claiming that subject expertise was very important to them, only 42% would be willing to wait for that expertise, and very few of them could quantify a specific amount of time to wait. Finally, near the end of each interview (question 11), VRS users were asked to compare their experiences of working with a librarian FtF and in the virtual space, with justification for their response. Many did not indicate a clear preference, though among those respondents several again mentioned the convenience and immediacy of the chat medium, and a few expressed a negative opinion of FtF reference ("… the convenience is still better online than in person, you don't have to make trips to the library" UTI-24). Among the respondents who indicated a preference for VRS, even more expressed the convenience of VRS in a positive light, and the lack of convenience in FtF as negative. Demographic differences in these data were negligible.

TABLE 11: SEEKING SYNCHRONICITY PHASE IV—TELEPHONE INTERVIEW VRS USER COMMENTS ABOUT CONVENIENCE

VRS users:	N=76
When recommending chat reference (question 10), they recommend based on:	
Speed and efficiency	32%
Convenience	22%
After-hours availability	7%
Getting answers in the online workflow	3%
When chat is first choice for information (question 3), they describe their reasons:	
Convenient	30%
Quick help-speedy answers	18%
After-hours, can't get to library	12%
Already at-in use of a computer	10%
Don't have to leave home-office	7%
Reliable information-sources	7%
Easier to go on-line	4%
How much time might you wait for a specialist (question 9)?	
Waiting only a specific amount of time	11%
Ten to fifteen minutes	4%
Half hour	3%
One to two hours	3%
Half a day	1%
In comparing chat to other formats (question 11),	
Positive immediacy-convenience-efficiency of VRS (prefer VRS)	14%
Positive Immediacy-convenience-efficiency of VRS (no clear preference)	11%

VRS users:	N=76
Negative immediacy-convenience-efficiency of FtF (prefer VRS)	5%
Negative immediacy-convenience-efficiency of FtF (no clear preference)	3%

Responses by VRS non-users to four questions in their telephone interviews also provided data related to convenience as a major factor in their individual choices while seeking information (see table 12 for results, and appendix 4 for the complete interview questions). When asked in the most general sense to "Think about a time you needed to know something" (question 2), a large majority responded that they would find the information themselves, potentially a very convenient and easy choice. Almost all of the remaining interviewees (with some overlap to the "find myself" answer) responded with some form of electronic resource; this is not explicitly a convenience choice, but implicitly. Similarly, when asked to consider times when they chose an alternative to the library (question 3), the largest number of respondents mentioned the Internet as a resource, with numerous references to specific online (and implicitly more convenient) resources.

When asked to hypothesize about what might convince them to try asking a librarian for help using a chat reference service (question 6), the single greatest factor was some form of convenience ("It would be convenient, because if I was sitting at a computer and I could ask a question and they would answer immediately ... that would be good. Convenience is why I do something as opposed to something else." N-131). This included a large number of respondents who could foresee an immediate need for answers, those who would value using VRS from home in a variety of circumstances, and those who would use the service at a time that was after library hours. Finally, in the follow-up to a question about the non-users' experience using electronic formats for personal and academic or professional purposes (question 5), the VRS non-users were asked to give some reasons for their use. Among the less-than-cohesive data from their responses, convenience emerged in a few cases. As with the VRS users in the telephone interviews, significant demographic differences were not present.

TABLE 12: SEEKING SYNCHRONICITY PHASE IV—TELEPHONE INTERVIEW VRS NON-USER COMMENTS ABOUT CONVENIENCE

VRS non-users:	N=107
Choices in an information source (question 2):	
Start with Internet (Internet first)	30%
Start with Google (Google first)	15%
Google	11%
Wikipedia	5%
Google Scholar	4%
Start with Wikipedia (Wikipedia first)	3%
Concerning alternatives to the library, and why (question 3),	
Alternative source is the Internet:	41%
Reason: personal convenience	**28%**
Google	11%
Databases associated with Internet (EBSCO, LexisNexis, etc.)	6%
Reason: Inconvenience of the library	**5%**
Google Scholar	3%
Wikipedia	3%
Expert web sites	3%
Yahoo!	2%
Reason: Internet as starting point	2%
Journals associated with Internet	1%
Online book sellers	1%
Possible reasons for trying chat include (question 6):	
Convenience	**62%**

VRS non-users:	N=107
Needing immediate answers	25%
Unable to get to the library	7%
Using the service after hours	7%
Perceiving chat reference as faster than email	4%
Valuing using chat reference from home	4%
Unable to telephone the library	4%
Citing general ease of use	2%
Experiencing bad weather	2%
Avoiding a long distance call	1%
Preferring chat to holding on the phone	1%
Reasons for using electronic communication formats (question 5):	
Convenience or speed	7%
Expectation of electronic formats' immediacy	6%
More convenient than in person	1%
Expecting electronic formats convenient to access	1%

Discussion

Between the two studies, empirical data identifies convenience as central to information-seeking behaviors. The centrality of convenience is especially prevalent among the younger ("Millennial") subjects in both studies, but is true across all demographic categories—age, gender, academic role, user or non-user of VRS.

These two studies indicate that convenience is a factor for making choices in all situations, both academic information seeking and everyday-life information seeking (though it plays different roles in different situations). The study data on convenience come from both prompted survey response language, and from free-response data in interviews and critical incident data (data regarding subjects' memories of a single successful or unsuccessful incident; Flanagan, 1954). Most importantly, the data on convenience are consistent across the longitudinal period between the two studies, indicating that the need for convenience is not new.

Convenience emerges from the data around three particular aspects of the concept. Ease of access to resources is one measure of convenience when making rational choices in information seeking. The most convenient sources of information might be Internet search engines, electronic databases, virtual reference, or online e-reserves, e-books, and online booksellers; findings indicate that Google is especially important to the younger generations. However, in addition to electronic resources which carry the convenience of desktop or home access, data emerged about the convenience of human resources as information sources, as well as the convenience of having a personal library on hand. Convenience also plays into the data regarding choices to use (or not to use) the brick-and-mortar library, or how to access library resources after hours or on the weekend. Convenience as expressed in ease of access was a repeated complaint made against library OPACs. This finding was reiterated in the Seeking Synchronicity study of VRS. The "magic wand" enhancements to library systems in the Sense-Making study differed by academic role of the participant, but these tended to relate to convenience of access to resources.

Different contexts and situations for information needs did not detract from the centrality of convenience in making choices, though the convenience factor acted differently depending on context: students faced with lengthy imposed academic tasks, for instance, and professional scholars, valued the most convenient access to the library's great store of resources, but acknowledged that their longer academic tasks would be more involved. In the Sense-Making study, in fact, convenience emerged as even more important to the subjects' discussion of academic tasks than to their discussion of everyday-life information needs. But convenience—in this case more often associated with speed of electronic search engines or the like—remained important in the more immediate everyday-life situations, and this finding was also repeated in the Seeking Synchronicity study. Convenience was a leading feature every time VRS users were asked in surveys and interviews to evaluate reasons for choosing the service, or for recommending it to others.

Finally, the data in both studies explored time as an important situation factor in convenience choices. The time-span of longer academic tasks featured in the "satisficing" behavior of the Sense-Making study's academic users, as well as the responses from the Seeking Synchronicity respondents describing their use of VRS for academic tasks. In both studies, the temporal context of an information need also might relate to library hours—experiencing an information need late at night, or on weekends. The Seeking Synchronicity study especially illuminated the kind of information need expressed as a "desperate need for immediate answers." Such highly time-oriented information needs were most often expressed by younger subjects, but featured in all demographic categories.

Implications for practice and conclusion

The image of libraries as a quiet place to access books, rather than to access electronic sources still is prevalent today (Connaway, & Dickey, 2010, p. 39). In order to entice people to use libraries and to change their perceptions of libraries, the library experience needs to become more like that available on the web (e.g., Google, Amazon.com, iTunes, etc.) and to be embedded in individual workflows. The web environment is familiar to users; therefore, they are comfortable and confident choosing to search for information there. Librarians need to adapt or seek to purchase services and systems that are designed to replicate the web environment so that they are perceived as convenient and easy to use.

Access to sources, not the discovery of sources, is the concern of information-seekers. People lack patience to wade through content silos and indexing and abstracting databases. They expect seamless access to resources such as full text e-journals, online foreign-language materials, ebooks, a variety of electronic publishers' platforms, and virtual reference desk services (Connaway & Dickey, 2010, p. 46–47). To meet these expectations, it is recommended that librarians should provide more authoritative, reliable digital sources through the library systems and services, from e-journals to curated data sets, as well as emerging services such as virtual research environments (VREs), open source materials, non-text-based and multimedia objects, and blogs.

Librarians also must advertise the library brand and its resources better to academics, researchers, students, and the general public. Demonstrating the library's value can be accomplished by identifying and promoting collections and services. One size does not fit all for library services, which need to be offered in multiple delivery modes to meet the different information needs of users in different situations. This versatility and flexibility is difficult in the current economic environment, but warrants further investigation.

The development of an economic model for the allocation of resources for the different delivery modes for library services would benefit all types of libraries. This would not only enable optimal scheduling of human resources for services but also the allocation of funds for both electronic and print resources based on user preferences.

There is a need for a user behavior study to address how library users find information in different contexts and situations. Vakkari (1997) calls for "studies which will concentrate more on contextual factors, and then combine the results with those of studies using more individual factors" (p.463). An approach like this would provide theoretical research that combines both the 11 individual and social factors that influence information-seeking behaviors (Connaway & Dickey, 2010).

As seen above, in some situations information seekers will readily sacrifice content for convenience. Convenience is thus one of the primary criteria used for making choices during the information-seeking process. Convenience includes the choice of the information source (is it readily available online or in print), the satisfaction with the source (does it contain the needed information and is it easy to use), and the time it will take to access and use the information source (how long will it take to access). In the current environment, most people do not have time to spend searching for information or for learning how to use a new information source or access method. In order to be one of the first choices for information, library systems and interfaces need to look familiar to people by resembling popular web interfaces and library services need to be easily accessible and to require little or no training to use. Convenience is a critical factor for users across all demographic categories, and is liable to remain so going forward.

REFERENCES

Agosto, D. 2002. "Bounded rationality and satisficing in young people's Web-based decision making." *Journal of the American Society for Information Science & Technology* 53, no. 1: 18–27.

Antell, K., & Engel, D. 2006. "Conduciveness to scholarship: The essence of academic library as place." *College & Research Libraries* 67, no. 6: 536–560.

Bawden, D., & Vilar, P. 2006. "Digital libraries: To meet or manage user expectations." *Aslib Proceedings: New Information Perspectives* 58: 346–354.

Chatman, E. 1991. "Life in a small world: Applicability of gratification theory to information-seeking behavior." *Journal of the American Society for Information Science & Technology* 42, no. 6: 438–449.

Connaway, L. S. 2007. "Mountains, valleys, and pathways: Serials users' needs and steps to meet them. Part I: Preliminary analysis of focus group and semi-structured interviews at colleges and universities." *Serials Librarian* 52, no. 1/2: 223–236.

Connaway, L. S., & Dickey, T. J. 2010. *The digital information seeker: Report of findings from selected OCLC, RIN and JISC user behaviour projects.* London: HEFCE on behalf of the JISC.

Connaway, L. S., Prabha, C., & Dickey, T. J. 2006. *Sense-making the information confluence: The whys and hows of college and university user satisficing of information needs. Phase III: Focus group interview study. Report on National Leadership Grant LG-02-03-0062-03, to Institute of Museum and Library Services, Washington, D.C.* Columbus, Ohio: School of Communication, The Ohio State University. http://imlsproject.comm.ohio-state.edu/imls_reports/PHASE_III/PH_III_report.pdf. (accessed 26 April 2010) (inaccessible 26 October 2015).

Connaway, L. S., Radford, M. L., & Dickey, T. J. 2008. "On the trail of the elusive nonuser: What research in virtual reference environments reveals." *ASIS&T Bulletin* 34, no. 2: 25–28. http://www.asis.org/Bulletin/Dec-07/Bulletin_DecJan08.pdf. (accessed 26 April 2010).

Connaway, L. S., Radford, M. L., Dickey, T. J., Williams, J. D., & Confer, P. 2008. "Sensemaking and synchronicity: Information-seeking behaviors of millennials and baby boomers." *Libri* 58: 123–135.

Cool, C. 2001. "The concept of situation in information science." M. E. Williams (Ed.). *Annual Review of Information Science and Technology* 35: 5–42. Medford, NJ: Information Today, Inc.

Dervin, B. 1977. "Useful theory for librarianship: Communication, not information." *Drexel Library Quarterly* 13: 16–32.

Dervin, B., and Reinhard, C. D. 2006. "Executive summary." B. Dervin, C.D. Reinhard, Z.Y. Kerr, M. Song, & F.C. Shen (Eds.). *Sense-making the information confluence: The whys and hows of college and university user satisficing of information needs. Phase II: Sense-making online survey and phone interview study. Report on National Leadership Grant LG-02-03-0062-03 to Institute of Museum and Library Services, Washington, D.C.* School of Communication, Ohio State University: Columbus, Ohio. http://imlsproject.comm.ohio-state.edu/imls_reports/imls_PH_II_report_list.html. (accessed 26 April 2010) (inaccessible 26 October 2015).

Dervin, B., Connaway, L. S., & Prabha, C. 2006. *Sense-making the information confluence: The whys and hows of college and university user satisficing of information needs.* http://imlsosuoclcproject.jcomm.ohio-state.edu (accessed 26 April 2010) (inaccessible 26 October 2015).

Dervin, B., & Vilan, M. 1986. "Information needs and uses." *Annual Review of Information Science & Technology* 21: 3–33.

Fast, K. V., & Campbell, D. G. 2004. "'I still like Google:' University student perceptions of searching OPACs and the Web." *Proceedings of the 67th ASIS&T Annual Meeting* 41: 138–146.

Fischer, K. E., Naumer, C., Durrance, J. C., Stromsky, L., & Christiansen, T. 2006. "Something old, something new: Preliminary findings from an exploratory study about people's information habits and information grounds." *Information Research* 10(2). http://informationr.net/ir/10-2/paper223.html. (accessed 26 April 2010).

Flanagan, J. C. 1954. "The critical incident technique." *Psychological Bulletin* 51: 327–358.

Friedman, D., & Hechter, M. 1998. "The contribution of rational choice theory to macro sociological research." *Sociological Theory* 6, no. 2: 201–218.

Green, S. L. 2002. *Rational choice theory: An overview. Waco, TX:* Baylor University. Retrieved http://business.baylor.edu/steve_green/green1.doc. (accessed 26 April 2010).

Griffiths, J. M., & King, D. W. 2008. *InterConnections: The IMLS national study on the use of libraries, museums and the Internet: General information report.* Institute of Museum and Library Services: Washington, DC.

Gross, M., & Latham, D. 2009. "Undergraduate perceptions of information literacy: Defining, attaining, and self-assessing skills." *College & Research Libraries* 70, no. 4: 336–350.

Head, A. J., & Eisenberg, M. B. 2010. "How today's college students use *Wikipedia* for course-related research." *First Monday* 15, no. 3. http://www.uic.edu/htbin/cgiwrap/bin/ojs/index.php/fm/article/viewArticle/2830/2476. (accessed 26 April 2010).

Idaho Commission for Libraries. 2007. *Perceptions of Idaho's digital natives on public libraries: Statewide focus group findings.* Institute of Museum and Library Services: Washington, DC.

Julien, H. E., & Michels, D. 2004. "Intra-individual information behavior in daily life." *Information Processing & Management* 40, no. 3: 547–562.

Lombardo, S. V., & Condic, K. S. 2001. "Convenience or content: A study of undergraduate periodical use." *Reference Services Review* 29, no. 4: 327–337.

Niu, X., Hemminger, B. M., Lown, C., Adams, S., Brown, C., Level, A., McLure, M., Powers, A., Tennant, M. R., & Cataldo, T. 2010. "National study of information seeking behavior of academic researchers in the United States." *Journal of the American Society for Information Science & Technology* 61, no. 5: 869–890.

Prabha, C., Connaway, L. S., & Dickey, T. J. 2006. *Sense-making the information confluence: The whys and hows of college and university user satisficing of information needs. Phase IV: Semi-structured interview study. Report on National Leadership Grant LG-02-03-0062-03, to Institute of Museum and Library Services, Washington, D.C.* Columbus, Ohio: School of Communication, The Ohio State University. http://imlsproject.comm.ohio-state.edu/imls_reports/PHASE_IV/PH_IV_report.pdf. (accessed 26 April 2010) (inaccessible 26 October 2015).

Prabha, C., Connaway, L. S., Olszewski, L., & Jenkins, L. 2007. "What is enough? Satisficing information needs." *Journal of Documentation* 63, no. 1: 74–89.

Prensky, M. 2001. "Digital natives, digital immigrants." *On the Horizon* 9, no. 5. http://www.marcprensky.com/writing. (accessed 26 April 2010) (inaccessible 26 October 2015).

> Alternative URL http://marcprensky.com/articles-in-publications/ (accessed 26 October 2015).

Pullinger, D. 1999. "Academics and the new information environment: The impact of local factors on use of electronic journals." *Journal of Information Science* 25, no. 2: 164–172.

Radford, M. L., & Connaway, L. S. 2008. *Seeking synchronicity: Evaluating virtual reference services from user, non-user, and librarian perspectives: IMLS final performance report. Report on Grant LG-06-05-0109-05, to Institute of Museum and Library Services, Washington, D.C.* Dublin, Ohio: OCLC Online Computer Library Center. http://www.oclc.org/research/activities/synchronicity/reports/20080626-final.pdf. (accessed 26 April 2010).

Savolainen, R. 1995. "Everyday life information seeking: Approaching information seeking in the context of 'way of life.'" *Library & Information Science Research* 17, no. 3: 259–294.

_____. 2006. "Time as a context of information seeking." *Library & Information Science Research* 28, no. 1: 110–127.

_____. 2008. *Everyday information practices.* Lanham, MD: Scarecrow.

Simon, H. A. 1955. "A behavioral model of rational choice." *Quarterly Journal of Economics* 69, no. 1: 99–118.

_____. (1979). *Models of thought.* New Haven, CT: Yale University Press.

Vakkari, P. (1997). "Information seeking in context: A challenging metatheory." P. Vakkari, R. Savolainen, & B. Dervin (Eds.). *Information seeking in context: Proceedings of a meeting in Finland 14–16 August 1996*, 451–463. London: Taylor Graham.

7

User-centered Decision Making: A New Model for Developing Academic Library Services and Systems

Lynn Silipigni Connaway, Ph.D.
OCLC Research

Donna Lanclos, Ph.D.
University of North Carolina, Charlotte

David White
University of Oxford

Alison Le Cornu, Ph.D.
The Higher Education Academy

Erin M. Hood
OCLC Research

A reprint of:

Connaway, Lynn Silipigni, Erin M. Hood, Donna Lanclos, David White, and Alison Le Cornu. 2012. "User-centered Decision Making: A New Model for Developing Academic Library Services and Systems," in *World Library and Information Congress. 78 (2012: Helsinki). Proceedings.* The Hague, Netherlands: IFLA. http://conference.ifla.org/past-wlic/2012/76-connaway-en.pdf

INTRODUCTION

There are many different ways to engage in the information environment making physical and digital libraries one of many options available to the information seeker. Library resources often are not the first choice of the academic community, who often choose the more convenient, easier to use open-access sources (Beetham, McGill, and Littlejohn 2009; Centre for Information Behaviour and the Evaluation of Research [CIBER] 2008; Connaway and Dickey 2010; Warwick, Galina, Terras, Huntington, and Pappa 2008). This could be attributed to the fact that resources used to be scarce, making attention abundant. However, attention currently is scarce because resources are abundant (Dempsey 2009, 2010). This means that "library users now have many opportunities to meet their information needs, and they have many demands on their attention. No single site is the sole focus of attention and convenience is important" (Dempsey 2010).

Connaway, Dickey, and Radford (2011) identified convenience as the number one factor for individuals selecting a service or system to find information. To make it more difficult, convenience is often determined by the situation and context of the specific information need.

In order to develop library systems and services that will meet the varied needs and situations of today's information seekers, it is necessary to identify how, why, and under what circumstances individuals use the various available systems and services.

Objectives and research questions

In an attempt to identify engagement with technology and information, the Digital Visitors and Residents (V&R) study involves working with users during a 3-year period, and tracking the shifts in their motivations and forms of engagement as they transition between four identified educational stages—Emerging (Late stage secondary school – first year undergraduate); Establishing (Second/third year undergraduate); Embedding (Postgraduates, PhD students); and Experienced (Scholars). It is based on the V&R framework proposed by White and Le Cornu (2011) as a method of contextualizing participants' motivations to engage with the digital environment.

The study is based on the following key research questions:
- What are the most significant factors for novice and experienced researchers in choosing their modes of engagement with the information environment?
- Do individuals develop personal engagement strategies which evolve over time and for specific needs and goals, or are the educational contexts (or, in the context of this study, "educational stages") the primary influence on their engagement strategies?
- Are modes of engagement shifting over the course of time, influenced by emergent web culture and the availability of "new" ways to engage, or are the underlying trends and motivations relatively static within particular educational stages?

Methodology and data collection techniques

The study is comprised of four phases.

- Phase 1: recruited and interviewed 30 individuals in the Emerging educational stage: 15 from the US and 15 from the UK. Eleven were male, 19 female. See figure 1. Since the participants mostly were drawn from the last year of secondary/high school and first year of university, the majority of the students were aged 18 and 19, but there was a small sample of younger (17) and older (34, 36 and 57) interviewees. See figure 2.

- Phase 2: recruited and interviewed 30 individuals from the Establishing (second/third year undergraduate), Embedding (postgraduates, PhD students), and Experienced (Scholars) stages: 5 from each of the three stages from both the US and the UK. Fourteen of the Phase 1 participants agreed to submit a monthly diary for 3 months during the summer of 2011 (8 US and 6 UK). The US participants were more faithful than the UK participants in submitting the dairies. At the end of Phase 1, there were 7 complete sets of diaries, including videos from one US participant from the Establishing educational stage. Several participants submitted intermittent monthly diaries, while others have failed to submit diaries. Although a thorough analysis of the diaries has not been completed, the team has begun to discuss whether they have been as effective a way as anticipated. The researchers are discussing several options in lieu of the diaries, which may include individual monthly conversations or IM sessions with participants or video submissions.

- Phase 3 (planned for May 2011–May 2013): test the interview and diary results with an in-depth survey of 50 participants from each of the four educational stages (total of 400 participants—200 each from the UK and US). Code, analyze, and compare data from the 4 educational stages to refine the emerging findings and explore possible trends across larger groupings, such as the stages themselves, discipline, and socioeconomic status.

- Phase 4: (planned for January 2013–May 2013): interview a second group of 6 students (3 students from each of the two types of institutions from both the US and UK) in the Emerging stage. This will help to determine if methods of engagement are changing over time as well as through the educational stages.

FIGURE 1: US VS. UK PARTICIPANT

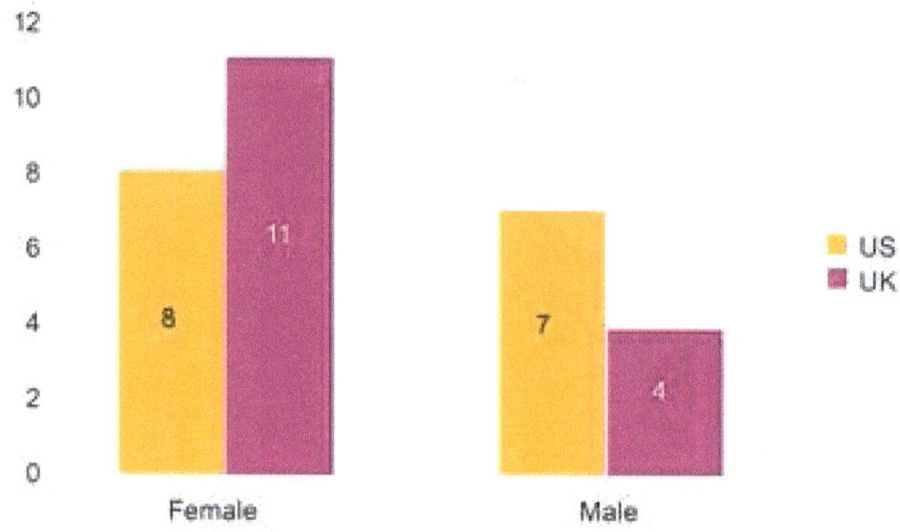

FIGURE 2: US VS. UK PARTICIPANT AGES

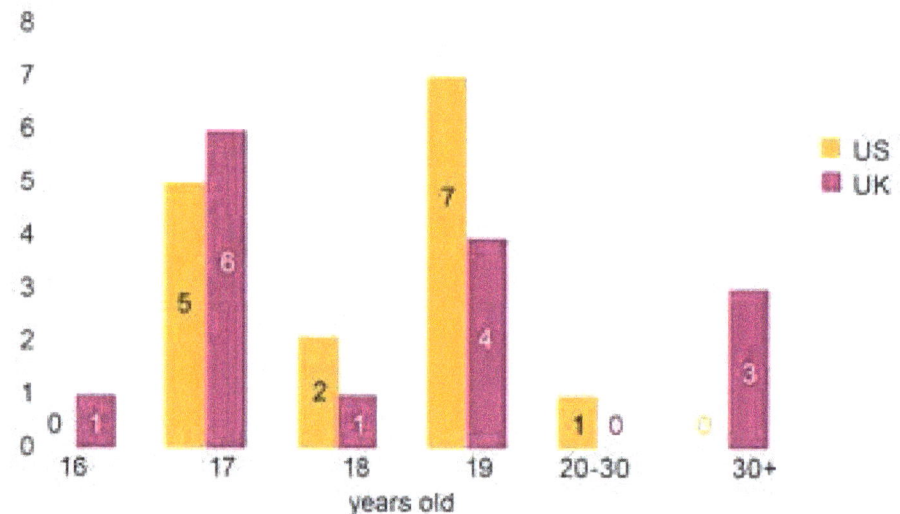

In the US the project worked in close partnership with the University of North Carolina, Charlotte (UNCC) to recruit participants, from different socio-economic groups from both private and public secondary schools as well as from the university. In the UK participants were drawn from Oxford Brooks University, Warwick University, and secondary schools in Oxford and Leicester. It was a purposive sample with the assumption that the students and scholars at these institutions were typical of other institutions (Connaway and Powell 2010). Although the subjects were a convenience sample (using contacts to connect the researchers with individuals within the 4 educational phases) and snowball sampling with participants recruiting their colleagues who fit the demographics of the 4 educational phases (Connaway and Powell 2010), they deliberately were selected to represent US and UK participants from various cultural, socio-economic, and disciplinary backgrounds. See table 1 for the subjects' disciplinary backgrounds.

TABLE 1: US VS. UK PARTICIPANT UNIVERSITY MAJORS

US (9 of 16)	UK (7 of 16)
5 Engineering	3 Teaching
1 Political Science	1 Chemical Biology
1 Pre-Business	1 Chemistry
2 Undeclared	1 History
	1 Languages

Several methods of data collection are being utilized in this study: semi-structured interviews, diaries, and an online survey. The multi-method design enables triangulation, which provides a cross examination of the data analysis and results. The quantitative and qualitative methods, including ethnographic methods that devote individual attention to the subjects, yield a very rich data set enabling multiple methods of analysis.

Interviews were selected as a technique of collecting data because they allow the interviewee to take time to provide thoughtful answers and for the interviewer to probe, follow up, and ask more focused questions. "It is generally believed that the interview is better at revealing information that is complex or emotionally laden" (Connaway and Powell 2010, 172).

A set of questions was developed for the individual semi-structured interviews. The same questions were asked of all participants. These questions were developed based on the literature and prior research and addressed the participants' needs and behaviors in both personal and academic situations and contexts. See appendix A.

Because this study is longitudinal, there needed to be follow-up with research subjects after the initial interview. Once individuals consented to be interviewed, researchers in the project asked them if they would also be interested in keeping research diaries, wherein they detailed their information-seeking behaviors month-to-month. The collection of such diaries was inspired in part by Carol Kuhlthau's (2003) work using self-reported written records from high school students. Such documents can potentially provide great depth and detail, but as Connaway and Powell (2010, 222) caution,

> "Among their obvious disadvantages are the tendency to reveal only what the participants choose to share with the researcher and the tendency to be incomplete (due to factors such as time, stress, or shame) on those points of extreme difficulty which are often most crucial to the researcher. To minimize these weaknesses, self-reported documents are often used in careful conjunction with other data-gathering techniques."

These diaries are not stand-alone, but are designed to provide time-depth as well as additional detail on the behaviors described by interviewees during Phases 1 and 2 of the project.

The diaries are a form of ethnographic data collection techniques. The goal of ethnography is to establish rapport with target communities, via a flexible toolkit of methods including participant observation, structured and unstructured interviews, reliance on selected research participants as "key informants," and keeping diaries. The analytical intellectual work of ethnography involves being able to engage in a particular way of seeing (Wolcott 2008) that is informed by the ethnographer's immersion in the reality of other people's existence. Such qualitative data must be approached and interpreted in a way that recognizes and retains this richness (Connaway and Powell 2010).

Interviewees were given a choice as to which format they wanted to use in submitting their monthly information diaries: email, follow-up face-to-face interview, blog, phone call, or video. Initially, nearly all of the diarists chose to submit via email messages (possibly because email was characterized as "formal" communication, and all of the Phase 1 diarists were in the Emerging phase). In Phase 2, the researchers provided a Google doc form to make diary submission easier (see appendix B), and they also started to get video-diary submissions via Vimeo from at least one participant. The diaries are a form of event sampling, which can focus participant attention on those areas which most interest researchers. Connaway and Powell (2010) point out that instruments (like diaries) that are intended to get people to describe what has just happened to them may be affected by distortions of memory and retrospection. They recommend that the question under review "center on discrete, defined events or moments so that such recording effort becomes reasonable and recall efforts are relatively straightforward" (Connaway and Powell 2010, 222).

A code book for analyzing the interview transcripts and diaries was developed. The code book emerged from the themes identified in the interview transcripts. Content analysis was used to tally mentions of the specific themes identified in the code book. All five of the researchers coded two of the same interview transcripts (1 US and 1 UK) to calculate intercoder reliability. The US transcript received a Kappa score of 0.63 (98% agreement), while the UK transcript received a Kappa score of 0.64 (97.78% agreement).[1] The researchers then discussed any differences to reach agreement and modified the code book to better reflect the themes emerging from the interview transcripts. All of the interview transcripts and diaries from Phases 1 and 2 were coded in NVivo[2] for further analysis.

The questionnaire is another technique or instrument for collecting survey data from a large number of respondents in a relatively short period of time (Connaway and Powell 2010). In the online survey in Phase 3, the participants will be asked questions derived from the collection and analysis of data from the semi-structured interviews and diaries during the first two phases of the project. Since the longitudinal study sample is small, the online survey is a way to involve more participants to validate the results of the analysis of the semistructured interviews and diaries.

Emerging findings

The preliminary analysis of the Emerging educational stage semi-structured interviews data suggest

- Learners' use of technology for both their academic and personal lives can be mapped against the concepts of V&R, where each is a mode of behavior, not necessarily a kind of individual. The data have revealed particular characteristics of V&R modes of behavior:
  — Residents: significant online presence and usage; high level of collaborative activity online; contributions to the online environment in the form of uploading materials, photos, videos; high dependence on a mobile device (smart phone, laptop, etc.); more than 10 hours a week spent online;
  — Visitors: functional use of technology, often linked to formal need (such as use of software for specific coursework, or organising meetings through email contact); less visible/more passive online presence, more likely to favour face-to-face interactions (even as they use the Internet to organize/ schedule those interactions); fewer than 6 hours spent online a week;
- There are a number of "covert" online study habits. For example, Wikipedia is widely used but almost always with a sense of guilt or an eagerness to convey awareness of its "unreliability;" there is an assumption by students that teachers and lecturers value the authenticity of paper-based books rather than information found online through a browser, such as Google. The data also indicate that this assumption is unfounded;
- Some changes are made when transitioning from one stage of academic life to another. For example, one interviewee cleared his Facebook site of his previous high school friends when he went to University, where he replaced them with new contacts; and
- A number of interviewees spoke about the way they evaluated information and sites from the Internet. A typical way of doing this was to judge sites by their popularity (as shown by their placement in the Google results list), i.e., popular = correct.

The V&R theory has developed over a period of years, finding formal expression in a recent publication by White and Le Cornu (2011). The paper suggests the following characteristics.

Visitors	Residents
• See web as untidy garden tool shed • Defined goal or task • Select most appropriate tool for task • Need to see concrete benefit from use of platform • No persistent online profile • Anonymous • Actively reject creation of digital identity • Caution: identity theft, privacy • Sense that online social networking is banal and egotistical • Will use technology to maintain relationships • Web offers set of tools to deliver or manipulate content (including conversations) • Tendency to respect (and seek out) authoritative sources • Thinking takes place offline • Users, not members, of the web • See no value of belonging online	• See web as place (park, building) where clusters of friends and colleagues meet • Live out a proportion of their life online • Distinction between online and offline increasingly blurred • Sense of belonging to a community • Have a profile in social networking platforms • Comfortable expressing their identity using SN platforms • Web is a place to express opinions, to form and extend relationships, maintain and develop a digital identity • Aspect of their persona remains once logged off • See web as networks or clusters of individuals who generate content • No clear distinction between concepts of persona and content • Popularity as one important measure of reliability

During the past year the researchers have been able to add characteristics which seem to accompany or elucidate each of the V&R approaches, as outlined in the table below.

Visitors	Residents
• Unseen • Instrumental • Functional • Individual	• Visible • Networked • Communicative • Communal

Convenience is a major factor in the decisions made by students in the Emerging educational stage. This is similar to findings of Connaway, Dickey, and Radford (2011), in which convenience was the primary factor in choosing or getting information. Convenience was determined by the specific context or situation, so the solution students identified as "convenient" did not always look the same.

Analysis of the diaries is just beginning. However, they appear to confirm tendencies identified in the interviews that participants look for convenient digital sources first and use a wide variety of digital sources in both their academic and everyday lives.

Convenience and authority are not always mutually exclusive in the data set. Some of the student participants choose the most convenient option out of a set of "legitimate" sources (those they have been directed to by their tutors or by library staff). It also is the case that students were generally positive about syllabus-based websites that had been recommended to them by tutors or were being used directly as part of the curriculum.

Convenience may be why the data indicate that Google and Wikipedia are the most popular search engine and information source respectively. While much of the discussion below specifically refers to Google and/or Wikipedia, these are exemplars of a search engine, and a form of crowd-sourced[3] information.

Almost without exception, the participants use Google as a starting point to seek information when they do not already know much about a topic. Many go no further, and it was not uncommon for them simply to accept the first Google site listed.

> *"I always stick with the first thing that comes up on Google because I think that's the most popular site which means that's the most correct." **(USS1)**[4]*

> *"Go to Google first thing. I mean, it's so easy; Internet, Google, type in book about or, you know, type in the author and the title and see if it comes up." **(USU4)***

Wikipedia would often be one of the top results returned by Google:

> *"My friends and I wanted to know the history of bloody Mary. I searched 'the history of bloody Mary' in the Google search box and the first website was Wikipedia." **(USU7)***

Google's "convenience" had other effects, since it presented students with a huge number of potential avenues to pursue. Faced with the challenges of available time and evaluative skills, a number of interviewees, when asked about what would be an "ideal" way to seek information, expressed a deep desire for an easier and more reliable way to ascertain quickly what is "right" and "wrong": in other words, to validate efficiently and effectively. There was a desire amongst participants for Google search and similar services to be more accurate and always to return a "correct" answer at the required academic level and length. In essence, many students were hoping that technology would evolve to become capable of returning the perfect answer and that they would not have to critically evaluate. This notion is very much in tension with academic notions of what it means to "learn" and how this differs from simply providing a "correct" answer.

> *"Like at first it was just Google and just research papers. And then, I don't have all the time, I just want a direct answer, I don't want to read about everyone's problems and symptoms."* **(USU2)**

> *"Well I'd probably be like running like something like magic laptop, that had all the answers to the world. I could just punch in, that would be amazing."* **(USU2)**

The web itself and all the information available on it may be branded as "suspect" unless created and managed by a trusted source. In the case of our Emerging interviewees, trusted sources were generally specifically-designed discipline and exam sites, together with reputable and well-known sites such as that of the BBC, and specialist sites such as those of a university.

One of the US participants in the Emerging educational stage discussed that his tutor thought that Wikipedia was "too convenient."

> *"The problem with Wikipedia is it's too easy. You can go to Wikipedia, you can get an answer, you don't actually learn anything, you just get an answer. Whereas if you have to do the rest of the research and, especially, when the reason you have to have three sources, even though the three sources may have the same sets of information, they may have different analysis of it, and they may have somewhat conflicting information, or information that appears to be conflicting until you do more research, and that's how you come to the understanding."* **(USU6)**

The student thinks that the reason his lecturer doesn't like Wikipedia is that the convenience of Wikipedia reduces students' ability to conduct other important academic searching and evaluation activities. US participants, in particular, seemed to consider Wikipedia at worst as invalid, and at best as a suspect source of information. Some students believe that their instructors think that Wikipedia is untrustworthy because it is crowdsourced.

There is evidence to suggest that on the whole Wikipedia is a high quality resource[5] and useful for what has been described as "presearch."[6] For many students in the Emerging educational stage the academic level of Wikipedia seems appropriate. It is frequently used for school and assessment purposes and provides the student interviewees not only with useful factual information, but also with an initial introduction to a topic, together with further references.

> *"Probably not the best, but I think it's the simplest and easiest way to get going. So if I needed to produce a much more detailed and developed essay I would probably explore further on the Internet."* **(UKS1-addressing using Wikipedia to start)**

The data suggest something similar to a "learning black market" (or "grey" market) as students make regular use of Wikipedia but are often uncomfortable about revealing this to their teachers.[7] One US interviewee expressed bluntly what their reaction would be.

> *"They don't fail you but you get ridiculed in front of everyone for sourcing Wikipedia."* **(USS3)**

Some participants used the references cited in a Wikipedia article, without citing the article itself, as a way of taking advantage of the online encyclopaedia without mentioning it directly, and some teachers seemed to authorize their students' use of Wikipedia in this way. However, it needs to be further investigated whether students' perceptions that instructors' disregard Wikipedia and similar sites is encouraging students to hide their successful and often sophisticated approaches towards information gathering using non-traditional online sources.

The ways in which sources such as Wikipedia and search engines such as Google are used could be taken into account as a part of students' information-seeking approaches. Librarians could consider how to advise students on how to position these types of information sources and tools within larger information-seeking strategies, which include more traditional sources. Those who are certain they have identified inaccuracies in Wikipedia articles (or in similar sites) could be encouraged to correct them to develop editorial skills and a part of the process of becoming "legitimate participants" in the generation of knowledge online.[8] It also will develop their realization that knowledge is not (or no longer) a fixed, black-and-white, right-or-wrong entity.

Attention needs to be given to searching techniques. If students generally accept Google's first recommended source because of the source's popularity, librarians need to equip them with ways of evaluating these sources *before* the link is followed. Information about how search engines operate (accompanied potentially by comparative exercises) also will be necessary. Calhoun, Cantrell, Gallagher, and Hawk (2009) report that when individuals were discussing library online catalogues, they were concerned that they had no idea how the system ranked their retrieval results and wanted this information provided to them. However, this was not mentioned when discussing Google's ranking system. There seems to be an innate trust of Google.

Institutions need to be better informed about the range of critical evaluation skills that students need to access and acquire information and sources regardless of format. This will enable them to adapt these literacies to any technologies or formats that may become available in the future. "Don't trust Wikipedia" or the US tendency to warn students not "to trust anything on a .com site" is probably unlikely to change students' practices. The quotes below suggest that these behaviors only may push the students' practices underground.

*"I feel really guilty about it. If I have absolutely nowhere else to go I have scoured Google, there is nothing in the library then I will have a quick look at Wikipedia and see what Wikipedia has to say about it. Then use maybe some of its other links or how it links onto other articles a bit like that." **(UKU3)***

Librarians could consider teaching online critical evaluation skills to students very early (possibly earlier than was typical when the institutional library was the key source of information) in their education. The comparative information "safety" of the institutional library has been superseded by the web, leaving students nervous as to which sources are valid.

The extent to which students successfully can complete assignments without engaging with institutionally-provided information sources is not yet clear. However, there are indications that the majority of information (and the learning that supports students' use) is drawn from sources from the open web. In the Emerging group this is heavily influenced by Wikipedia and by syllabus-based sites recommended by their tutors. One implication of this is that institutionally-provided information services could consider how to position themselves and what services are most needed when they are more often than not second to the open web in students' information-seeking practices.

The students in the study perceive institutionally-provided information as having a level of authority or validity above and beyond sources from the open web. They regularly check the URL of a source to assess its potential validity and often will imply that physical books from the library are the most valid of all sources (even if for convenience they choose not to use them). This indicates that the expert curation of links and media (whether locally produced or not) by institutions under a trusted URL is of great value.

There is little evidence of Emerging educational stage students seeking out librarians and other support staff specifically for advice on critically evaluating sources. Students appear not to see staff in these roles as a route to information. One useful response might be to suggest that staff attempt to convene an open discussion around students' actual information-seeking habits so that they can indicate where they will be of help.

Next steps

The researchers will continue to collect and analyze the diaries. They also will administer the online survey, and analyze these data as well as the data collected from the semi-structured interviews with the other three educational stage participants. Semistructured interviews with a new group of Emerging educational stage participants will be the final data collection activity. All of the collected data will be analyzed and compared to portray the engagement of students and faculty with technology and information over a 3-year period.

Conclusion

Instead of reporting general information-seeking habits and technology use, this study explores how the subjects get their information based on the context and situation of their needs during an extended period of time, identifying if and how their behaviors change. The study uses both quantitative and qualitative data collection techniques that enable triangulation of the data analysis results.

The findings from this research can inform libraries of current and perspective users' expectations of services and systems based on their engagement and motivation with technology. The findings also can be used to develop options for designing and delivering digital platforms and services, which will enable educators and service providers to make informed decisions relative to engagement and motivation for individuals as they progress through the educational stages. The project will position the role of the library within emergent information-seeking patterns of both students and faculty by investigating and describing user-owned digital literacies.

NOTES

1. Cohen's kappa coefficient, a measurement method used for calculating inter-coder reliability, considers not just agreement, but what agreement may have taken place by chance.

2. NVivo 9, a qualitative software package, is a product of QSR International Pty Ltd. Further information on NVivo can be found on their website: http://www.qsrinternational.com/products_nvivo.aspx.

3. The term crowdsourced implies "free for all" when in fact Wikipedia has stringent "verifiability" rules (http://en.wikipedia.org/wiki/Wikipedia:Verifiability) which are closely policed, especially on the types of articles that are likely to relate to academic assignments.

4. For anonymity, participants are designated with tags which indicate their country (UK or US), their educational stage (S for Secondary school/High school, U for University, G for Grads, or F for Faculty), and then an individual number.

5. Jimmy Wales recently claimed that the decline in Wikipedia editors was due to the fact that many entries were now so accurate that only "experts" could contribute to them (http://midea.nmc.org/2011/08/wikimania-recap/). Sir Harry Kroto, Nobel laureate in chemistry was recently quoted as saying that in his field, Wikipedia was more accurate than the textbooks (http://twitter.com/#!/jimmy_wales/status/132464444235186176).

6. See a reference to "presearch" relating to Wikipedia and Google Scholar at: http://blogs.ubc.ca/googlescholar/2009/02/wikipedia-google-scholar-as-pre-search/. (inaccessible 26 October 2015).

7. This concept of "The Learning Black Market" has been well received through blogging and presentations at events such as NetSkills seminars and the JISC online conference. These events have been used as opportunities to refine our thinking as well as to disseminate the project's activity.

8. This already is happening in some institutions. At Davidson College in North Carolina, a psychology professor partnered with Wikipedia as a part of their Education Program (http://outreach.wikimedia.org/wiki/Wikipedia_Education_Program), and had her students edit Wikipedia articles as a part of her capstone senior class (Munger, http://www.psychologicalscience.org/index.php/members/aps-wikipedia-initiative/having-undergraduates-write-for-wikipedia). At University College London, for example, one lecturer requires his students to compose and post Wikipedia articles. In so doing it would seem that Wikipedia has been lifted from black-market territory into a "teachable moment." This is the sort of initiative which could usefully be developed and expanded.

REFERENCES

Beetham, Helen, Lou McGill, and Allison Littlejohn. 2009. *Thriving in the 21st century: Learning literacies for the digital age (LLiDA Project)*. The Caledonian Academy, Glasgow Caledonian University: Glasgow. http://www.academy.gcal.ac.uk/llida/LLiDAReportJune2009.pdf. (inaccessible 26 October 2015).

 Alternative URL http://www.jisc.ac.uk/media/documents/projects/llidaexecsumjune2009.pdf (accessed 26 October 2015).

Calhoun, Karen, Joanne Cantrell, Peggy Callagher, and Janet Hawk. 2009. *Online catalogs: What users and librarians want: An OCLC report*. Dublin, OH: OCLC Online Computer Library Center.

Centre for Information Behaviour and the Evaluation of Research [CIBER]. 2008. *Information behaviour of the researcher of the future: A CIBER briefing paper*. London: CIBER. http://www.jisc.ac.uk/media/documents/programmes/reppres/gg_final_keynote_11012008.pdf.

Connaway, Lynn Silipigni, and Timothy J. Dickey. 2010. *The Digital Information Seeker: Report of the findings from selected OCLC, RIN, and JISC user behaviour projects*. http://www.jisc.ac.uk/media/documents/publications/reports/2010/digitalinformationseekerreport.pdf.

Connaway, Lynn Silipigni, Timothy J. Dickey, and Marie L. Radford. 2011. "'If it is too inconvenient I'm not going after it:' Convenience as a critical factor in information-seeking behaviors." *Library & Information Science Research* 33, no. 3: 179–90.

Connaway, Lynn Silipigni, and Ronald R. Powell. 2010. *Basic research methods for librarians*. Fifth edition. Littleton, CO: Libraries Unlimited.

Dempsey, Lorcan. 2009. "Always on: Libraries in a world of permanent connectivity." *First Monday* 14, no. 1 (5 January). http://firstmonday.org/htbin/cgiwrap/bin/ojs/index.php/fm/article/view/2291/2070.

Dempsey, Lorcan. 2010. "3 switches." *Lorcan Dempsey's Weblog* (blog), 13 June 2010. http://orweblog.oclc.org/archives/002104.html.

Kuhltahu, Carol C. 2003. "Rethinking libraries for the Information Age school: Vital roles in inquiry learning." *School Libraries in Canada* 22, no. 4: 3–5.

Warwick, Claire, Isabel Galina, Melissa Terras, Paul Huntington, and Nikoleta Pappa. 2008. "The master builders: LAIRAH research on good practice in the construction of digital humanities projects." *Literary and Linguistic Computing* 23, no. 3: 383–96. http://discovery.ucl.ac.uk/13810/.

White, David S., and Alison Le Cornu. 2011. "Visitors and Residents: A new typology for online engagement." *First Monday* 16, no. 9. http://firstmonday.org/htbin/cgiwrap/bin/ojs/index.php/fm/article/view/3171/3049.

Wolcott, Harry F. 2008. *Ethnography: A way of seeing*. Lanham, MD: Altamira Press.

APPENDIX A:

Participant interview questions—Secondary/High school and University level

1. Describe the things you enjoy doing with technology and the web each week.

    This is a conversational start in order to put the interviewees at their ease. We are trying to get a sense of their overall digital literacy so that we can set their information seeking behaviors within a broader context. Do they socialize online? (See probe.) Do they "contribute" online in the form of pictures, video, blogs, etc.?

    [PROBES: How important is the web for your social life, do you use it to keep in touch with your friends? What gadgets/devices/things do you use the most, is there anything you "couldn't live without"? How much time on average do you spend online each week? Is there anything that bothers you about being online?]

2. Think of the ways you have used technology and the web for your studies. Describe a typical week.

    We are looking at interviewees' use of educational technologies more specifically for study. We hope they will start to introduce informal learning, self-directed study, peer to peer learning, etc. We anticipate they will (or may not) mention Facebook, MySpace, etc.

    [PROBES: How do you keep track of things? What systems for learning online do you have? Can you give us any examples of when you've asked your friends for help on assignments/homework online? What kind of online resources have you found that help you with your studies? How did you find them? What other gadgets or devices do you use for your studies?]

3. Think about the next stage of your education. Tell me what you think this will be like. [Alternative University Student Interviews: What did you think university studies would be like when you were in high school? How is your experience different from what you thought it would be? Describe what you think the next stage of your education will be. Tell me what you think this will be like.]

    This will hopefully encourage them to reflect on what they envisage their role will be in the next stage. What they imagine the next educational-stage to be like will be something we can cross check as we follow them through the project.

    [PROBES: How do you think you will use technology in the next part of your education? If you think you will need to adapt the way you use technology, what sort of changes do you think you'll make?]

4. Think of a time when you had a situation where you needed answers or solutions and you did a quick search and made do with it. You knew there were other sources but you decided not to use them. Please include sources such as friends, family, teachers, TAs, tutors, coaches, etc.

    Prompt for both academic and informal (domestic, personal ...) examples.

    [PROBES: Did you simply take the first answer/solution you were able to find? What was the situation? What sources did you use? What led you to use them...and not others? Did they help? How? What sources did you decide not to use? What led to this/these decision/s? What did source A give you that you thought source B could not? Are there situations where source B would be a better choice for you? How did you decide when it was time to stop looking? How did you assess what was good enough?]

5. Have there been times when you were told to use a library or virtual learning environment (or learning platform), and used other source(s) instead?

    [PROBE: What made you decide not to use what you were asked to use? What kinds of things do your instructors want you to do when you're looking for information? Does what you do look like that, and if not, what does it look like?]

6. If you had a magic wand, what would your ideal way of getting information be? How would you go about using the systems and services? When? Where? How?

7. What comments or questions do you have for me? Is there anything you would like me to explain? What would you like to tell me that you've thought about during this interview?

APPENDIX B:

Google diary questions

1. In your general use of technology for your coursework/research over the past weeks what would you say has gone particularly well? Why?

2. What would you say has not gone as well as you'd hoped or anticipated?

3. Have you any examples of when you used technology to help you with something that wasn't directly to do with your studies?

4. Have you got any examples where you didn't use technology to help with a problem or a project?

5. Have you picked up any new ways of doing things with technology?

6. Have you found that an approach to doing something that you've used in the past no longer works?

7. Have you found any new sources of useful information?

8. Is there anything else that you think would be useful for us to know about?

8

Visitors and Residents: What Motivates Engagement with the Digital Information Environment?

Lynn Silipigni Connaway, Ph.D.
OCLC Research

David White
University of Oxford

Donna Lanclos, Ph.D.
University of North Carolina, Charlotte

Alison Le Cornu, Ph.D.
The Higher Education Academy

A reprint of:

Connaway, Lynn Silipigni, Donna Lanclos, David White, and Alison Le Cornu. 2012. "Visitors and Residents: What Motivates Engagement with the Digital Information Environment?" *Information Research*. http://InformationR.net/ir/18-1/paper556.html

© 2013 OCLC Online Computer Library Center, Inc., David White, Donna Lanclos, and Alison Le Cornu.

This work is licensed under a Creative Commons Attribution-NonCommercial-NoDerivs 3.0 Unported License.

http://creativecommons.org/licenses/by-nc-nd/3.0/

INTRODUCTION

We have little understanding of what motivates individuals to use particular technologies or spaces when engaging with the information environment. As a result people tend to adopt simplistic but culturally panicked ideas in their attempts to grasp the problem while others delve into specifics to the extent that little substantive conclusions can be drawn. This lack of understanding also makes the task of facilitating digital literacy skills challenging, as any form of literacy has to be defined against the motivations and goals of those individuals being taught.

There is now a multiplicity of ways to engage in the information environment. Both physical and digital libraries are among the options available to the information seeker. The large number of available open-access choices creates a competitive information environment for schools and universities that expend a great amount of resources on the information environment in the form of academic staff, print and digital sources and physical space (such as laboratories, libraries and classrooms). The school or university resources are not necessarily the first or even second choices of the students and academic community, who often choose the more convenient, easier to use open-access sources (Beetham et al. 2009; Centre for Information Behaviour... 2008; Connaway and Dickey 2010; Warwick et al. 2008).

Objectives

This three-year longitudinal study is conducted in four iterations of a sample of students and scholars representing different stages of the educational lifecycle:

1. Emerging (late stage secondary school-first year undergraduate);
2. Establishing (second and third year undergraduate);
3. Embedding (postgraduates, Ph.D. students);
4. Experienced (scholars).

The design of the study is an attempt to eliminate any assumed links between age and technological engagement by working with users over time, tracking the shifts in their motivations and forms of engagement as they transition between these educational stages. The study is using the visitors and residents principle proposed by White and Le Cornu (2011) as an overarching framework to contextualize participants' motivations to engage with the digital environment. The findings will be used to create a matrix of implementation options, allowing those designing and delivering digital platforms and services to make informed decisions relative to engagement and motivation for individuals at each of the educational stages.

The quantitative and qualitative methods, including ethnographic methods and the individual attention devoted to the subjects will yield a very rich data set enabling multiple methods of analysis. Instead of reporting the general information-seeking habits of the Google Generation and their use of technology, this study explores how the subjects get their information based on the context and situation of their needs during an extended period of time, identifying if and how their behaviour changes. The project is user-centred, not platform- or discipline-centred. There is a history of research conducted on university campuses among undergraduates and faculty, in attempts by libraries and information scientists to learn about how people search for the information they need to live their lives, both in and out of academic environments (e.g., Bartley et al. 2006; Connaway 2008; Connaway et al. 2008; Delcore et al. 2009; Dervin et al. 2003; Foster and Gibbons 2007; Fister 1992; Gabridge et al. 2008; Head and Eisenberg 2009; Jordan and Ziebell 2009; Malvasi et al. 2009; Maybee 2006; Prabha et al. 2007; Suarez 2007; Valentine 2001; White and Le Cornu 2011; Witt and Gearhart 2003). Previous ethnographic studies of students (Bartley et al. 2006; Connaway 2007, Connaway 2008; Delcore et al. 2009; Dervin et al. 2003; Foster and Gibbons 2007; Gabridge et al. 2008; Wu and Lanclos 2011, and the Ethnographic Research in Illinois Academic Libraries (ERIAL) Project), in addition to focusing on university students, also have tended to be limited in time, gathering information from a given semester, or even during the course of a single project within the semester. The literature reviewed includes no longitudinal research studying individuals' information use and search behaviour within a contextual framework in the different educational stages. Another problem with previous studies is that there is very little attention paid to where information-gathering habits originally form in students; doing research exclusively among people who already are in university—either as students or as faculty—does not tell researchers where and how they learned to gather and evaluate information.

The *emerging* stage, then, is of particular interest as it bridges what is traditionally seen as a distinct divide between higher and tertiary education. We believe that this divide is notional and that the student's information-gathering techniques are unlikely to change in the few months between secondary school and university. By including the emerging educational stage the project will generate outputs which will enable universities to make informed decisions for planning services and systems for entering students; therefore, proactively planning rather than haphazardly reacting to passing trends.

Methodology and research questions

As participants transition through the educational system, they are demarcated by the educational stages mentioned above. In addition, participants will be chosen to draw out engagement factors relative to:

1. Cultural background: participants were recruited from matching educational-stages in both the UK and the USA.

2. Socio-economic background: participants were recruited to represent a range of socio-economic backgrounds.

3. Disciplinary focus: participants were recruited from the arts and humanities, social sciences and sciences.

Selecting participants on this basis allows the researchers to distinguish generic engagement factors from those that are specific to particular groups.

A set of questions were developed for the individual interviews with the participants. The same questions were asked of all participants. These questions were developed based on the literature and previous research and addressed the participants' needs and behaviour in both personal and academic situations and contexts. See appendix A for the questions.

Using the visitors and residents principle as a framework, a subset of individuals from each of the educational stages is being tracked (through the monthly interviews, review of diaries, etc.) to identify their changing approaches to the information environment as they move through the educational stages. The participants were given a choice of communication methods, such as instant messenger interviews, email, Facebook, paper or electronic diaries, blogs, face-to-face, or telephone, with the research team. The choice they make provides additional information about the different participants' preferred forms of communication and insight into how services need to be presented as context and expectations shift during the educational lifecycle.

The three-year, four-phased study is based on the following key research questions:

- What are the most significant factors for novice and experienced researchers in choosing their modes of engagement with the information environment?
- Do individuals develop personal engagement strategies which evolve over time and for specific needs and goals, or are the educational contexts (or, in the context of this study, *educational stages)* the primary influence on their engagement strategies?
- Are modes of engagement shifting over the course of time, influenced by emergent Web culture and the availability of new ways to engage, or are the underlying trends and motivations relatively static within particular educational stages?

PHASE 1: PILOT STAGE, MONTHS 1–6

The initial six-month pilot stage has focused on the emerging educational stage to refine the research methodology and to establish the value of the work to the funders and other supporters. In the USA the project worked in close partnership with the University of North Carolina, Charlotte (UNCC) to recruit participants from different socio-economic groups, from both private and public secondary schools as well as first-year university students. In the UK participants were drawn from Oxford Brooks University, Warwick University and secondary schools in Oxford and Leicester.

PARTICIPANTS

Thirty-one individuals in the *emerging* educational stage (late stage secondary or high school and first-year university) were recruited: sixteen in the USA and fifteen in the UK and ranged in age from 16 years old to middle age. See tables 1 and 2. Of the sixteen first-year university students, nine were in the USA and seven in the UK. Five of the USA students had chosen an engineering major, one was in political science, one in pre-business and two were undeclared. From the UK, three had chosen teaching, one was in chemical biology, one in chemistry, one in history and one in languages.

Of the thirty-one participants recruited, fourteen (eight in the USA and six in the UK) were asked to document their information-seeking activities for a three-month period. They were closely facilitated through this process and communicated with the research team in the medium of their choice during this period.

DATA

The information collected from the interviews and monthly correspondence with the selected fourteen students provide rich data that have been analysed and reported both quantitatively and qualitatively.

- The quantitative data include demographics; number of occurrences for different types of technologies, sources and behaviour.
- The qualitative data provide themes that identify behaviour and sources for different contexts and situations and include direct quotations and behaviour. Examples of direct quotations:

> "...our generation isn't technology orientated. I think it's always a stereotype."
>
> (Participant UKS4)

> "I just type it into Google and see what comes-up..."
>
> (Participant UKS2)

> "I always stick with the first thing that comes up on Google because I think that's the most popular site which means that's the most correct."
>
> (Participant USAS1)

A code book was developed from the emerging themes of the interview transcripts. Then the data were manually coded using theme analysis based on the code book and input into the NVivo software program. This enabled the researchers to analyse and report the data not only by themes and demographics but also by the number of respondents and percentiles.

Note: For anonymity, participants are designated with tags which indicate their country (UK or USA), their educational stage (S for Secondary school/High school, U for University, G for Grads, or F for Faculty) and then an individual number.

PHASE 2: MONTHS 7–12

The study has been extended to include ten participants from the other three educational stages (five USA and five UK). Building on the principle of Phase 1, the additional participants have been recruited from a post-1992 institution, such as Oxford Brookes University and a Russell Group university, such as Warwick University in order to more accurately portray typical UK students and scholars. This brings the total number of participants, including those from the pilot phase to sixty-one. In the USA, recruiting has continued at UNC Charlotte, which has a history of non-traditional students (especially returning students and transfer students), but has recently begun recruiting larger percentages of students directly from high school, providing an opportunity to have a broader sample of USA students and scholars.

Although the researchers only will discuss the findings from the first two phases of the study, it is important to explain the other two phases of the study to fully understand the scope of the project and the possible impact the findings may have on planning services and systems for students entering universities; therefore, the following phases are outlined to set the pilot phase in the context of the overall longitudinal study. These phases are likely to be iteratively modified to account for ongoing findings and to ensure that the overall study remains as relevant to the stakeholders as possible over time.

PHASE 3: MONTHS 13–24

In addition to the tracking of the fourteen diarists during the second phase of the study, an online survey will be developed and disseminated to a total of 400 students and scholars—split equally between the USA and the UK. Fifty participants from each of the four educational stages will be selected from each of the universities. The participants will be asked questions derived from the collection and analysis of data collected from the sixty-one participants during the first two phases of the project. Since the longitudinal study sample is small, the online survey is a way to involve more participants in the study to compare with the data collected from the individuals who participate in the three-year study.

PHASE 4: MONTHS 25–36

In the third year the project will work with a second group of six students (three students from each of the two types of universities) in the *emerging* stage. This will help to determine if methods of engagement are changing over time as well as through the educational stages.

It is not anticipated that the expectations of the members of the four educational stages will be met by the educational institutions. The educational process should, at times, be challenging and possibly disruptive; there should be a healthy tension between the educational institution and those it is there to serve. However, if a clear picture of student expectations, motivations and behaviour can be identified, informed decisions can be instrumental in determining what expectations should be challenged and the benefit to the learners that these challenges deliver.

Emerging findings

The analysis of phase 1 and 2 data is in its early stages. The development of the code book is a major finding, since it was grounded in the data; notably, to date, the word *librarian* was never mentioned by title as a source of information. However, Participant USAU5 did so indirectly by referring to *'a lady in the library who helps you find things.'*

The project is identifying *learner owned* digital and information literacies that are little understood by educational institutions. Examples of these include:

- The practice of citing the references attached to a Wikipedia article but not the article itself to avoid potential ridicule from tutors and peers.

- The basic methods employed by students when assessing the validity of a source returned by a Google search. As Participant UKS4 stated, *'I simply just type it into Google and just see what comes up'* and then later, *'I knew that the Internet wouldn't give me a wrong answer.'* This collaborates with Taylor (2012) who found that only 16% of the subjects in his study went through a verifying stage, instead performing evaluation at the end, demonstrating procrastination. Additionally, he found that the subjects were not as concerned with quality and authority as with other factors such as quantity or currency.
- The manner in which *emerging* stage students rely on the residency of their peers in social media, allowing them to discuss assignments the night before they are due. Participants in the *emerging* educational stage often wanted to talk to a fellow student about an assignment using Facebook. If the person they were hoping to connect with in Facebook was not online then some participants would text the person in question to request that they login. This level of Residency meant that students could discuss an assignment at a time that was convenient to them. At the *emerging* stage that was often the night before a deadline. All the participants who talked about this claimed that they did not 'do' the assignments in this manner but merely confirmed exactly what was required from them or sought specific information such as a maths formula or a reference.
- The importance of *convenience* and how the Web often will be chosen as an information source by students even when they know higher quality sources are available elsewhere. For example, the information is available in text books or by asking a tutor or parent, yet Google is used instead. We suspect that convenience is a large part of why our data indicate that Google and Wikipedia are the most popular search engine and information source respectively. While much of the discussion below specifically refers to Google and/or Wikipedia, we are treating these as exemplars of a search engine and a form of crowd-sourced information. Almost without exception, our participants use Google as a starting point to seek out information when they do not already know much about a topic. Many go no further and it was not uncommon for interviewees simply to accept the first Google site listed.
- A portion of the *emerging* educational stage participants were uncomfortable about the addictive nature of social media and the extent to which it wasted their time.
- The multi-tab environment that students have on screen represents a convergence of the social and the academic. In this context, the mode of an activity is no longer based on the physical space in which it occurs since any access to a network provided almost every aspect of life to those with a Resident approach to the Web. Some participants had developed methods of separating Resident modes of engagement from the more Visitor-style approaches required of them to complete or revise assignments.

The researchers have been experimenting with mapping individual participant's data to the visitors and residents framework as a way of identifying modes of engagement. See appendix B for an example mapping. (The numbers on the dark blue blocks in the mapping diagram represent the time-code point in the interview at which the participant discussed an activity or approach. A number of quotes have been added to the maps to give a sense of the data that are being plotted and of the character of the participant in terms of the visitors and residents continuum).

A goal of the project is to develop a method which will programmatically produce simple mappings of this type which draw on interview and survey data to indicate engagement trends across key groups. This prototype mapping system can be used as a tool to visually communicate the modes of engagement within the visitors and residents framework as well as a broad model of how digital and information literacies evolve across the educational stages.

The project also is attempting to define the transition points when individuals are most likely to change their mode of participation. For example:

- A geographical move (moving country or state) is likely to encourage more *resident* behaviour as individuals attempt to maintain relationships at a distance by using social media.
- Some participants begrudgingly visit *resident*-style platforms when they discover that their non-participation is constricting their social or intellectual life. Often in these cases the participant uses social media in a *visitor* mode.
- The specific requirements of a programme of study will occasionally encourage students to change modes. This could occur, if students are asked to reflect on their learning in blog posts or to improve or update a Wikipedia page. Mode changes in these circumstances tend to be sort-lived and acted-out rather than incorporated into the participants' on-going practice.

Conclusion

The findings from this research can inform institutions of higher education of current and perspective students' expectations of services and systems based on their engagement with technology and their information-seeking behaviour in different contexts and situations. The research uses both quantitative and qualitative data collection methods, which enable triangulation of the data to provide a more nuanced understanding of students' and scholars' engagement with technology.

Although this project is a multi-phased longitudinal study funded by four institutions, it can be used as a model for single institutions to study and learn about their user groups. This study is not limited to any one organization within the university community; therefore, it can be easily adapted to many different situations. This type of research can be initiated by professionals to collect data that can help organizations make planning decisions based on evidence.

The research findings to date and the research methodology provides others, including those who are new to research, the opportunity to replicate all or selected phases of the research. The more that researchers replicate the methodology used for this project, the better chance there is of making sense of how individuals engage with technology for their information-seeking behaviour, while transitioning between the different educational stages.

ACKNOWLEDGMENTS

The authors want to thank Erin Hood, Research Assistant, OCLC Research, for her assistance in analysing the data and preparing the manuscript.

ABOUT THE AUTHORS

Lynn Silipigni Connaway, Ph.D., is a Senior Research Scientist at OCLC Research. She has experience in academic, public and school libraries, as well as library and information science education. She can be contacted at: connawal@oclc.org.

David White co-manages Technology-Assisted Lifelong Learning (TALL), an award-winning e-learning research and development group in the University of Oxford. He can be contacted at: david.white@conted.ox.ac.uk.

Donna Lanclos, Ph.D., is currently the Library Ethnographer at the University of North Carolina, Charlotte, directing projects on the ethnography of academic work in Optical Engineering, as well as UNC Charlotte student and faculty academic work and information gathering practices in and out of the library. She can be contacted at: dlanclos@uncc.edu.

Alison Le Cornu, Ph.D., is Academic Lead for Flexible Learning with the Higher Education Academy in the UK. She was previously a member of the Technology-Assisted Lifelong Learning team in the Department for Continuing Education at Oxford University where she was co-investigator with the Visitors and Residents project. She can be contacted at: alison@alisonlecornu.co.uk.

REFERENCES

Bartley, M., Duke, D., Gabridge, T., Gaskell, M., Hennig, N., Quirion, C., Skuce, S., Stout, A. & Duranceau, E. F. (2006). *User needs assessment of information seeking activities of MIT students-spring 2006.* http://dspace.mit.edu/bitstream/handle/1721.1/33456/userneeds-report.pdf?sequence=1 (accessed 15 February 2013) (Archived by WebCite® at http://www.webcitation.org/6ESNylOP8) (inaccessible 26 October 2015).

Beetham, H., McGill, L. & Littlejohn, A. (2009). *Thriving in the 21st century: Learning literacies for the digital age (LLiDA Project).* The Caledonian Academy, Glasgow Caledonian University: Glasgow. http://www.jisc.ac.uk/media/documents/projects/llidaexecsumjune2009.pdf (accessed 16 February 2013) (Archived by WebCite® at http://www.webcitation.org/6EThMAE7o).

Centre for Information Behaviour and the Evaluation of Research [CIBER]. (2008). *Information behaviour of the researcher of the future: A CIBER briefing paper.* London: CIBER. http://www.jisc.ac.uk/media/documents/programmes/reppres/gg_final_keynote_11012008.pdf (accessed 15 February 2013) (Archived by WebCite® at http://www.webcitation.org/6ESOA3gax).

Connaway, L. S. (2007). "Mountains, valleys and pathways: serials users' needs and steps to meet them. Part I: Preliminary analysis of focus group and semi-structured interviews at colleges and universities." *Serials Librarian* 52, no. 1/2: 223–236. http://www.oclc.org/research/publications/archive/2007/connaway-serialslibrarian.pdf (accessed 15 February 2013) (Archived by WebCite® at http://www.webcitation.org/6ESOGuHv4).

Connaway, L. S. & Dickey, T. J. 2010. *The digital information seeker: report of the findings from selected OCLC, RIN and JISC user behaviour projects.* http://www.jisc.ac.uk/media/documents/publications/reports/2010/digitalinformationseekerreport.pdf (accessed 15 February 2013) (Archived by WebCite® at http://www.webcitation.org/6ESOU9yX6).

Connaway, L. S., Radford, M. L., Dickey, T. J., Williams, J. D. & Confer, P. 2008. "Sense-making and synchronicity: information-seeking behaviors of millennials and baby boomers." *Libri* 58, no. 2: 123–135. http://www.oclc.org/research/publications/archive/2008/connaway-libri.pdf (accessed 15 February 2013) (Archived by WebCite® at http://www.webcitation.org/6ESOYYz2O).

Delcore, H. D., Mullooly, J. & Scroggins, M. (with Arnold, K., Franco, E. & Gaspar, J.). 2009. *The library study at Fresno State.* Institute of Public Anthropology, California State University: Fresno, CA. http://www.fresnostate.edu/socialsciences/anthropology/documents/ipa/TheLibraryStudy(DelcoreMulloolyScroggins).pdf (accessed 15 February 2013) (Archived by WebCite® at http://www.webcitation.org/6ESOcM74i).

Dervin, B., Connaway, L. S. & Prabha, C. 2003. *Sense-making the information confluence: the whys and hows of college and university user satisficing of information needs.* http://www.oclc.org/research/activities/imls.html.

Fister, B. (1992). "The research process of undergraduate students." *The Journal of Academic Librarianship* 18, no. 3: 163–169.

Foster, N. F. & Gibbons, S. 2007. *Studying students: The undergraduate research project at the University of Rochester.* Chicago: Association of College and Research Libraries.

Gabridge, T., Gaskell, M. & Stout, A. 2008. "Information seeking through students' eyes: The MIT photo diary study." *College and Research Libraries* 69, no. 6: 510–522.

Head, A. & Eisenberg, M. B. 2009. *Lessons learned: How college students seek information in the digital age.* The Information School, University of Washington: Seattle, WA.

Jordan, E. & Ziebell, T. 2009. *Learning in the spaces: A comparative study of the use of traditional and 'new generation' library learning spaces by various disciplinary cohorts.* The University of Queensland: Queensland, Australia. http://espace.library.uq.edu.au/eserv/UQ:157791/NextGenLearningSpacesPaper.pdf (accessed 15 February 2013) (Archived by WebCite® at http://www.webcitation.org/6ESOiVKIz).

Malvasi, M., Rudowsky, C. & Valencia, J. M. 2009. *Library Rx: Measuring and treating library anxiety. A research study.* Chicago: Association of College and Research Libraries.

Maybee, C. 2006. "Undergraduate perceptions of information use: The basis for creating user-centred student information literacy instruction." *The Journal of Academic Librarianship* 32, no. 1: 79–85.

Prabha, C., Connaway, L. S., Olszewski, L. & Jenkins, L. R. 2007. "What is enough? Satisficing information needs." *Journal of Documentation* 63, no. 1: 74–89.

Suarez, D. 2007. "What students do when they study in the library: Using ethnographic methods to observe student behavior." *Electronic Journal of Academic and Special Librarianship* 8(3). http://southernlibrarianship.icaap.org/content/v08n03/suarez_d01.html (accessed 15 February 2013) (Archived by WebCite® at http://www.webcitation.org/6ESOmHTF9).

Taylor, A. 2012. "A study of the information search behaviour of the millennial generation." *Information Research,* 17, no. 1, paper 508. http://informationr.net/ir/17-1/paper508.html (accessed 15 February 2013) (Archived by WebCite® at http://www.webcitation.org/6ESOpKfvZ).

Valentine, B. 2001. "The legitimate effort in research papers: Student commitment versus faculty expectations." *The Journal of Academic Librarianship* 27, no. 2: 107–115.

Warwick, C., Galina, I., Terras, M., Huntington, P. & Pappa, N. 2008. "The master builders: LAIRAH research on good practice in the construction of digital humanities projects." *Literary and Linguistic Computing* 23, no. 3: 383–396. http://discovery.ucl.ac.uk/13810/1/13810.pdf (accessed 15 February 2013) (Archived by WebCite® at http://www.webcitation.org/6ESOurK0l).

White, D. & Le Cornu, A. 2011. "Visitors and residents: A new typology for online engagement." *First Monday* 16, no. 9. http://firstmonday.org/htbin/cgiwrap/bin/ojs/index.php/fm/article/viewArticle/3171/3049 (accessed 15 February 2013) (Archived by WebCite® at http://www.webcitation.org/6ESRHzkxq).

Witt, S. & Gearhart, R. 2003. "Ethnography and information literacy: An assessment project." E. F. Avery (Ed.). *Assessing student learning outcomes for information literacy instruction in academic institutions,* p. 265–278. Chicago: Association of College and Research Libraries.

Wu, S. K. & Lanclos, D. (2011). "Re-imagining the users' experience: an ethnographic approach to web usability and space design." *Reference Services Review* 39, no. 3: 369–389.

How to cite this paper

Connaway, L. S., White, D., Lanclos, D. & Le Cornu, A. 2012. "Visitors and residents: What motivates engagement with the digital information environment?" *Information Research,* 18(1) paper 556. Retrieved from http://InformationR.net/ir/18-1/paper556.html.

APPENDIX A

Participant interview questions—Secondary/High school and University level

1. Describe the things you enjoy doing with technology and the web each week.

   This is a conversational start in order to put the interviewees at their ease. We are trying to get a sense of their overall digital literacy so that we can set their information seeking behaviors within a broader context. Do they socialize online? (See probe.) Do they 'contribute' online in the form of pictures, video, blogs, etc.?

   [PROBES: How important is the web for your social life, do you use it to keep in touch with your friends? What gadgets/devices/things do you use the most, is there anything you 'couldn't live without'? How much time on average do you spend online each week? Is there anything that bothers you about being online?]

2. Think of the ways you have used technology and the web for your studies. Describe a typical week.

   We are looking at interviewees' use of educational technologies more specifically for study. We hope they will start to introduce informal learning, self-directed study, peer to peer learning, etc. We anticipate they will (or may not) mention Facebook, MySpace, etc.

   [PROBES: How do you keep track of things? What systems for learning online do you have? Can you give us any examples of when you've asked your friends for help on assignments/homework online? What kind of online resources have you found that help you with your studies? How did you find them? What other gadgets or devices do you use for your studies?]

3. Think about the next stage of your education. Tell me what you think this will be like. [Alternative University Student Interviews: What did you think university studies would be like when you were in high school? How is your experience different from what you thought it would be? Describe what you think the next stage of your education will be. Tell me what you think this will be like.]

   This will hopefully encourage them to reflect on what they envisage their role will be in the next stage. What they imagine the next educational-stage to be like will be something we can cross check as we follow them through the project.

   [PROBES: How do you think you will use technology in the next part of your education? If you think you will need to adapt the way you use technology, what sort of changes do you think you'll make?]

4. Think of a time when you had a situation where you needed answers or solutions and you did a quick search and made do with it. You knew there were other sources but you decided not to use them. Please include sources such as friends, family, teachers, TAs, tutors, coaches, etc.

    Prompt for both academic and informal (domestic, personal...) examples.

    [PROBES: Did you simply take the first answer/solution you were able to find? What was the situation? What sources did you use? What led you to use them...and not others? Did they help? How? What sources did you decide not to use? What led to this/these decision/s? What did source A give you that you thought source B could not? Are there situations where source B would 'be a better choice for you? How did you decide when it was time to stop looking? How did you assess what was good enough?]

5. Have there been times when you were told to use a library or virtual learning environment (or learning platform), and used other source(s) instead?

    [PROBE: What made you decide not to use what you were asked to use?
    What kinds of things do your instructors want you to do when you're looking for information? Does what you do look like that, and if not, what does it look like?]

6. If you had a magic wand, what would your ideal way of getting information be? How would you go about using the systems and services? When? Where? How?

7. What comments or questions do you have for me? Is there anything you would like me to explain? What would you like to tell me that you've thought about during this interview?

APPENDIX B

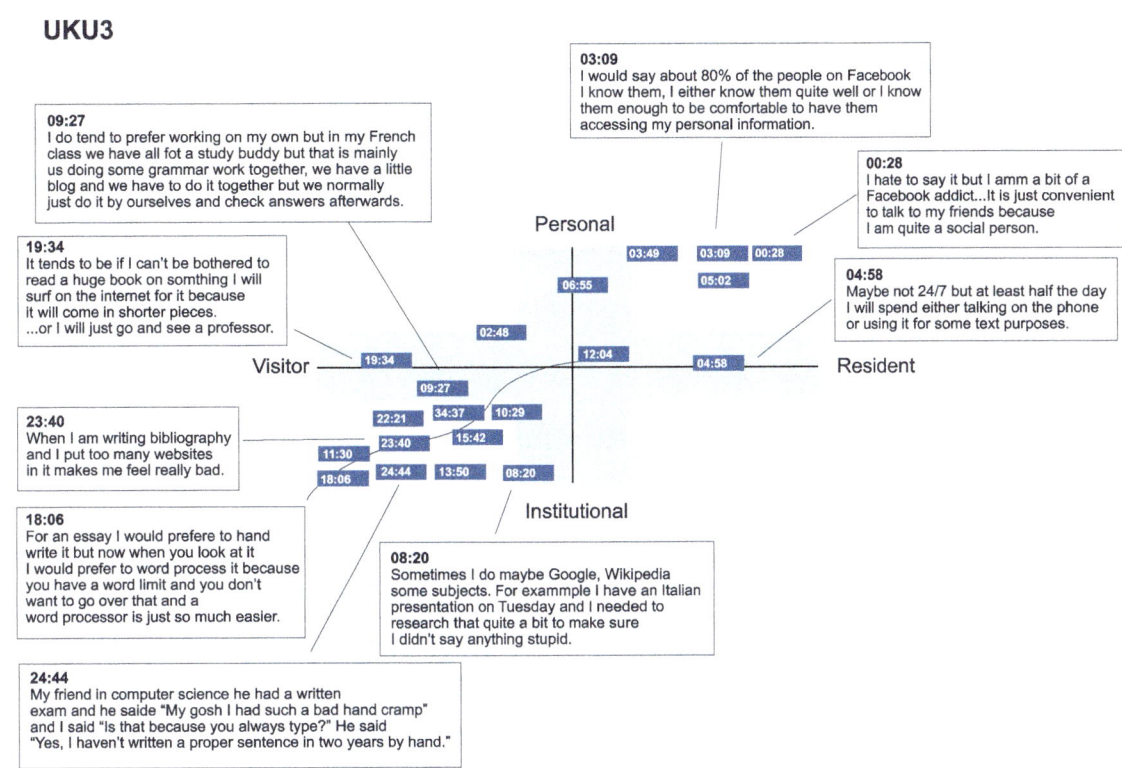

Example mapping of a participant's modes of engagement using the Visitors and Residents framework (including selected direct quotes)

9

"I always stick with the first thing that comes up on Google..." Where People Go for Information, What They Use, and Why

Lynn Silipigni Connaway, Ph.D.
OCLC Research

Donna M. Lanclos, Ph.D.
University of North Carolina, Charlotte

Erin M. Hood
OCLC Research

A reprint of:

Connaway, Lynn Silipigni, Donna M. Lanclos, and Erin M. Hood. 2013. "'I always stick with the first thing that comes up on Google...' Where People Go for Information, What They Use, and Why." *EDUCAUSE Review Online*.

http://www.educause.edu/ero/article/i-always-stick-first-thing-comes-google-where-people-go-information-what-they-use-and-why

© 2013 OCLC Online Computer Library Center, Inc. and Donna M. Lanclos.

This work is licensed under a Creative Commons Attribution 3.0 Unported License.

http://creativecommons.org/licenses/by/3.0/

KEY TAKEAWAYS

The Visitors and Residents project seeks to identify and recommend strategies that IT staff and library professionals can adopt to **help students and faculty** members better **discover, access, and evaluate digital information.**

The project team interviewed participants from **four educational stages**—from emerging (high school/secondary school seniors and first-year college students) through experiencing (faculty members)—that **focus on context and motive** rather than age as **a determining factor in information-seeking behaviors.**

In addition to identifying **how and why individuals engage with technology** to acquire the information, the project offers recommendations on **how to build relationships with community members** and **how to study user behavior** to better test and develop library systems.

Note: The quote in the title was made by a participant in the study reported on in this article.[1]

Lynn Silipigni Connaway is a senior research scientist and Erin M. Hood is a research support specialist at the Online Computer Library Center. Donna Lanclos is associate professor for Anthropological Research at the University of North Carolina, Charlotte, J. Murrey Atkins Library.

To better meet the needs of the academic community, education IT staff and library and information science (LIS) professionals must know the extent to which people are engaged with their institution's technologies and sources. What is behind the choices that people make about the information they consume? How do they determine whether or not a source is authoritative? What fluencies (digital, information, and computer) are relevant to people's choices? What are the motives behind choosing one source or plan of action over another?

The Visitors and Residents (V&R) project, started in 2010, proposes that context and motive matter more than age or skill level when it comes to people's decisions about technology and digital spaces. This new understanding of technology engagement offers a balanced alternative to Marc Prensky's "digital natives" metaphor.[2] The V&R project's emerging research results uncover the contexts in which individuals use technology (in homes, at institutions, and so on) and how this engagement changes as people transition between educational stages, from the final year of high school to faculty positions at universities.

Although people historically have depended on institutionally provided resources and technology, today's affordable connectivity and devices have enabled access to the open web and its numerous free information sources. Thus, the need for local infrastructure has declined.[3] Individuals are not limited to an institution's online catalog, but rather have access to information at a much broader level, such as through web browsers and online services. Also, the convenience of finding information online does not directly equate with the information's quality.

The V&R project results help identify ways to aid academic community members develop their skills in discovering, accessing, and evaluating digital information.

Here, we focus on three primary areas:

- Where people go when looking for information,
- What sources they use the most, and
- Why they choose and return to these sources instead of other sources.

We also include specific recommendations for organizations based on our preliminary research results, which are drawn primarily from structured interviews conducted since 2010.[4]

The Visitors and Residents framework

The V&R project is a collaboration between the Online Computer Library Center (OCLC) and the University of Oxford, in partnership with the University of North Carolina, Charlotte; it has been underway for the past two years with partial funding from JISC.[5] The project outlines learners' modes of engagement within four educational stages and how these learners intersect with institutional services.

The V&R premise is a continuum: individuals' modes of engagement will be more *visitor* or more *resident*, depending on their personal motivations and context,[6] and individuals frequently move between the two modes. In visitor mode, people treat the web as a series of tools. They decide what they want to achieve, choose an appropriate online tool, and then log off. They leave no social trace of themselves online. In resident mode, people live a portion of their lives online and approach the web as a place where they can express themselves and spend time with people. When acting as residents, people visit social networking platforms, and aspects of their digital identity maintain a presence even when they're not online through their social media profiles.

The V&R project's intent is to identify how and why individuals engage with technology to acquire the information they need. To uncover the hows and whys, we recruited individuals from four project-defined educational stages:

- **Emerging:** last-year high school/secondary and first-year undergraduate college/university students
- **Establishing:** upper division undergraduate college/university students
- **Embedding:** graduate students
- **Experiencing:** faculty

We use these stages because they reflect the behavioral commonalities among high school seniors and college freshmen, as well as the differences that emerge when people transition to upper-division undergraduate status and beyond. First-year college students' information-seeking practices seem to mimic habits they acquired in high school. Changes to those habits will be embedded in the practices and relationships that individuals engage in during their remaining time in college and later on in professional contexts.

To date, findings indicate that the behavior patterns revealed in the V&R research noticeably vary by the participants' educational stage rather than by age, which can vary broadly within each stage. This categorization by educational stages rather than age contrasts with Prensky's "natives and immigrants" paradigm. However, the visitors and residents notion more accurately reflects the reality that individual choices about technology and information seeking derive from context—that is, from individuals' educational and professional priorities—rather than from their age.

MAPPING THE V&R FRAMEWORK

During an EDUCAUSE 2012 session and two expert sessions at the 2013 American Library Association (ALA) Conference, education IT staff and LIS professionals mapped their own activities and their perceptions of one of their user groups' activities onto a V&R pole map with two axes: the horizontal Visitor-Resident (V, R) axis, and the vertical Personal-Institutional (P, I) axis.

Figure 1 shows an example of a librarian's activities: high-level visitor mode within the institutional context, with a great deal of Google searching, as well as some Facebook, Flickr, and Vimeo use. Resident behavior is shown in both institutional and personal contexts through the use of Pinterest, blogging, texting, and Google docs. Figure 2 shows the same librarian's perception of undergraduate engagement with a heavy emphasis on resident mode in the personal context: Facebook, blogs, twitter, Instagram, texting, and Flickr. She mapped e-mail for undergraduates on the visitor end of the continuum and divided it in two to represent use of two different e-mail addresses—one institutional and one personal.

FIGURE 1. THE V&R MAP OF A LIBRARY PROFESSIONAL

FIGURE 2. THE SAME LIBRARIAN'S PERCEPTION OF UNDERGRADUATE ENGAGEMENT

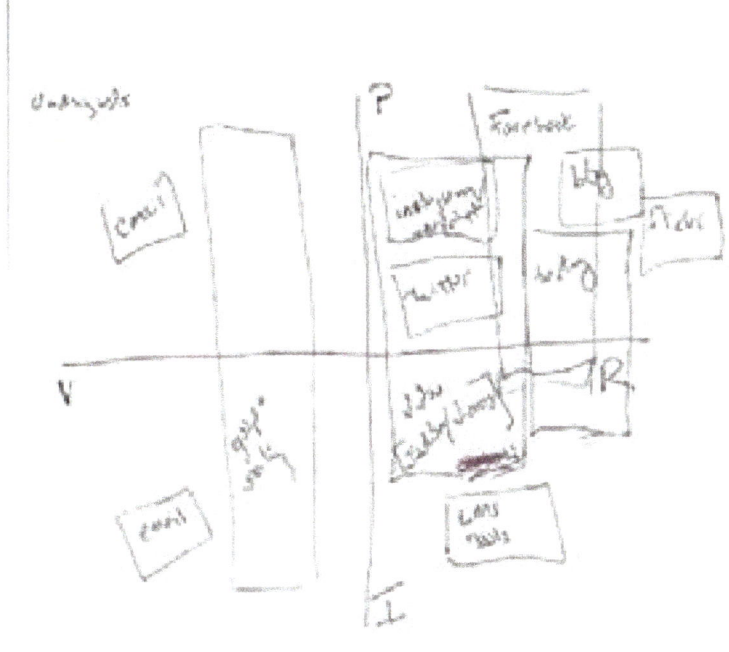

These mapping exercises illustrate the tools/digital space that people use/inhabit, which is less important than what they are doing in that space with that tool. That is, it is not enough to count how many students are on Twitter or Facebook; further qualitative inquiry is necessary to determine what they might be doing with these tools in these environments. For example, some people use Facebook to periodically connect with people, others post everything to their Facebook wall, and still others use Facebook as a clearinghouse to track their events and organizations. Ideally, the analysis of what people are doing to engage with resources should be tool-agnostic, just as IT support should be device-agnostic (individuals on campus should be able to do their work whether they have a Mac or a PC, a netbook, or a mobile phone). Further, an outreach/engagement strategy that simply provides an institutional presence on Facebook or Twitter, without providing information of interest to the academic community, is unlikely to succeed.

Research design and methods

The V&R uses both quantitative and qualitative methods for a mixed methods approach, which can increase the validity of our findings.[7] We use the qualitative methods of semi-structured interviews, sometimes accompanied by monthly diaries and follow-up interviews, to create a rich, descriptive longitudinal study of preselected individuals who represent the four educational stages. Qualitative methods are fitting when the phenomena being studied are social in nature, complex, and unquantifiable.[8] It is acceptable for qualitative research to use small samples, as it is not always necessary to generalize the data to wider populations.[9] Using this type of research is best when the topic is personal, when the researcher wants to go into greater detail about a small unit, or when there is little previous knowledge about the topic.[10] This method can be significantly useful in exploratory research.[11]

All individuals in the four educational stages participated in the semi-structured interviews, and a subset of each stage also participated in monthly diary submissions and follow-up interviews. (Our interview questions, along with the written diary submission questions and outline and the diary follow-up questions, are available elsewhere.[12]) The stratified, purposive, nonprobability sampling methods and the small sample size restrict our ability to generalize on the results of these interviews and diary entries. However, the findings offer a glimpse at how a specific group of individuals engaged with technology and how their behaviors changed (or not) over a three-year period.

In Phase 1 of the V&R project, we conducted semi-structured interviews with participants in the four educational stages in the US and UK.[13] Including a sample of participants from outside the US allows for a more effective answer to questions such as: Do the behaviors occur because of the technology? Are the behaviors characteristic of people who are in university settings? Do geographic and cultural differences between participants in the UK and the US influence the way individuals engage with technology and get information?

In Phase 2 of the project, we selected a subset of the interviewees to participate in monthly information diaries.[14] Each diarist submitted, in the form of their choice, descriptions of the types of activities they did online, both in academic and nonacademic settings. Diaries were primarily submitted via e-mail messages (because they were "formal communication" with researchers), but a few participants also submitted video logs.[15] We intended the diary entries and follow-up interviews to provide time-depth to the study. They also reveal changes that might occur as participants transition from one educational stage to another or as new digital innovations emerge or become more widely available in both educational and personal settings. Figure 3 shows a chart of the project's phases and participants' educational stages from 2010–2013.

FIGURE 3. THE VISITOR AND RESIDENTS PROJECT PHASES

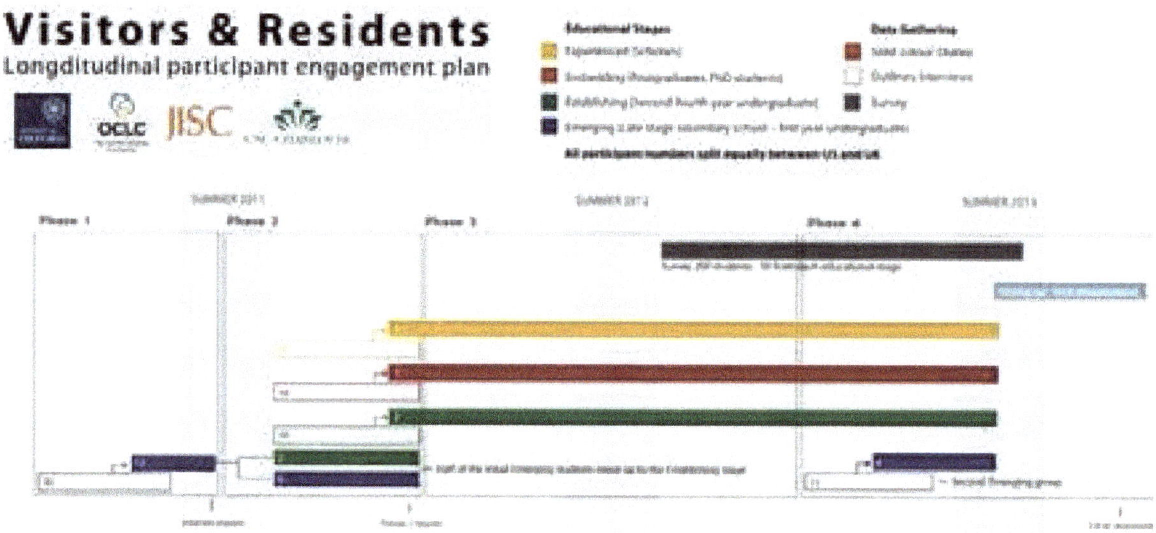

To compare and verify the qualitative method results, we use quantitative methods. Specifically, we are distributing an online survey of a broader population selected by the quota sampling method; this survey will be both generalizable and comparative. For the survey, which is scheduled to be disseminated before the end of 2013, we will choose 25 participants from each educational stage from both the US and the UK. If the sample of 100 individuals does not reach saturation, we will select another sample of 100 individuals.

Content analysis is a critical and time-consuming aspect of any qualitative research study. In our case, it consisted heavily of coding interview transcripts and the various types of follow-up diary submissions. Once we completed the initial interview round in V&R Phase 1, we used the emerging themes identified in the interview data to develop a codebook for analysing the project data.[16] After each research team member tested the codebook's first iteration, we discussed and reached agreements on any differences and modified the codebook to better reflect the emerging themes. After the codebook was completed and refined, we progressively coded both the interviews and diaries through each phase. For this study, the codebook focused on several themes, including place, sources, tools, agency, situation/context, and contact.[17] Some of the themes of interest were not present in the original interviews with the emerging-stage students. For example, none of them mentioned "librarians." Because we were interested in discussing the role of librarians in information-seeking situations, we added a code for "Librarian" so that we could talk about the relative absence of that theme in the data. (Participants in the other educational stages did mention librarians in their individual interviews.)

Using qualitative methods with a small sample size and a quantitative method with the large sample size gave us rich, thick data descriptions as well as numerical analyses and comparisons. If the quantitative and qualitative data show little variance, it will be possible to generalize all of our findings. Here, however, we report only some of the findings from the qualitative data collection methods.

ANALYSIS

To interpret the V&R data, we must examine how individuals acquire the information-seeking behaviors and technology-centered practices of their respective communities within and outside of academia. We drew insights from the community of practice literature, especially the works of Jean Lave and Etienne Wenger and Barbara Rogoff and Wenger, which outline and analyze what happens when people learn how to be members of groups.[18] The literature describes a wide variety of groups, including vocational, educational, and recovery. Central to Lave and Wenger's 1991 discussion is the idea of legitimate peripheral participation:

> We intend for the concept to be taken as a whole. Each of the aspects is indispensable in defining the others and cannot be considered in isolation.... Thus, in the terms proposed here there may very well be no such thing as an "illegitimate peripheral participant." The form that the legitimacy of participation takes is a defining characteristic of ways of belonging, and is therefore not only a crucial condition for learning, but a constitutive element of its content. Similarly, with regard to "peripherality" there may well be no such simple thing as "central participation" in a community of practice. Peripherality suggests that there are multiple, varied, more- or less-engaged and -inclusive ways of being located in the fields of participation defined by a community. Peripheral participation is about being located in the social world. Changing locations and perspectives are part of actors' learning trajectories, developing identities, and forms of membership.[19]

Lave and Wenger further point out that legitimate peripheral participation occurs within social structures that involve power relations. So, different power relations can serve as barriers to or facilitators of participation. No inevitable progress toward a "center" exists in their structure; rather, it is an attempt to give a theoretical structure to a changeable social phenomenon. They emphasize that their concept is not "itself an educational form, much less a pedagogical strategy or a teaching technique. It is an analytical viewpoint on learning, a way of understanding learning."[20]

Participants in our V&R interviews engage in practices that they acquired in social matrices of friends, family, peers, teachers, co-workers, and supervisors. Participants' relationships with people from whom they learn practices in turn inform the relationships they have to those practices, the resources they choose to consult, and the resources they reject. Their confidence in the acquired practices appears to be directly related to the strength of their connection to the community in which they are participating. That connection has less to do with abstract notions of best practices than it does with the *familiar*—not to be confused with the convenient, although that comes into it as well—which we define as those practices engaged in by people the participants trust, and with whom they have existing relationships.

The V&R paradigm is based on the assumption that individuals' engagement with technology is related to whether they regard the platforms they use as tools or places. The manner in which individuals engage with technology and access information is influenced by context and situation. In today's environment, people often are inundated with information sources and might make choices based on the source's appearance or familiarity—or on how much time they think accessing that information will take, which is a significant context in information seeking.[21] Time is related to convenience, which is a recurring theme in information-seeking behavior research.[22] When asked about using information systems, individuals repeatedly state that they want to find information conveniently and quickly.[23] Research also suggests that convenient service often is more important to people than quick service.[24] Convenience can be either physical or virtual, based on the particular context and situation.[25] Campus information commons—with 24/7 access to materials and facilities and cafes—are popular because they are convenient for individuals in specific situations.[26]

Situation is related to context but is somewhat narrower. "Situation refers to the time-space concept in which sense is constructed."[27] Context provides the background for that which individuals want to understand and explain.[28] "Convenience is a situational criterion in people's choices and actions during all stages of the information-seeking process. The concept of convenience can include their choice of an information source, their satisfaction with the source and its ease of use, and their time horizon in information seeking."[29]

LOCATION: WHERE DO PEOPLE GO FOR INFORMATION?

When talking about places they went for information, interviewees mentioned Internet resources, such as search engines and social media sites, far more often than physical places. This reliance on digital spaces coexists with a persistent need to be in contact with other people both online and face to face. Personal networks, and the relationships that comprise them, were important factors in participants' information-seeking strategies across educational stages.[30] This is a key point to remember when thinking about how to attract people to institutional information and technology resources.

MODES AND MODE COMBINATIONS

Participants' varied modes of digital contact combined visitor modes (texting, private messaging, and e-mail) and resident modes (Twitter and media postings). It is therefore not enough to get individuals to want to access services/resources; you must make such access available in a wide variety of platforms. Representative quotes from the interview data illustrate this nicely[31]:

> "I don't use Twitter, partially because a lot of my friends—there's a certain negative connotation with Twitter that it's online presence taken too far, taken to the extreme among people my age, I suppose."
>
> —UKG2, Embedding, 0:25:47, Female, Age 22

> "I get on Twitter a whole bunch …. Twitter or Facebook are what I usually use the most to talk to my friends."
>
> —USS1, Emerging, 0:09:28, Female, Age 17

> "No, no. I think Twitter's a bit bizarre because it seems to be people just declaring what they think rather than socializing really with other people. I mean, you can choose to comment upon what other people are saying, but in general it's sort of like a declaration of your status, and I don't really see why it's—well I see why it's so popular, but it's not for me, I don't think."
>
> —UKU12, Establishing, 0:03:16, Female, Age 21

Of course, even Twitter and blogs can be approached in the less-visible visitor mode when people use them to consume rather than produce Internet content. Because people use various platforms in a range of modes, you need a broad commitment to multiple technology modes for information seeking and communication.

In the case of e-mail, however, people seem to conform readily to the current expectation that e-mail is where official communication occurs. Individuals in the emerging stage mentioned e-mail much less than individuals in the establishing stage. When these emerging-stage students did mention using e-mail, it was to communicate with teachers or for other school business, such as school activities and administration. Clearly, as people move through the educational stages, they become more reliant upon e-mail and recognize the consequences of not checking their accounts regularly.

"So, I find that a lot of the time, it's easier for me just to e-mail them [lecturers], and they would get back to me pretty … pretty quick."

—2UKU2, Emerging, 08:29, Male, Age 18

"I talk to all of my lecturers if I don't understand something. And they're usually very good at replying. Also, the good thing about Exeter is all of them [have] contacts. Everyone has the ability to contact everyone. So you have advertisements, um, good opportunities for anyone and, actually, study abroad came through on the e-mails."

—2UKU3, Emerging, 8:05, Female, Age 19

"Oh yeah. Like, if I don't get something, I usually just e-mail them [teachers]. And hopefully they e-mail me like maybe an hour after—but sometimes they don't. I just find that helpful."

—2USS2, Emerging, 09:03, Female, Age 17

"I usually e-mail the professor or ask somebody in my class."

—2USU3, Emerging, 11:11, Female, Age 19

DEVICES

The frequent mentions of texting, telephone calls, and private messaging by emerging- and establishing-stage interviewees correlates with the technologies they said they could not live without: cellphones, smart phones, and laptops. They used these not only for communicating and contacting individuals but also for searching the Internet and organizing their time and activities using calendars.

"It's the cell phone … you can do so much with it, it is not something you want to really lose or get rid of. I mean, if I break my phone

I'll get a replacement the next day just because they are that important. It's the biggest way to get in contact with people."

—USU3, Emerging, 00:09:23, Male, Age 19

"If I had to—if I could only pick one, it would be … it would be the MacBook, just because these are for convenience, these are mobile and 'net on the go, but, really, as far as continuing to facilitate efficiency and life, the MacBook is where it is. This is just a slightly less computer on the go, but I can still do my homework, I can still get on Facebook, and I can still connect and e-mail people with the MacBook."

—USU5, Emerging, 0:15:45, Male, Age 19

"I could probably live without my phone. But I could probably not live without the computer and, you know, the Internet. Because work and the e-mails … yes."

—USU2, Emerging, 0:11:50, Female, Age 19

"I'd say it would have to be my phone because I keep in contact with people on it. I've got things like the Internet, so I can use Facebook, I can check my e-mails. I can download apps and stuff, I have got a SatNav on my phone, so if I ever get lost—which happens a lot—I can just check to see where I am and where I'm going."

—UKU6, Emerging, 00:03:39, Female, Age 19

"My laptop. It's got to be my laptop … yes. Everything's on there, like just everything that I use. All the programs that I use and kind of all my work I like to back up on my laptop and stuff. If it went down I'd be very, very unhappy." (Laughter)

—UKU5, Emerging, 0:03:06, Female, Age 19

> "I think my phone …. I just—it's just the easiest way to keep in contact with people. And also with phones these days, it's like a mini computer to be honest. Smart phones—so, yes."
>
> —UKS7, Emerging, 0:06:22, Female, Age 17

As these quotes show, the "most important" device varied from individual to individual. Some could not live without their phones, others their laptops. Such results reinforce the importance of device-agnostic services and resources. The results also demonstrate that, as portable devices gain functionality traditionally available only on a laptop or desktop, individuals will adopt the technology that is most convenient for their situation. The individuals who participated in this study expect to use their own technology to connect with institutional (and other) resources, and also to engage in resident modes of behavior.

NAVIGATION AND IDEAL SOLUTIONS

Also important are digital places unmediated by personal networks; ease of navigation for such places is essential. In this typically visitor mode of engagement, people do not seek to connect with other people, but rather with resources.

> "Yes, for many journals it's [go] directly …. I don't go through [academic library name] as much anymore because I have the journals I look at bookmarked. But usually, it's a couple of different search engines that are used for looking for an article or just what's new on this topic."
>
> I used to make regular trips to the library to read journals, and I haven't been to [academic library name] to read a journal [in] many years. If I go there, it's for meetings. "
>
> —USF4, Experiencing, 0:22:02-0:27:15, Male, Age 54

Interviewees frequently described digital solutions in response to the questions, "If you had a magic wand, what would be your ideal way of getting information? How would you go about using the systems and services? When? Where? How?" (Many of the respondents seemed to be describing a better Google—that is, a better way of identifying more accurate and relevant information and sources). A UK university student responded in the following way:[32]

> "My ideal way I think definitely would have to be a mixture of digital and analogue sort of research, well finding things …. Basically sort of what you do in the natural world like go into a library and picking books off a shelf. But if you had a virtual reality sort of version of that in which you didn't have to physically necessarily go to a library or you

> could physically go to … or you could digitally go to a library that had everything you could possibly want but you didn't need to necessarily go wandering around it forever. I think that would be the best, that would be the ideal sort of way of doing it, yes. Certainly the ease of the Internet and the ease of everything, having everything digitally is brilliant. I mean obviously you can store several thousand libraries worth of information on the Internet. And to have that accessible—but also … in a more instinctual way. … There's a certain sort of, I don't know, a certain sort of nice feeling about going into a library and picking a book off the shelf and going and sitting down and reading it. If you could do that in a digital environment, that'd be fantastic."
>
> —UKU11, Establishing, 0:36:10, Male, Age 33

Both in this study and in previous studies users did not consistently associate digital academic resources with academic libraries. People might recognize that the resources they are using are not popular or nonacademic resources, but they seem to be unaware (or think it is unimportant to note) that those resources are associated with a library.[33] Research also indicates that even the terminology used in libraries, such as the phrase, "Ask a Librarian," is not understood by library users.[34]

RECOMMENDATIONS: LOCATION

Institutional services and systems must be embedded within the academic community's workflow so that individuals are able to use critical skills for inquiry wherever they land in the information landscape.[35] Aggregating these services and systems into combined interfaces or portals might also entice individuals to use them. Following are some suggestions for university IT and LIS professionals who want to attract their user groups to institutional resources:

- **Provide a broad range of tools.** People make decisions in a variety of contexts, so the outcome of any given task is hard to predict. If we lock our patrons into one tool or mode of engagement (whether visitor or resident) and disregard other possibilities, we drive them away.
- **Create simple and convenient interface designs.** As an example of such a design, figure 4 shows Trove, the National Library of Australia's catalog. Another example is Finna, an online catalog that offers access to Finland's archives, libraries, and museums (see figure 5). Overly complex institutional interfaces will consistently drive patrons to the Internet resources they already know and trust, even if the solutions they offer are not as effective as those their institutions provide.

FIGURE 4. INTERFACE FOR TROVE, THE NATIONAL LIBRARY OF AUSTRALIA'S CATALOG

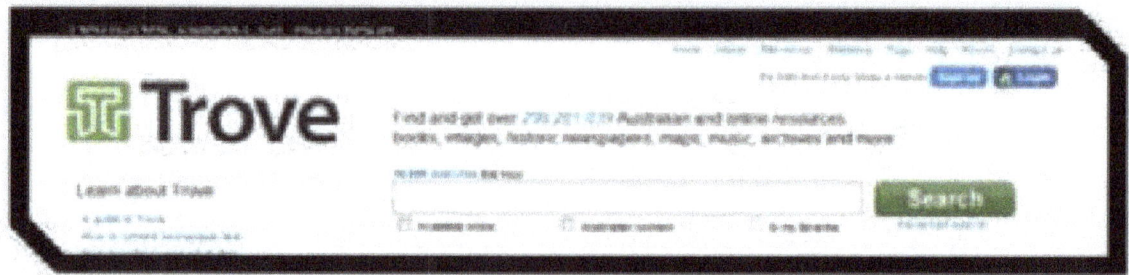

FIGURE 5. THE INTERFACE OF FINLAND'S FINNA

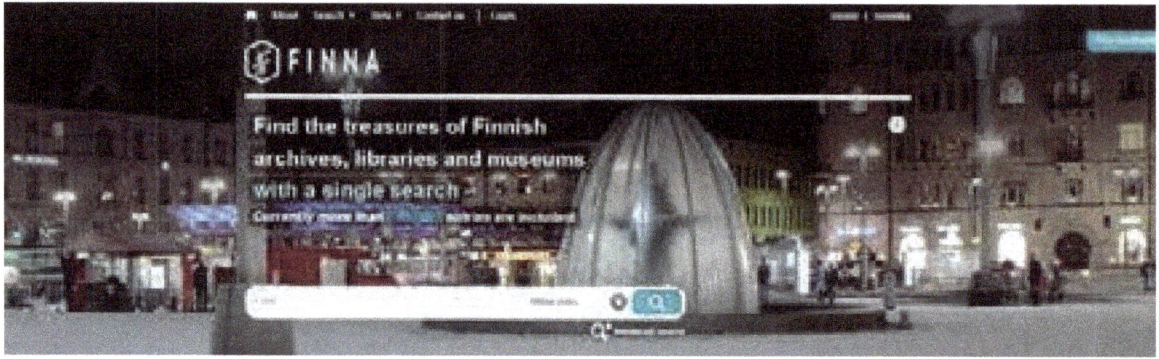

- **Remove barriers between information discovery and access.** You can do this by providing enough descriptive information about sources for individuals to easily determine whether a particular source has the information they need.
- **Promote and market services to the academic constituencies.** It is not enough to only provide services; people must know that these services are available.

These recommendations are not new, but our research results suggest that they remain important and have yet to be adequately addressed.

Sources: what are people finding and using?

Regardless of whether people get recommendations from personal networks (online or offline) or in digital locations such as Google, the sources they choose to use are overwhelmingly digital.

PRIMARY SOURCES

Databases were mentioned more than any kind of electronic books by a wide margin of participants in our study. Explicit mentions of databases are particularly characteristic of faculty and graduate students. The increase begins with undergraduates (because high school seniors rarely have access to university-provided databases), and the higher the participants' educational levels, the greater the number of database mentions. For people affiliated with universities, database use most closely mirrors the use of the free web (that is, content not paid for by institutions or individuals) in that they do not have to pay for the resource themselves (because their institutions pay for it) and because the items they find tend to be articles—a shorter and more convenient format than books. Participants viewed the library stereotypically, seeing it primarily as a place to access books rather than other sources or services; this view has been reported consistently in the literature as well.[36]

The significant number of database mentions by our study's participants shows how important they are within academic and library contexts to both embedding-stage (graduate student) and experiencing-stage (faculty) participants. Emerging- and establishing-stage participants did not talk about databases as explicitly as graduate students and faculty did, possibly because they did not know they were using academic databases (again underlining the importance of marketing). The emerging participants typically talked more generally about using the library's digital resources, without specifically mentioning databases. They also talked about social media such as Facebook in academic contexts. However, this was not unique to these early stage students, as the following quote from a UK graduate student indicates:

> "Our Learning and Technology group is trying to start a wiki because it's a useful way to develop our interests on each having a separate page and being able to share resources. We do that through Facebook currently. We do say, 'Hey, this is a resource about blogging that I'd like to pass onto you because I know you're interested in it.' We do that through Facebook, but we find it's very difficult to separate out. There's only one feed for different people's interests. So, we're looking at developing a wiki to kind of share ideas and resources between our different topic areas and force ourselves to develop our topic areas in a public forum, a forum where we'd have to write out what we're interested in online. But the Facebook group is extremely active also, if not for just complaining about an assignment or trying to find a particular reading, but also sharing current news articles with each other."
>
> —UKG2, Embedding, 0:15:35, Female, Age 22

Mentions of the free web, as represented by major media sites and Wikipedia, also far outnumbered mentions of university databases or course management systems such as Moodle, even among graduate students.[37] Wikipedia was heavily mentioned by participants in all educational stages, including half of the faculty/scholar participants. Mentions of major media sites were lowest among emerging students, increased with graduate students, and then declined among faculty—a pattern that directly contrasts with that of databases.

Although some disciplines strongly rely on peer-reviewed articles, other fields consider secondary and social media sources, such as newspaper articles and blogs, to be viable resources.[38] Helena Francke and Olof Sundin reported that educators would recommend the Internet and sources like Wikipedia as viable options because they are so up to date for researching "current trends, new technology, and popular phenomena."[39] This is supported in our data by relatively high faculty mentions of Wikipedia use for orienting themselves on unfamiliar topics. Laura Saunders also found that faculty are "concerned with students' reliance on Google and Wikipedia for information."[40] This might help explain why many of the emerging-stage participants expressed a reluctance to cite Wikipedia in their work for fear of being ridiculed by faculty or given a lower grade. This "learning black market" (a phrase coined by our colleague David S. White) is discussed in more detail elsewhere.[41]

RECOMMENDATIONS: SOURCES

Rather than perpetuating this "black market" traffic in resources, institutions should use individual Internet practices as a guide to linking institutional resources to those on the open web. Individuals use a broad range of tools to get information, and they engage with technology in multiple ways. It is therefore imperative to provide a broad range of tools and services in different media. One size cannot fit all; we should strive for a diversity of approaches based on how individuals engage with technology and get their information:

- **Converse with your academic constituencies** to identify their information-seeking and evaluation strategies in both library and open web contexts. It will then be possible to advise them on ways to improve their strategies and to integrate both environments into a broad information-seeking strategy.
- **Use what we already know about how people use Wikipedia** to link library content to Wikipedia articles. As figure 6 shows, the University of Washington library has done this with authoritative references and links to full text, open content in special collections, and other resources on salmon following Wikipedia community norms. Library and other information professionals are encouraged to add references to the most relevant resources in their collection as they relate to a particular topic. Engaging with Wikipedia can range from librarians attending local editathons for practical experience, to employing a Wikipedian in Residence as many institutions have done, including OCLC.[42] Lorcan Dempsey refers to this as the "inside-out" model of managing resources.[43]

FIGURE 6. THE UNIVERSITY OF WASHINGTON ACTIVELY LINKS ITS COLLECTIONS TO RELEVANT WIKIPEDIA ARTICLES

External links

- *Plea for the Wanderer*, an NFB documentary on West Coast salmon
- *Fish farms drive wild salmon populations toward extinction* Biology News Net. December 13, 2007.
- *Salmonid parasites* University of St Andrews Marine Ecology Research Group.
- Watershed Watch Salmon Society A British Columbia advocacy group for wild salmon
- Wild Salmon in Trouble *The Link Between Farmed Salmon, Sea Lice and Wild Salmon* -Watershed based on peer-reviewed scientific research, with subject background article Watching out for Wild Salm
- Aquacultural Revolution: *The scientific case for changing salmon farming* - Watershed Watch Salmon scientists and First Nation representatives speak their minds about the salmon farming industry and the populations.
- Genetic Status of Atlantic Salmon in Maine: Interim Report (2002) Online book
- University of Washington Libraries Digital Collections – Salmon Collection A collection of documents d
- Canned Salmon Recipes by Alaska Packers' Association 900 e-book with color illustrations, availabl
- Epicurean.com Salmon Recipes Collected recipes using Salmon at epicurean.com
- Low Sodium Salmon Recipe Recipe to make smoked salmon mousse.
- *Salmon-omics: Effect of Pacific Decadal Oscillation on Alaskan Chinook Harvests and Market Price*
- Salmon Nation A movement to create a bioregional community, based on the historic spawning area o

Why people choose: source evaluation, authority, and legitimacy

Relevance and reliability are highly important to emerging-stage students, perhaps because they lack subject expertise. As individuals progress through their educational stages, they become more familiar with subject-specific sources and learn how to navigate journals, publishers, databases, and human sources (such as authors). Even without subject expertise, however, emerging-stage participants were concerned about selecting reliable sources and often mentioned searching for web sites from domains such as .edu, .ac, and .gov, which they viewed as more reliable than commercial domains such as .com.

Participants also mentioned repetition of the same information from several different sources as a measure of reliability, as the following quote exemplifies:

> "And so it's kind of time really to stop once you've got information that corresponds with information from somewhere else—that's like if you've got two comparative sources that agree, then kind of the place to stop is really within the limits of that thing."
>
> —UKU4, Emerging, 0:26:22, Male, Age 19

Pickard and Logan reported finding this approach more common among senior undergraduate students than those of freshmen undergraduate students.[44]

Some study participants measured reliability based on a site's appearance:

> "It depends. It depends who's made the website or what I have been told about the website or whether I know about it at all. But—it sounds silly—but sometimes you can just tell whether a website looks reliable or not depending on how professional [it] looks and who's written it."
>
> —UKU6, Emerging, 00:16:04, Female, Age 19

Similarly, according to Pickard and Logan, their "freshmen interviewees used general terms such as 'scholarly,' 'reliable,' 'peer-reviewed,' 'written by professors,' and 'looks fancy'" to judge a source as scholarly or not.[45]

CONVENIENCE: THE KEY FACTOR

Not surprisingly, participants in all stages frequently mentioned convenience/ease of use as an important factor in obtaining information. Emerging students also consistently discussed authority/legitimacy, though mentions of this decreased among establishing students, only to increase again among embedded and experiencing participants.

Information science has long been concerned with how individuals evaluate a source's authority or legitimacy, yet the issue has increasing immediacy given the numerous information sources that are outside academic institutions or unvetted by the publishing review process. Harlan, Bruce, and Lupton found that, among teenaged participants, authority was established if the information came from a teacher or from a professional, popular, or helpful source—or if the source sounded self-confident.[46] Francke and Sundin reported that approaches for evaluating credibility depended on the discipline and subject.[47] Saunders observed that differences in approaches to evaluating authority occur as students become more immersed in their fields.[48]

These findings support the conclusions of Connaway, Dickey, and Radford, who reported that convenience trumps all other reasons for selecting and using a source. Convenience also is determined by the information seeker's context and situation.[49] Immediacy's relative lack of importance in choosing sources is striking—and counter to assumptions about people's desire for immediate gratification. Connaway, Dickey, and Radford corroborate this view of immediacy, finding that speed in getting information is less important than convenience.[50]

INFORMATION QUALITY

The V&R data indicate that evaluation is taking place—individuals are not using sources without considering information quality. The factors that most strongly influence the choice of sources, however, are issues other than quality, such as the amount of time available and the assignment's stakes:

> "I may have to use other sources than the Internet. Right now, I use a lot of the Internet. When you walked in, I was reading—we have a workbook that came with our AP Biology book, and then, for AP Stats, I bought the [Barron's] test prep book, and I used that. I'll probably have to use more books in college, I'm thinking, than just the Internet. There are some things that for college you can't find on the Internet. You're doing a research paper or something, and it's on a subject that's further in the past—you'd have more reliable resources outside of the Internet."
>
> —USS7, Emerging, 0:17:53, Female, Age 17

"Last semester, I was writing a paper on Brazil and there was a book in the library that I just did not want to leave my house to go to. It is a 50-minute drive, I didn't want to do that, but I was writing my paper and so I used Google books instead and really they only had a section of the book available but that was the section I used. So, you know, doing that instead of coming here physically and going to get the whole book. And it saved time, it saved gas, I got what I needed, and it wasn't a big deal."

—USG4, Embedding, 0:39:42, Female, Age 23

[Laughter] "And again … the lovely thing about the Internet is it's all instantly, it is all there, and so you can pick exactly what it is that you want to watch and just shove that on."

—UKS8, Emerging, 0:05:50.5, Male, Age 17

So, if it's possible, I will want some, like, intelligent device to filter everything for me. So I can just get everything that's essential to me. Useful to me. So I can save my time from, you know, wasting it on filtering everything by myself."

—UKG1, Embedding, 0:43:39, Female, Age 23

GATEKEEPING

When an individual is searching for information, various channels might be open and gatekeeping can occur.[51] "In the communications field, "gatekeeping" refers to a process in which numerous messages are reduced to just a few.[52] The entrance to each channel or section of channel is called a gate [and] movement from one channel selection to another is determined by human gatekeepers, or a set of impartial rules."[53] Positive and negative forces surround the gates; therefore, whether or not someone passes through a gate depends on the forces surrounding or guarding the gate.

For example, a student who wants to find a work by a specific author might have several channels available, including search engines, databases, professors, and peers. The student might choose a search engine because it has fewer negative forces at the gate—databases require login, and e-mailing or calling a professor or friend takes time. Essentially, the student perceives the search engine as the easiest channel for information. Also, some channels might have multiple gates, which increases the likelihood that the student will reject them.[54]

THE IMPORTANCE OF RELATIONSHIP

Sometimes, people turn to their personal networks to determine a source's legitimacy. The composition of those networks shifts as individuals move through the educational stages, as reflected in our interview data (see table 1). Emerging-stage students consulted parents, siblings, and friends about academic work. In Pickard and Logan's study, freshmen sought help from their friends/classmates and family members at a higher rate than seniors.[55] Establishing-stage students consulted roommates, classmates, and siblings who have taken similar classes before. Graduate students consulted graduate school peers and professors, but consulted far less than individuals in any other educational stage. Faculty most often consulted friends, colleagues, and peers.

TABLE 1. HUMAN SOURCES MENTIONED BY MORE THAN ONE-THIRD OF THE PARTICIPANTS

Human sources	Participant educational stages			
	Emerging	Establishing	Embedding	Experiencing
Mother	X	X	X	
Father	X	X	X	
Extended family	X	X		
Experts/professionals				
Friends/colleagues	X	X	X	X
Teachers/professors	X	X	X	
Peers	X	X	X	X
Librarians				
Other		X		X

The lack of consistent mentions for expert/professionals and librarians by participants across all educational stages differs slightly from the findings of Pickard and Logan; in their study, senior college/university students "referred to 'Reference Librarians' and the 'Circulation Desk.'"[56] In our study the highest mentions of these sources were from faculty/scholars, followed by emerging-stage students. However, the latter group often did not use the term *librarian*, as exemplified by one of the participants:

> "...a lady in the library who helps you find things."
>
> —USU5, Emerging, 0:37:17, Male, Age 19

This corroborates Pickard and Logan's findings that "...most freshmen often did not know that reference librarians existed, much less what they did."[57]

Clearly, individuals seek what they need within the relationships that surround them. As they move through the educational stages, their networks are increasingly populated with people who have relevant subject expertise. By the time people become faculty members, calling a "friend" about an article almost certainly means the friend is also an expert in the field. Relationships continue to be a major component in how individuals get information and whom they choose for collaboration. The desire to make contact with others also motivates people to engage with technology.[58]

In the V&R interviews, collaboration was most common with emerging-stage participants, decreased sharply for both establishing and embedding participants, and then increased for experiencing participants. This might reflect not only the need for collaboration among emerging students, but also the emphasis on individual/isolating work for more advanced students. The high level of faculty collaboration is an interesting contrast to the training that graduate students apparently receive. Given that scholars need to work with colleagues in teaching and research contexts after graduate school, the dip in collaboration as a motive for contact in graduate school is both a red flag and an opportunity. Identifying ways to help graduate students connect with their peers in other institutions is important because these individuals might become professional colleagues and collaborators as they gain specialized knowledge in their fields. Social media can be a tool for decreasing isolation among graduate students and better preparing them to be senior scholars and knowledgeable professionals.

RECOMMENDATIONS: EVALUATION, AUTHORITY, AND LEGITIMACY

We cannot overestimate the importance of embedding services and resources within the spaces where people build trusted relationships with individuals. Institutions should consider digital and face-to-face community building as a cornerstone of their enterprise-wide policies. Individuals will turn to libraries or librarians for resources only if they are a part of the individuals' networks. As the following recommendations show, social media tools can be used obliquely to build such relationships.

- Ensure that your library has a diverse presence in both digital and physical spaces. Because academic constituencies need help in a variety of situations, you should offer services in multiple formats and at different hours of the day and night. Offer help at the time of need, such as pop-up chat in your online library catalogs for no retrievals and on institutional web pages within 10 seconds of visitor inactivity. Also, education IT staff and LIS professionals should be embedded in online and physical classes, and possibly have offices in their respective academic departments.
- Engage in interesting discussions and innovative strategies for promoting and making collections come to life using social media. A great example here is the University of Nevada, Reno, which offers a lively special collections presence on Facebook.[59]

Conclusions

Our recommendations here are not revenue neutral; they require expertise, time, and resources. Given the current economic climate and the resulting shortfall of university resources due to state budget cuts and decreasing endowments, how can institutions recalibrate their services as outlined above?

One way is to engage with academic community members, which offers the opportunity to better assess their needs and to provide services and systems that they'll actually use. Our study results indicate that individuals do contact other people when they need help or specific information; initiating and developing relationships is therefore necessary. As Mathews states, "By focusing on relationship building instead of service excellence, organizations can uncover new needs and be in position to make a stronger impact."[60]

However, to engage with users and potential users of our systems and services, we must be present and available in the spaces in which they dwell. We cannot simply create a social media account for the library; we must become an involved and interactive presence within the social media venue. This means becoming personally involved in promoting the library collections by spotlighting special collections, archival materials, and the digital library.

Connecting with students in the library's physical spaces also builds relationships. For example, at the University of North Carolina, Charlotte, the J. Murrey Atkins Library stages an exam break room with games, art supplies, snacks, comfortable chairs, and even pillows.[61] Close to where they study, the room lets students take a break from the intensity of studying for final exams without completely losing their focus. Marketing materials and social media engagement made it clear that the library was responsible for the break room, associating the library staff with concern for students and their well-being.

Hosting special programs and adding links to special collections in Wikipedia can promote the physical library, its services, and its collections. Also, embedding librarians both physically and virtually within academic departments or classes also promotes the library as an active participant in the learning and teaching environments.

Finally, studying user behavior can enhance the development and testing of library systems. Our findings suggest that people prefer easy-to-use, familiar systems with a simple interface design. To ensure that your library catalog and website interfaces best meet users' needs, you can analyze catalog and web logs to identify their information-seeking and evaluation strategies. Such an analysis will also help librarians better advise users on ways to improve their search and evaluation practices. These strategies will in turn give you new opportunities to market institutional systems and services and encourage users' engagement with them. Finally—and critically, in these times—such strategies can help libraries both assess and define their value to the larger academic institution.

ACKNOWLEDGMENTS

This study was part of the Digital Visitors and Residents: What Motivates Engagement with the Digital Information Environment? project, which was funded by JISC, University of Oxford, and OCLC, in partnership with the University of North Carolina, Charlotte. Special thanks to David S. White, University of Oxford, and Carrie Vass, our research assistant.

NOTES

1. Direct quote from USS1, Emerging, 0:21:57, Female, Age 18.

2. For more in-depth information on the methods used for this study, see Lynn Silipigni Connaway, David White, Donna Lanclos, and Alison Le Cornu, "Visitors and Residents: What Motivates Engagement with the Digital Information Environment?" *Information Research,* vol. 18, no. 1, 2013; Lynn Silipigni Connaway, Donna Lanclos, and Erin M. Hood, "'I find Google a lot easier than going to the library website.' Imagine Ways to Innovate and Inspire Students to Use the Academic Library," *Proceedings of the Association of College & Research Libraries (ACRL) 2013 Conference, April 10–13, 2013;* David White, *Digital Visitors and Residents: The Video,* video presentation; David S. White and Alison Le Cornu, "Visitors and Residents: A New Typology for Online Engagement," *First Monday,* vol. 16, no. 9, 2011; and Marc Prensky, "Digital Natives, Digital Immigrants," *On the Horizon,* vol. 9, no. 5 (October 2001).

3. Lorcan Dempsey, "Thirteen Ways of Looking at Libraries, Discovery, and the Catalog: Scale, Workflow, Attention," *EDUCAUSE Review Online,* 10 December 2012.

4. In our analysis of interview data, we use frequency of mentions as a proxy for issues that should be addressed by academic institutions. Each theme is the unit of analysis and the frequency of occurrence merits further analytical attention; for instance, if there are many mentions of Wikipedia, it is not enough to say, "Wikipedia is important," but to analyze the content of the interviews to identify why and how the interviewees were using Wikipedia.

5. JISC, *Visitors and Residents: What Motivates Engagement with the Digital Information Environment,* David White, Oxford University, and Lynn Silipigni Connaway, OCLC Research, Project Managers, 2011–2012.

6. Lynn Silipigni Connaway, Donna Lanclos, David White, Alison Le Cornu, and Erin M. Hood, "User-Centered Decision Making: A New Model for Developing Academic Library Services and Systems," *IFLA Journal,* 2013, vol. 39(1): p. 30–36; Connaway, White, Lanclos, and Le Cornu, "Visitors and Residents: What Motivates Engagement with the Digital Information Environment?"; JISC, *Visitors and Residents: What Motivates Engagement.*

7. Lynn Silipigni Connaway and Ronald R. Powell, *Basic Research Methods for Librarians,* 5th ed., Libraries Unlimited, 2010.

8. Ibid.

9. Ibid; Christine S. Davis, Heather L. Powell, and Kenneth L. Lachlan, *Straight Talk about Communication Research Methods,* Kendall Hunt Publishing Company, 2013.

10. Davis, Powell, and Lachlan, *Straight Talk about Communication.*

11. Connaway and Powell, *Basic Research Methods for Librarians.*

12. Ibid.

13. Online are the full list of semi-structured interview questions for emerging, establishing, and embedding; the full list of semi-structured interview questions for experiencing; and the full list of questions for monthly diary submissions.

14. For more detailed information about the research methodology, see Connaway, White, Lanclos, and Le Cornu, "Visitors and Residents: What Motivates Engagement with the Digital Information Environment?" *ISIC 2012 Conference Proceedings,* 2012; and Connaway, Lanclos, and Hood, "'I find Google a lot easier ... ,'"p. 289–300; the full list of diarist follow-up interview questions is online.

15. Connaway, Lanclos, White, Le Cornu, and Hood, "User-Centered Decision Making," p. 30–36.

16. A minimum of 85 percent in inter-coder reliability levels of agreement is emphasized for most projects. An initial inter-coder reliability test was run to ensure high levels of agreement and again each time another coder was trained and brought in. Looking at two transcripts (one from the US and one from the UK), levels of agreement for the initial ICR tests were at 97.78 percent (0.6442 Kappa) for the UK transcript and 98.39 percent (0.6319 Kappa) for the US transcript. Following ICRs for new coders maintained the same high levels of agreement.

17. The complete codebook is available online.

18. Jean Lave and Etienne Wenger, *Situated Learning: Legitimate Peripheral Participation,* University of Cambridge Press, 1991; Barbara Rogoff, *Apprenticeship in Thinking: Cognitive Development in Social Context,* Oxford University Press, 1990; and Etienne Wenger, *Communities of Practice: Learning, Meaning, and Identity,* University of Cambridge Press, 1998.

19. Lave and Wenger, Situated Learning, p. 35–36.

20. Ibid, p. 40.

21. Reijo Savolainen, "Time as a Context of Information Seeking," *Library & Information Science Research,* vol. 28, no. 1, 2006, p. 110–127; Lynn Silipigni Connaway, Timothy J. Dickey, and Marie L. Radford, "'If it is too inconvenient I'm not going after it': Convenience as a Critical Factor in Information-Seeking Behaviors," *Library & Information Science Research,* vol. 33, no. 3, 2011, p. 179–190.

22. Connaway, Dickey, and Radford, "'If it is too inconvenient ...,'" p. 179–190; Connaway, White, Lanclos, and Le Cornu, "*Visitors and Residents: What Motivates Engagement with the Digital Information Environment?*"; and Connaway, Lanclos, and Hood, "'I find Google a lot easier ...,'" p. 289–300.

23. Connaway, Dickey, and Radford, "'If it is too inconvenient ...,'" p. 179–190; Connaway and Radford, *Seeking Synchronicity: Revelations and Recommendations for Virtual Reference,* OCLC Research, 2011; Connaway, Lanclos, and Hood, "'I find Google a lot easier ...,'" p. 289–300; Connaway, Lanclos, White, Le Cornu, and Hood, "User-Centered Decision Making," p. 30–36; and Connaway, White, Lanclos, and Le Cornu, "Visitors and Residents: What Motivates Engagement with the Digital Information Environment?."

24. Connaway, Dickey, and Radford, "'If it is too inconvenient ...,'" p. 179–190; and Connaway, Lanclos, and Hood, "'I find Google a lot easier ...,'" p. 289–300.

25. Lynn Silipigni Connaway, "Findings from User Behavior Studies: A User's World," presentation made at *ALA Midwinter Meeting and Exhibits,* Seattle, WA, 28 January 2012; Connaway, Lanclos, White, Le Cornu, and Hood, "User-Centered Decision Making," p. 30–36; and Connaway, White, Lanclos, and Le Cornu, "Visitors and Residents: What Motivates Engagement with the Digital Information Environment?."

26. Connaway, "Findings from User Behavior Studies."

27. Reijo Savolainen, "The Sense-Making Theory: Reviewing the Interests of a User-centered Approach to Information Seeking and Use," *Information Processing & Management,* vol. 29, no. 1, 1993, p. 17.

28. Sanna Talja, Heidi Keso, and Tarja Pietilainen, "The Production of 'Context' in Information Seeking Research: A Metatheoretical View," *Information Processing & Management,* vol. 35, no. 6, 1999, p. 751–763.

29. Connaway, Dickey, and Radford, "'If it is too inconvenient …,'" p. 180.

30. For a more detailed discussion of individuals' interactions with humans as sources of information, see Connaway, Lanclos, and Hood, "'I find Google a lot easier ….'"

31. Interviews were transcribed to include pauses and utterances such as "ah" and "um" (a few of which were removed for readability here). For anonymity, we assigned participants tags to indicate their country (UK or US) and educational stage ("S" for secondary school/high school, "U" for university, "G" for graduate students, and "F" for faculty), and gave each participant an identification number.

32. Institute of Museum and Library Services Research Grant, "Sense-Making the Information Confluence: The Hows and the Whys of College and University User Satisficing of Information Needs," Brenda Dervin, Ohio State University, Principal Investigator, and Lynn Silipigni Connaway and Chandra Prabha, OCLC Research, Co-Investigators, 2003–2005; and JISC, *Visitors and Residents: What Motivates Engagement?*.

33. Institute of Museum and Library Services Research Grant, "Seeking Synchronicity: Evaluating Virtual Reference Services from User, Non-User, and Librarian Perspectives," Lynn Silipigni Connaway, OCLC Research, and Marie L. Radford, Rutgers University, Co-Principal Investigators, 2005–2007; Institute of Museum and Library Services Research Grant, "Sense-Making the Information Confluence: The Hows and the Whys of College and University User Satisficing of Information Needs," Cathy De Rosa, Joanne Cantrell, Diane Cellentani, Janet Hawk, Lillie Jenkins, and Alane Wilson, *Perceptions of Libraries and Information Resources: A Report to the OCLC Membership,* OCLC Online Computer Library Center, 2005; and Cathy De Rosa, Joanne Cantrell, Matthew Carlson, Peggy Gallagher, Janet Hawk, and Charlotte Sturtz, *Perceptions of Libraries, 2010: Context and Community: A Report to the OCLC Membership,* OCLC Online Computer Library Center, 2011.

34. Institute of Museum and Library Services Research Grant, "Seeking Synchronicity: Evaluating Virtual Reference Services from User, Non-User, and Librarian Perspectives," Lynn Silipigni Connaway, OCLC Research, and Marie L. Radford, Rutgers University, Co-Principal Investigators, 2005–2007.

35. Lorcan Dempsey, "Always On: Libraries in a World of Permanent Connectivity," *First Monday,* vol. 14, no. 1, 2008; and Dempsey, "Thirteen Ways of Looking at Libraries."

36. Lynn Silipigni Connaway and Timothy J. Dickey, *The Digital Information Seeker: Report of Findings from Selected OCLC, RIN and JISC User Behaviour Projects,* Higher Education Funding Council for England, 2010; Elizabeth Pickard and Firouzeh Logan, "The Research Process and the Library: First-Generation College Seniors vs. Freshmen," College & Research Libraries, vol. 74, no. 4, 2013, p. 399–415; De Rosa et al., *Perceptions of Libraries and Information Resources: A Report to the OCLC Membership;* and De Rosa et al., *Perceptions of Libraries, 2010: Context and Community: A Report to the OCLC Membership.*

37. This bias for Moodle in the data could be attributed to the fact that it is the CMS used at the University of North Carolina, Charlotte, and students who talked about technology in their classes would have to talk about or at least mention Moodle.
38. Ibid.
39. Helena Francke and Olof Sundin, "Negotiating the Role of Sources: Educators' Conceptions of Credibility in Participatory Media," *Library & Information Science Research,* vol. 34, no. 3, 2012, p. 173.
40. Laura Saunders, "Faculty Perspectives on Information Literacy as a Student Learning Outcome," *The Journal of Academic Librarianship,* vol. 38, no. 4, 2012, p. 231.
41. Connaway, Lanclos, and Hood, "'I find Google a lot easier ....,'" p. 289–300, and David White, "The Learning Black Market," *TALL blog,* 30 September 2011.
42. OCLC Research, "Max Klein Named OCLC Research Wikipedian in Residence," OCLC.org. An early case study on these efforts was provided by Ann M. Lally and Carolyn E. Dunford, "Using Wikipedia to Extend Digital Collections," *D-Lib Magazine,* vol. 13, no. 5/6, 2007. Information professionals seeking guidance on how to get started should consult the GLAM Wiki portal.
43. Dempsey, "Thirteen Ways of Looking at Libraries."
44. Pickard and Logan, "The Research Process and the Library," p. 399–415.
45. Ibid.
46. Mary Ann Harlan, Christine Bruce, and Mandy Lupton, "Teen Content Creators: Experiences of Using Information to Learn," *Library Trends,* vol. 60, no. 3, 2012, p. 569–587.
47. Helena Francke and Olof Sundin, "Negotiating the Role of Sources: Educators' Conceptions of Credibility in Participatory Media," *Library & Information Science Research,* vol. 34, no. 3, 2012, p. 169–175.
48. Saunders, "Faculty Perspectives on Information Literacy," p. 231.
49. Connaway, Dickey, and Radford, "'If it is too inconvenient ...,'" p. 179–190.
50. Ibid.
51. Kurt Lewin, *Field Theory in Social Science: Selected Theoretical Papers,* Harper, 1951.
52. Lewin, *Field Theory in Social Science*; and Pamela Shoemaker and Tim P. Vos, *Gatekeeping Theory* (New York: Routledge, 2009).
53. Lewin, *Field Theory in Social Science,* p. 186; and Shoemaker and Vos, *Gatekeeping Theory,* p. 80.
54. Lewin, *Field Theory in Social Science*; and Shoemaker and Vos, *Gatekeeping Theory.*
55. Pickard and Logan, "The Research Process and the Library," p. 408.
56. Ibid., p. 403.
57. Ibid., p. 403.
58. Connaway and Radford, *Seeking Synchronicity.*
59. Nick DeSantis, "On Facebook, Librarian Brings 2 Students From the Early 1900s to Life," *Chronicle of Higher Education,* 6 January 2012. Joe McDonald's Facebook page is currently available along with Leola Lewis's page.

60. Brian Mathews, *Think Like a Startup: A White Paper to Inspire Library Entrepreneurialism,* white paper, The Ubiquitous Librarian, 4 April 2012.
61. Jean Hiebert and Shelly Theriault, "BLASTing the Zombies! Creative Ideas to Fight Finals Fatigue," *College & Research Libraries News,* vol. 73, no. 9, 2012, p. 540–569.

10

Meeting the Expectations of the Community: The Engagement-Centered Library

Lynn Silipigni Connaway, Ph.D.
OCLC Research

A reprint of:

Lynn Silipigni Connaway. "Meeting the Expectations of the Community: The Engagement-centered Library." *Library 2020: Today's Leading Visionaries Describe Tomorrow's Library*, ed. Joe Janes. (Lanham, MD: Scarecrow Press, 2013), 83–88.

Used by arrangement with Rowman & Littlefield. All rights reserved. No part of this excerpt may be reproduced or printed without permission in writing from the publisher.

The library in 2020 will be engagement-centered.

In 2008, Lorcan Dempsey stated that it used to be that users built their workflows around the library, resources were scarce, therefore, the users' attention was abundant. He went on to say that the library now must build its service around the users' workflow because their attention is scarce and the available resources are abundant. This scenario most likely will intensify. As Mitchell Kapor said, "Getting information off the Internet is like taking a drink from a fire hydrant."[1]

The library of the future needs to be constantly changing or it will not survive. Regardless of whether the library is public or academic, in order to remain relevant in a rapidly changing global environment, it will need to provide an environment for "innovation, productivity, collaboration, and knowledge" (Mathews 2012).

Libraries traditionally have been most concerned with access to information and content (Mathews 2011). Accessing information is no longer an issue. Librarians can fill a niche in the use, creation, and curation of information and content. Librarians in 2020 will be assisting users in the creation, evaluation, and production of content. We will not only need to create repositories for content but also to engage and motivate researchers, scholars, and business people to contribute, share, and reuse the content. Librarians will need to develop partnerships with the individuals who create, collect, and analyze data sets in order to provide policies, systems, and services for the storage, access, preservation, and shared use of these data.

Something that often is difficult for library and information professionals to comprehend is that the majority of the population does not use libraries to get information. Many people get their information from human resources (family, teachers, professors, colleagues, peers) and the Internet (Connaway and Dickey 2010; Head and Eisenberg 2010; Prabha, Connaway, and Dickey 2006; Connaway, Prabha, and Dickey 2006; Connaway, Lanclos, White, Le Cornu, and Hood 2012; Connaway, White, Lanclos, and Le Cornu 2012). Google and Wikipedia often are the first places individuals go for information regardless of age or educational background (Head and Eisenberg 2010; Head and Eisenberg 2009; Connaway, Lanclos, White, Le Cornu, and Hood 2012; Connaway, White, Lanclos, and Le Cornu 2012). Why? Because people go for what's convenient (Connaway, Dickey, and Radford 2011; Connaway and Dickey 2010).

If this is the case, why not gear library services and systems to those who actually use them? This also may be more efficient for the library. Andy Priestner and Elizabeth Tilley propose this in the concept of boutique academic libraries (Priestner and Tilley 2010; Priestner and Tilley, 2012). They equate the boutique library with the boutique hotel—personalized service. It's a customer-focused approach that will utilize the skills and knowledge of professional librarians, possibly eliminating the more clerical responsibilities of some current library positions. Subject librarians will collaboratively work with users and develop relationships with them to create services specifically geared to their needs.

Relationships are important to both librarians and users. Research in virtual reference services (VRS) reported that both VRS librarians and reference service users value the relationships developed in both face-to-face (FtF) and virtual environments. Even though VRS is more convenient, users often prefer FtF reference because of the relationships they develop with librarians (Connaway and Radford 2011).

Felicia A. Smith coins the term, Helicopter Librarians, based on the concept of Helicopter Parents. She describes Helicopter Librarianship as "a holistic approach to a human interaction based on individuality and genuine compassion" (Smith 2012). She stresses the importance of building relationships during instruction sessions and reference encounters, and by embracing "new and unconventional methods" for users to contact and interact with librarians when they need help (Smith 2012).

This may call for a new type of librarian and information professional—one who embraces change and possesses a willingness and eagerness to try new technologies and modes of communication and delivery of services. When users visit our online catalogs and web sites, they often find them confusing and difficult to use (Connaway and Dickey 2010; Connaway, Prabha, and Dickey 2006). Why not provide a pop-up chat box that asks, "What can I help you find?"? We need to be where our users need us, when they need us. If the majority of our users prefer to communicate via mobile phone texting, chat, or IM; to learn through gaming; by accessing the library's unique collections and materials via social media, such as Facebook[2] and Wikipedia; or to meet with us FtF outside of the library, we need to be there!

Today it's not unusual for librarians to make themselves physically available within the academic departments, student unions, and cafeterias. This is referred to as embedded librarianship. Kessleman and Watstein (2009, p. 385) stated that "bringing the library and the librarian to the user, wherever they are—office, laboratory, home, or even on their mobile device is at the forefront of what it means to be embedded." Some academic librarians embed themselves in both FtF and online classes, which provides them with the opportunity to interact with the students and faculty on a regular basis.

A more innovative example of embedded librarianship was the October 2011 announcement that the William H. Welch Medical Library at Johns Hopkins University in Baltimore, Maryland, would close its physical doors to patrons on 1 January 2012.[3] The plan was for the library to continue to provide resources completely online. One of the main reasons for the closing of the library was the decrease in use and circulation of physical materials and the exponential increase in the use of electronic materials. The librarians have been embedded within the academic departments for the past 6 years and are available to students and faculty via email or phone (Kelley 2011).

Embedded librarianship also is an important aspect of public library engagement with the community. Many public libraries are providing kiosks in public spaces, such as train and bus stations and parks, for users to check-out and return print, audio, and electronic books, magazines, newspapers, and journals.

I was visiting Washington, DC several years ago and as I walked down the street, there were several individuals who were wearing yellow shirts, with the word information printed on them, standing on the street corners. I decided to ask for directions (although I did not need them). The person was very pleasant, gave me directions, and offered me a map as well. I immediately thought that this would be a perfect venue for public librarians to engage with the community and to communicate the library's value, although I am not advocating yellow shirts!

A similar idea occurred to me several months ago when a friend, who is very involved in local politics in Aspen, Colorado, called me to discuss the Pitkin County Library's request for funds to renovate and expand the library. Although he had no idea of the library's impact on the community or how the library and its services are used, he felt that the request was unwarranted since the library occupied a beautiful space that was sufficiently staffed and funded to meet the needs of the community. I immediately thought of the information kiosk at the corner of the pedestrian mall in Aspen that is staffed by local volunteers and that I often frequent to find out about daily events, restaurants, and shops. Wouldn't this be the perfect outpost for the library? It would give the library visibility in a bustling small town and would demonstrate the library's engagement with and contributions to the community.

My mother works in retail and always says that "one size fits no one." This pertains to library services and systems as well. No one service or system will meet the needs of every individual. We need to develop an economic model for the allocation of resources for the various modes of user engagement based on the specific user groups' needs and expectations.

The library of 2020 will provide user-centered services and systems that will meet the expectations of the community. The library staff will need to develop relationships with their users and partner with other organizations in order to produce, store, and preserve content and data sets and to provide personalized services. Recruiting and retaining innovative, creative individuals who are willing to engage with users and to embrace new technologies and modes of communication will be imperative for the success of the library of 2020. Access to the library and its resources when and where users need them (which may involve being accessible in multiple physical and virtual locations), will be essential since convenient access to resources, whether human, print, or electronic is the most critical factor for users. As stated by one of our study participants, "If it is too inconvenient I'm not going after it" (Connaway, Dickey, and Radford 2011). Ultimately, the library must develop strategic plans and continually change and innovate in order to respond proactively instead of reactively to community needs and engagement opportunities.

NOTES

1. Taken from Image: http://www.flickr.com/photos/will-lion/2595497078/; http://giveupinternet.com/2009/01/14/mitchell-kapor-getting-information-off-the-internet-is-like-taking-a-drink-from-a-fire-hydrant-pic/.

2. The Director of Research Collections and Services at the University of Nevada, Reno created Facebook profiles for Joe McDonald, a sophomore at the university in 1913, and his girlfriend and future wife, Leola Lewis, to promote the library's special collections. Although Facebook made the library remove the profiles since the two individuals are no longer alive, the site is still active and has attracted thousands to the special collections (DeSantis, 2012).

3. The library did not close its physical doors on 1 January 2012. The Board is still reviewing the options to determine which will best provide services to its users.

REFERENCES

Connaway, Lynn Silipigni, and Timothy J. Dickey. 2010. *The Digital Information Seeker: Report of Findings from Selected OCLC, RIN, and JISC User Behavior Projects*. Bristol: HEFCE. http://www.jisc.ac.uk/media/documents/publications/reports/2010/digitalinformationseekerreport.pdf (accessed 11 October 2012).

Connaway, Lynn Silipigni, Timothy J. Dickey, and Marie L. Radford 2011. "'If it is too inconvenient I'm not going after it:' Convenience as a Critical Factor in Information-seeking Behaviors." *Library & Information Science Research* 33, no. 3: 179–90.

Connaway, Lynn Silipigni, Donna Lanclos, David White, Alison Le Cornu, and Erin M. Hood. 2012. "User-centered Decision Making: A New Model for Developing Academic Library Services and Systems." *IFLA World Library and Information Congress 2012 Helsinki Proceedings: "Libraries Now! Inspiring, Surprising, Empowering."* http://conference.ifla.org/sites/default/files/files/papers/wlic2012/76-connaway-en.pdf.

Connaway, Lynn Silipigni, Chandra Prabha, and Timothy J. Dickey. 2006. *Sense-making the Information Confluence: The Whys and Hows of College and University User Satisficing of Information Needs. Phase III: Focus Group Interview Study*. Report on National Leadership Grant LG-02-03-0062-03, to Institute of Museum and Library Services, Washington, DC. Columbus, OH: School of Communication, The Ohio State University.

Connaway, Lynn Silipigni, and Marie L. Radford. 2011. *Seeking Synchronicity: Revelations and Recommendations for Virtual Reference*. Dublin, OH: OCLC Research. http://www.oclc.org/reports/synchronicity/full.pdf.

Connaway, Lynn Silipigni, David White, Donna Lanclos, and Alison Le Cornu. 2012. "Visitors and Residents: What Motivates Engagement with the Digital Information Environment?" *ISIC 2012 Conference Proceedings*, 5–7 September 2012, Tokyo, Japan.

Dempsey, Lorcan. 2008. "Always On: Libraries in a World of Permanent Connectivity." *First Monday* 14, no. 1. http://www.firstmonday.org/htbin/cgiwrap/bin/ojs/index.php/fm/article/view/2291/207 (accessed 12 October 2012).

DeSantis, Nick 2012. "On Facebook, Librarian Brings 2 Students from the Early 1900s to Life." *Chronicle of Higher Education*, 6 Jan. 2012. http://chronicle.com/blogs/wiredcampus/on-facebook-librarian-brings-two-students-from-the-early-1900s-to-life/34845 (accessed 12 October 2012).

Head, Alison J., and Michael B. Eisenberg. 2010. "How Today's College Students Use Wikipedia for Course-related Research." *First Monday* 15, no. 3. http://www.uic.edu/htbin/cgiwrap/bin/ojs/index.php/fm/article/viewArticle/2830/2476 (accessed. 11 October 2012).

Head, Alison J., and Michael B. Eisenberg. 2009. *Lessons Learned: How College Students Seek Information in the Digital Age*. Seattle, WA: The Information School, University of Washington.

Kelley, Michael 2012. "Major Medical Library Closing Its Doors to Patrons and Moving to Digital Model." *The Digital Shift,* 27 Oct. 2011. http://www.thedigitalshift.com/2011/10/research/major-medical-library-closing-its-doors-to-patrons-and-moving-to-digital-model/ (accessed 12 October 2012).

Kesselman, Martin A., and Sarah Barbara Watstein. 2009. "Creating Opportunities: Embedded Librarians." *Journal of Library Administration* 49, no. 4: 383–400.

Mathews, Brian. 2012. "Our Strategy: Be Regenerative." The Ubiquitous Librarian. *The Chronicle,* 4 Oct. 2012. http://chronicle.com/blognetwork/theubiquitouslibrarian/2012/10/04/our-strategy-be-regenerative/ (accessed 12 October 2012).

Mathews, Brian. 2010. *Think Like a Startup: A White Paper to Inspire Library Entrepreneurialism.* Blacksburg: Virginia Teach University. http://vtechworks.lib.vt.edu/handle/10919/18649 (accessed 11 October 2012).

Prabha, Chandra, Lynn Silipigni Connaway, and Timothy J. Dickey 2006. *Sense-making the Information Confluence: The Whys and Hows of College and University User Satisficing of Information Needs. Phase IV: Semi-structured Interview Study.* Report on National Leadership Grant LG-02-03-0062-03, to Institute of Museum and Library Services, Washington, DC. Columbus (Ohio): School of Communication, The Ohio State University, 2006.

Priestner, Andy, and Elizabeth Tilley. 2010. "Boutique Libraries at Your Service." *Library & Information Update* 9, no. 6: 36–39. http://personalisedlibraries.files.wordpress.com/2011/01/boutiquelibraries.pdf (accessed 12 October 2012).

Priestner, Andy, and Elizabeth Tilley (Eds.). 2012. *Personalizing Library Services in Higher Education: The Boutique Approach.* Burlington, VT: Ashgate.

Smith, Felicia A. 2012. "Helicopter Librarian: Expect the Unexpected Backtalk." *Library Journal,* 28 Aug. 2012. http://lj.libraryjournal.com/2012/08/opinion/backtalk/helicopter-librarian-expect-the-unexpected-backtalk/#_ (accessed 12 October 2012).

www.ingramcontent.com/pod-product-compliance
Lightning Source LLC
Chambersburg PA
CBHW060940170426
43195CB00025B/2986